HISPANIC FOUNDATION
BIBLIOGRAPHICAL SERIES NO. 13

Latin America, spain, and portugal
an *Annotated Bibliography of* paperback books

Compiled by
GEORGETTE M. DORN
Hispanic Foundation, Reference Department

Library of Congress   •   Washington : 1971

Library of Congress Cataloging in Publication Data

Dorn, Georgette M
    Latin America, Spain, and Portugal.

    (Hispanic Foundation bibliographical series, no. 13)
    Originally compiled in 1964 by D. H. Andrews,
under title: Latin America; a bibliography of paper-
back books.
    1. Latin America--Bibliography. 2. Spain--Bibli-
ography. 3. Portugal--Bibliography. 4. Bibliography
--Paperback editions. I. Andrews, David H. Latin
America; a bibliography of paperback books. II. U. S.
Library of Congress. Hispanic Foundation. III. Title.
IV. Series.
Z2685.H5 no. 13 [Z1601] 016.918   71-37945
ISBN 0-8444-0013-0

For sale by the Superintendent of Documents, U.S. Government Printing Office
Washington, D.C. 20402 - Price 75 cents
Stock Number 3013-0005

CONTENTS

INTRODUCTION

The increasing demand for information on relatively inexpensive paperback books about Latin America, primarily from students and teachers,
prompted the Hispanic Foundation, in cooperation with the State Education
Department of the University of the State of New York, to publish in 1964
<u>Latin America: A Bibliography of Paperback Books</u>. Sales of this reference
and teaching tool exceeded all expectations and encouraged a second revised
edition, <u>Latin America: An Annotated Bibliography of Paperback Books</u>, which
appeared in 1967.

Spain and Portugal have been added to the present edition. Travel guides
are now included in the Latin America and Iberian Peninsula sections. A new
category has been created for a selection of outstanding grammars, language
readers, dictionaries, and textbooks.

The bibliography lists 1,512 paperback books currently in print on the
social sciences and humanities, generally available at newsstands and
college bookstores. The entries are arranged alphabetically by author within
each section and include full bibliographic information, price of the
publication, and a brief descriptive comment. To enhance the bibliography's
utility, a list of publishers and a subject index are appended.

A wide selection of sources were used in the preparation of the
bibliography, including <u>Paperback Books in Print</u> (New York, Bowker, 1971)
and various catalogs of university presses and commercial publishing houses.

Many individuals have generously aided Mrs. Dorn in preparing this work.
Dr. Charles Fleener of St. Louis University contributed many entries which
are identified accordingly. Thanks also go to Mrs. Josephita Boddie and
Miss Karen Oram, who helped with editorial tasks. Gratitude is due Mrs.
Julia Thomas and Miss Dorothy McNeal, who typed the manuscript.

Earl J. Pariseau
Acting Director
Hispanic Foundation
Library of Congress

LATIN AMERICA

1.

Abel, Elie. THE MISSILE CRISIS. New York, Bantam Books, 1966. 197p. $0.95
   This is a journalist's day-to-day account of the 1962 U.S.-Soviet confrontation over the missile sites in Cuba. The author seldom cites his
sources.

2.

Adams, Richard N., and others. SOCIAL CHANGE IN LATIN AMERICA TODAY: ITS
IMPLICATIONS FOR U.S. POLICY. New York, Random House, 1961. 353p. $1.45
   Includes essays by six scholars, with specific studies of Peru, Bolivia,
Brazil, Guatemala, and Mexico. The work was commissioned by the Council on
Foreign Relations.

3.

Aguilar, Alonso. PAN-AMERICANISM FROM MONROE TO THE PRESENT; A VIEW FROM
THE OTHER SIDE. Rev. ed. Translated by Asa Zatz. New York, Monthly Review
Press, 1968. 192p. $2.95
   An economist traces the history of U.S. relations with Latin America from
Presidents Monroe to Johnson. The major part of the book deals with the
20th century, and he stresses the aspects of what he terms "U.S. imperialism."
For North American readers this work provides an excellent example of one
aspect of Latin American radicalism. The original Spanish title in El pan-
americanismo de la doctrina Monroe a la doctrina Johnson (1965).

4.

Aguilar, Luis E., ed. MARXISM IN LATIN AMERICA. New York, Knopf, 1968. 271p.
$2.75
   Save for a brief excerpting from Marx' and Engles' own brief recognition
of Latin America, the bulk of the material presented here is by Latin
American authors. Prof. Aguilar's selection is very good, and he contri-
butes with an excellent introduction.

5.

Alba, Victor. THE LATIN AMERICANS. New York Praeger, 1970. 393p. $3.95
   An excellent introduction to Latin America, its history, politics, social
customs, cultural life, and its aspirations for the future by a long-time
student of Latin American problems.

6.

——————. THE MEXICANS. New York, Pegasus, 1970. 272p. illus. $2.45
   This is a perceptive history of Mexico after Porfirio Díaz. The author
points out the relevance of Mexico's geography in Mexico's history. The
division into regions is firm and regions are in turn divided into enclaves.
This work captures the very essence of Mexico.

7.

Albion, Robert G., ed. EXPLORATION AND DISCOVERY. New York, Macmillan,
1967. 151p. (Main themes in European history). $1.75
   Includes essays on exploration and discovery by J. H. Parry, Boies Penrose,
C. E. Nowell, and others. Prince Henry the Navigator, Vasco da Gama, and
Columbus are the subjects of major essays.

8.
Alden, Peter. FINDING BIRDS IN WESTERN MEXICO. Tucson, University of Arizona
Press, 1969. 138p. illus. maps. $5.95

9.
Alegría, Ciro. THE GOLDEN SERPENT. Translation and afterword by Harriet de
Onís. New York, New American Library, 1963. 190p. (Signet classics, CP-114)
$0.60
   One of the greatest novels of Peru, and indeed of Latin America, this is
the story about the remorseless Marañón country. The author's heroes are the
outcast, the humble, the Indian. This excellent English translation of La
serpiente de oro was first published in 1943.

10.
Alexander, Robert J. THE COMMUNIST PARTY OF VENEZUELA. Edited by Jan F.
Triska. Stanford, Calif., Hoover Institution Press, 1970. 246p. $2.80
   The author analyzes the Communist Party of Venezuela as it seeks power
through shifting national regimes and studies the party as party-out-of power
in a democratic nation-state. This book is one in a series which considers the
state of the non-ruling communist parties in the world.

11.
----------. LATIN AMERICAN POLITICS AND GOVERNMENT. New York, Harper and Row,
1966. 184p. $2.50
   A brief discussion of the historical background of politics and government
structure in Latin America. It is a review of this rapidly changing field,
intended for use in college courses.

12.
----------. TODAY'S LATIN AMERICA. 2d rev. ed. Garden City , N. Y. Doubleday, 1968. 261p. (Anchor books) $1.45
   Treats of contemporary Latin America placing undue emphasis on similarities
in culture, traditions, society, and not enough on the basic ecological,
historical, social, and cultural differences. Intended for the generalist.

13.
Alexandre, Marianne, ed. VIVA CHE! New York, Dutton, 1970. 128p. illus.
$1.75
   The editor provides a synopsis of the life of Ernesto Che Guevara in prose
and poetry. The authors include Jean-Paul Sartre, Thomas Merton, Stokely
Carmichael, Graham Greene, Fidel Castro, and others.

14.
Alisky, Marvin. WHO'S WHO IN MEXICAN GOVERNMENT. Tempe, Arizona State
University, 1969. 64p. $1.00
   Not since 1946 when Stanford University brought one out, has any institution
in the U.S. published a who's who for Mexico. Even textbooks on Mexican government do not include biographical data which trace the careers of Mexican
government officials. This is a useful and welcome work.

15.
Allen, J. LATIN AMERICA. Englewood Cliffs, N.J., Prentice-Hall, 1970. 190p.
illus. $1.60
   Presents a succinct overview of Latin America.

16.
Allison, Graham U. CONCEPTUAL MODELS AND THE CUBAN MISSILE CRISIA: NATIONAL
POLICIES, ORGANIZATIONAL PROCESS, AND BUREAUCRATIC POLITICS. Boston, Little,
Brown, 1971. 69p. Price not set
   Originally a Harvard doctoral thesis, this work became a Rand Corporation
report, and is now published in book form. It analyzes the many logistic and
technological facets of the Cuban Missile Crisis.

17.
Alvarez, J. H. RETURN MIGRATION TO PUERTO RICO. Introd. by K. Davis.
Berkeley, University of California, International Studies, 1969. 101p. $2.00
   This is a study of people who return to Puerto Rico from the U. S. main-
land.

18.
Alvarez, Luisa M., and Ruth W. Mulvey. GOOD FOOD FROM MEXICO. New rev. ed.
New York, Collier Books, 1962. 253p. (A Collier cookbook, AS-470). $0.95
   First published in 1950, this perennial favorite includes the better-
known dishes from Mexico.

19.
American Assembly. UNITED STATES AND LATIN AMERICA. Edited by Herbert L.
Matthews. 2d ed. Englewood Cliffs, N. J., Prentice-Hall, 1970. 179p.
illus. (A Spectrum book) $1.95

20.
American Universities Field Staff. New York. A SELECT BIBLIOGRAPHY: ASIA,
AFRICA, EASTERN EUROPE, LATIN AMERICA. Supplement 1969. New York, 1969.
97p. $3.00
   This is an annotated bibliography to assist college librarians in building their collections in area studies. Georgette M. Dorn contributed 203
entries on Latin America. The 1961, 1963, and 1967 supplements are also
available.

21.
---. A SELECT BIBLIOGRAPHY: ASIA,
AFRICA, EASTERN EUROPE, LATIN AMERICA. Supplement 1971. New York, 1971.
[In press] $3.50
   This annotated bibliography contains 212 English-language entries on
Latin America contributed by Georgette M. Dorn.

22.
ANCIENT PERUVIAN TEXTILES FROM THE COLLECTION OF THE TEXTILE MUSEUM, WASH-
INGTON, D.C.; THE MUSEUM OF PRIMITVE ART, NEW YORK, New York, New York
Graphic Art Society, 1965. 48p. illus. map. $3.75
   Mary Elizabeth King provides the brief introduction and the notes that
amplify the 44 illustrations of Peruvian textiles from the Paracas, Nazca,
Tiahuanaco, Inca, and Central coast cultures.

23.
Anderson, Charles W., Fred R. Van der Mehden, and Crawford Young. ISSUES
OF POLITICAL DEVELOPMENT. Englewood Cliffs, N. J., Prentice-Hall, 1967.
284p. maps. $4.75

24.
Anderson, Charles W. POLITICS AND ECONOMIC CHANGE IN LATIN AMERICA; THE
GOVERNING OF RESTLESS NATIONS. New York, Van Nostrand, 1967. 388p. $4.95
   This book analyzes the political element in economic change in contemporary Latin America. Part I studies development policy-making; Part II
deals with the specific experience of ten Latin American nations in formu-
lating an approach to developmental problems; and Part III outlines a con-
ception of political change.

25.
Anderson-Imbert, Enrique. FUGA. Edited by J. V. Falconieri. New York,
Macmillan, 1969. 110p. $2.25
   This is a short novel by the contemporary Argentine literary critic and
novelist who is well known for his avant-garde style.

26.
Anderson-Imbert, Enrique. SPANISH-AMERICAN LITERATURE; A HISTORY. Detroit,
Wayne State University Press, 1969. 2v. $3.95 each v.
    This is a comprehensive history of Spanish-American literature which has
become a major reference source since its first publication in 1963. It
includes all major and a great many lesser figures of Spanish-American
literature.

27.
----------, and Lawrence B. Kiddle. VEINTE CUENTOS HISPANO-AMERICANOS DEL
SIGLO VEINTE. New York, Appleton-Century-Crofts, 1960. 242p. $3.45
    This is a very good, brief anthology of Spanish-America. Includes authors
such as Leopoldo Lugones, Pedro Henríquez Ureña, Jorge Luis Borges, and Lino
Novás Calvo, among others.

28.
Andic, Fuat M., and Suphan Andic. FISCAL SURVEY OF THE FRENCH CARIBBEAN.
Rio Piedras, University of Puerto Rico, Institute of Caribbean Studies,
1965. 107p. tables. $3.00
    Analyzes the revenue system of the French Caribbean and evaluates its
importance within the general economic structure of the region. A section
deals with economic relations between France and the French Caribbean.

29.
----------. GOVERNMENT FINANCE AND PLANNED DEVELOPMENT. FISCAL SURVEYS OF
SURINAM AND THE NETHERLANDS ANTILLES. Rio Piedras, University of Puerto Rico,
Institute of Caribbean Studies, 1968. 395p. tables. $5.00
    Studies the size and structure of the budgets of the Netherlands Caribbean
countries in relation with the development objectives of these states.

30.
Andreski, Stanislav. PARASITISM AND SUBVERSION: THE CASE OF LATIN AMERICA.
New York, Schocken Books, 1966. 299p. tables. $2.45
    This is a Thoughtful   analysis of contemporary social and political
patterns in Latin America.

31.
Arce de Váquez, Margot. GABRIELA MISTRAL: THE POET AND HER WORK. Translated
from the Spanish by Helen Masslo Anderson. New York, New York University
Press, 1964. 158p. $1.75
    A brief biography and critical study of the Chilean poet who was awarded
the 1945 Nobel Prize in Literature. Gabriela Mistral emerges as an exceptional educator and social philosopher as well as a first-rate poet. The
greater part of the work is an analysis of Mistral's poetry.

32.
Armitage, Merle. PAGANS, CONQUISTADORES, HEROES, AND MARTYRS: THE SPIRIT
CONQUEST OF AMERICA, by Merle Armitage assisted by Peter Ribera Ortega.
Fresno, Calif., Academy Guild Press, 1966. 99p. illus. $2.75
    A simplified and readable account about the Spanish Conquistadors and
missionaries in the Spanish Southwest.

33.
Arnade, Charles, W. SIEGE OF ST. AUGUSTINE IN 1702. Gainesville, University
of Fla. Press, 1959. 67p. illus. $2.00
    An historical outline of St. Augustine during the early 18th century.

34.
Argentine-U.S. Commission on Foot-and-Mouth Disease. STUDIES IN FOOT AND
MOUTH DISEASE. Washington, National Academy of Sciences, 1969.
    Contains studies and reports by the Argentine-U.S. commission dealing with
this dreaded cattle disease.

35.
Arratia, Alejandro, and Carlos D. Hamilton, eds. DIEZ CUENTOS HISPANOAMERI-
CANOS, Illus. by Marjorie Auerbach. New York, Oxford University Press, 1958.
178p. illus. $2.95
   Includes short stories by Ricardo Palma, Rafael Delgado, Rubén Darío,
Baldomero Lillo, Horacio Quiroga, José Vasconcelos, Alfonso Hernández Catá.
Manuel Rojas, Jorge Luis Borges, and Arturo Uslar Pietri. The stories are
arranged chronologically and are designed to introduce the student to some
aspects of life in Spanish America. The introduction traces the history of
the Spanish-language short story from the 1335 romance Conde de Lucanor to
the present.

36.
Arreola, Juan José. CONFABULARIO TOTAL. Austin, University of Texas Press,
1964. 245p. illus. $1.95
   Arreola, born in 1918, is one of the principal novelists of contemporary
Mexico. Confabulario total appeared in 1962. In it the author shows his
penchant for fantastic stories and intellectual games rich in humor.

37.
Arriaga, Eduardo E. MORTALITY DECLINE AND ITS DEMOGRAPHIC EFFECTS IN LATIN
AMERICA. Foreword by Kingsley Davis. Berkeley, University of California,
Institute of International Studies, 1970. 232p. illus. $3.00
   New population data indicate that the mortality decline in Latin America
has been the fastest ever experienced by a major world region.

38.
----------. NEW LIFE TABLES FOR LATIN AMERICAN POPULATIONS IN THE NINETEENTH
AND TWENTIETH CENTURIES. Berkeley, University of California, Institute of
International Studies, 1968. 324p. tables. $2.75
   The author has compiled a very useful reference tool for the historian,
sociologist, political scientist, and economist, containing numerous tables
on vital statistics.

39.
Astuto, Philip Louis, and R. A. Leal. LATIN AMERICAN PROBLEMS. Jamaica,
N.Y., St. Johns University Press, 1970. 320p. $3.50
   A general study of contemporary Latin American problems.

40.
Atwater, James D., and Ruiz, Ramón Eduardo. OUT FROM UNDER: BENITO JUAREZ
AND MEXICO'S STRUGGLE FOR INDEPENDENCE. Illus. by Paul Hogar H. Garden
City, N.Y., Doubleday, 1969. 118p. illus. $2.95
   This book on Juárez and Mexican independence is intended for Chicano high
school and junior college students. It is one in a series of books which
aim to present the history of minority groups in the U.S. and their partici-
pation in the development of the country.

41.
Augier, F. R. and S. C. Gordon., eds. SOURCES OF WEST INDIAN HISTORY. A
COMPILATION OF WRITINGS OF HISTORICAL EVENTS IN THE WEST INDIES. New York,
Humanities Press, 1967. 308p. $1.25
   This selection of readings traces the history of the West Indies, partic-
ularly those areas where the English language is spoken, from 1492 to the
1950's.

42.
Azuela, Mariano. TWO NOVELS OF MEXICO: THE FLIES; THE BOSSES. Translated
from the Spanish by Lesley Byrd Simpson. Berkeley, University of California
Press, 1956. 194p. $1.25
   Originally published in Spanish as Las moscas (1918) and Los caciques
(1917), respectively, these are two remakable vignettes of the Mexican Revolution. They describe the people caught in the great social upheaval which
changed the course of Mexican history.

43.

----------. LOS DE ABAJO: NOVELA DE LA REVOLUCION MEXICANA. Edited by John
E. Englekirk and Lawrence B. Kiddle. New York, Appleton-Century-Crofts, 1966.
139p. fold. map. $2.45
     This is a Spanish edition of Azuela's classic novel first published in 1916
about the Mexican revolution. This edition contains notes and vocabulary.

44.

----------. THE UNDERDOGS: A NOVEL OF THE MEXICAN REVOLUTION. Translated by
E. Munguía, Jr. Foreword by Harriet de Onís. New York, New American Library,
1963. 151p. $0.75
     English translation of Los de abajo (1916), the great novel of the Mexican
Revolution. The novel covers the period between Madero's assassination and the
defeat of Pancho Villa's partisans in the battle of Celaya. Azuela presents
men and their lives with realism. His importance rests on being the founder
of the novel of the Revolution, yet those who judge Underdogs from a political
and not a literary point of view, considered it an anti-revolutionary work.

45.

Babian, Haig, and others. WORLD AREAS TODAY: LATIN AMERICA. New York, Harcourt, Brace and World, 1970. 100p. illus. $1.35
     This is a brief descriptive book about Latin America.

46.

Bachmura, Frank T., ed. HUMAN RESOURCES IN LATIN AMERICA; AN INTERDISCIPLINARY
FOCUS. Bloomington, Indiana University, Bureau of Business Research, 1968.
212p. $4.50
     The 1967 meeting of the Midwest Association for Latin American Studies
dealt with the human resources problem in Latin America. This volume contains
the papers delivered at the conference.

47.

Bakeless, John Edwin. THE EYES OF DISCOVERY: AMERICA AS SEEN BY THE FIRST
EXPLORERS. New York, Dover Publications, 1968. 439p. illus. $3.00
     This is a popularized description of North America as the first white men
saw it.

48.

Bannon, John Francis, ed. INDIAN LABOR IN THE SPANISH INDIES: WAS THERE
ANOTHER SOLUTION? Boston, Heath, 1966. 105p. (Problems in Latin American
civilization series) $2.25
     The editor has included essays by Charles Gibson, Bartolomé de las Casas,
Motolinia, Lewis Hanke, Lesley Byrd Simpson and others, dealing with pre-
Conquest labor practices, evolution of the post-Conquest labor system and
legislation to regulate Indian labor. The three interest groups studied are
the Crown, the Indians, and the colonists.

49.

----------. THE SPANISH CONQUISTADORES, MEN OR DEVILS? New York, Holt, Rinehart and Winston, 1966. 43p. (Source problems in world civilization) $0.95
     Contains a cross-section of selections, some from the writings of the Con-
quistadores and others from modern writers. The author attempts to show a
balanced picture of the 16th century explorers by presenting varied source
materials.

50.

Barager, Joseph. WHY PERON CAME TO POWER: THE BACKGROUND TO PERONISM IN
ARGENTINA. New York, Knopf, 1968. 274p. $2.75
     Includes a collection of essays on Argentine social and political history
by Ricardo Levene, James R. Scobie, Gino Germani, and others. The first
essay is taken from the writings of former Argentine president Domingo F.
Sarmiento. The last essay, by British historian George Pendle, present a re-
trospective view on the Peron era.

51.
Barbieri, Sante Uberto. LAND OF EL DORADO. New York, Friendship Press,
1961. 161p. illus. $1.50
    This is a study of the growth of Protestantism in Latin America.

52.
Barrenechea, Ana María. BORGES THE LABYRINTH MAKER. Edited and translated
by Robert Lima. New York, New York University Press, 1965. 175p. $1.95
    The author has added new materials to La expresión de la realidad en la
obra de Jorge Luis Borges (1957) co-authored with Borges. This work is a
perceptive analysis of Argentina's most gifted writer with special emphasis
on his approach to reality, symbolism, and transmutation of values.

53.
Batchelor, Courtnay Malcolm, ed. CUENTOS DE ACÁ Y ALLÁ. 2nd ed. Boston,
Houghton, Mifflin, 1968. 395p. $5.00
    Includes short stories by Juan Bosch, Vicente Blasco Ibañez, Manuel Rojas,
Rufino Blanco-Fombona, Juan Natalicio González, Gregorio López y Fuentes,
Azorín, and others. This is a useful book for college level advanced Spanish
courses.

54.
Bates, Henry W. THE NATURALIST ON THE RIVER AMAZON. Berkeley, University of
California Press, 1962. 462p. $2.45
    First published in 1863, in London, England, this is a lucid and interest-
ing account by an English naturalist of his 11 years of travel throughout the
Amazon region.

55.
Baughman, R. E. VIDA ABUNDANTE, Chicago, Moody Press, 1968. 150p. $0.75
    Translation of Abundant Jife.

56.
Beals, Carleton. NOMADS AND EMPIRE BUILDERS: NATIVE PEOPLES AND CULTURES OF
SOUTH AMERICA. New York, Citadel Press, 1965. 322p. illus. $2.25
    A general book on the Indians of South America written in a highly ro-
manticized manner. The author's polished literary style, however, fails to
compensate for the inaccuracy of much of his information.

57.
Beck, Warren A., and Ynez D. Haase. HISTORICAL ATLAS OF NEW MEXICO. Norman,
University of Oklahoma Press, 1969. 152p. maps $2.95
    In 62 maps with the accompanying text, a cartographer and a historian
trace the long history of New Mexico. The topics include Spanish and U.S.
expeditions, stagecoach and railroad lines, state and national parks as well
as geographical data.

58.
Beiler, Edna. TRES CASAS, TRES FAMILIAS, illustrated by Ezra Jack Keats.
New York, Friendship Press, 1964. 126p. illus. $2.25
    Three short stories about Spanish Americans, intended principally for high
school use.

59.
Bell, Wendell, ed. THE DEMOCRATIC REVOLUTION IN THE WEST INDIES: STUDIES IN
NATIONALISM, LEADERSHIP, AND THE BELIEF IN PROGRESS. Cambridge, Mass.,
Schenkman Pub. Co., 1967. 232p. illus., tables $3.95
    The results of a large research project of the West Indies Study Program,
University of California, Los Angeles, this is the first of a projected
four-volume set dealing with the upheavals and search for a national identity
as well economic survival of the West Indian islands.

60.
Bello, José Maria. A HISTORY OF MODERN BRAZIL, 1889-1964. Translated from the Portuguese by James L. Taylor with a new concluding chapter by Rollie W. Poppino. Stanford, Calif., Stanford University Press, 1966. 362p. $5.75
　　Translation of the 4th edition of História da República, 1889-1902 (1959), which is the basic political history on modern Brazil available in English. Professor Poppino's chapter entitled "Brazil since 1954" brings the book almost up to the present.

61.
Bemis, Samuel Flagg. THE LATIN AMERICAN POLICY OF THE UNITED STATES: AN HISTORICAL INTERPRETATION. New York, Norton, 1967. 470p. maps $3.45
　　The author traces the development of U.S.-Latin American relations from 1876 to the end of World War II. It was first published in 1943.

62.
Bennett, Wendell Clark, and Junius B. Bird. ANDEAN CULTURE HISTORY. Rev. ed. Garden City, N.Y., Natural History Press, 1964. 257p. illus., maps (American museum science books, B-9) $1.95
　　Originally published in 1947, this book reviews the archaeology of the Central Andes from early man to the Incas. It begins with a general discussion of South American archaeology and ethnology followed by a chronological review of the known archaeological cultures from Peru and northern Bolivia. Bird's contribution is an excellent exposition of the technology of Andean metallurgy, ceramics, and textiles. Includes a comprehensive bibliography.

63.
Benson, Elizabeth P. AN OLMEC FIGURE AT DUMBARTON OAKS. Washington, Dumbarton Oaks, 1971. 30p. illus. (Studies in pre-Columbian art and archaeology, 8) $2.00
　　This is an interesting study of an important Olmec figure.

64.
Benton, William, VOICE OF LATIN AMERICA. Rev. ed. New York, Harper & Row, 1965. 202p. illus., maps. $1.60
　　This is a thoughtful book about social conditions and politics in Latin America by a former coordinator of Inter-American Affairs. Includes a bibliography.

65.
Berle, Adolf A., Jr., LATIN AMERICA: DIPLOMACY AND REALITY. New York, Published for the Council on Foreign Relations by Harper and Row, 1962. 144p. $1.95
　　In this brief book, a long-time officer of the Department of State and student of inter-American affairs, discusses his understanding of Latin America's domestic and foreign policy problems.

66.
Bernal, Ignacio. MEXICAN WALL PAINTINGS OF THE MAYA AND AZTEC PERIODS. New York, New American Library, 1963. 24p. illus. 28 color plates. $0.95
　　Bernal has assembled an attractive edition of Aztec and Maya mural paintings, and has added an excellent explanatory text. The work includes a bibliography.

67.
-----------. MEXICO BEFORE CORTEZ: ART, HISTORY, LEGEND. Translated by Willis Barnstone. New York, Doubleday, 1963. 135p. illus. $1.45
　　This is a translation of Tenochtitlán en una isla (1959). The author focuses on the Toltec city of Tula and the Aztec city of Tenochtitlan, giving us a sharp insight into the spiritual and aesthetic qualities of Indian life prior to the arrival of the Spaniards.

68.
 ----------. THREE THOUSAND YEARS OF ART AND LIFE IN MEXICO AS SEEN IN THE
NATIONAL MUSEUM OF ANTHROPOLOGY OF MEXICO CITY. Translated by Carolyn B.
Czitrom. New York, New American Library, 1968. 216p. illus. $3.95
 An excellent guide to Mexico's outstanding National Museum of Anthropology.

69.
Bernstein, Harry. VENEZUELA AND COLOMBIA. Englewood Cliffs, N.J., Prentice-
Hall, 1964. 152p. maps. $1.95
 Owing to space limitation, the author had to limit coverage of the colonial
and national periods to some 80 pages per country, resulting in two compact,
barely-annotated essays. A slim bibliography is included.

70.
Bernstein, Marvin D., ed. FOREIGN INVESTMENT IN LATIN AMERICA: CASES AND
ATTITUDES. New York, Knopf, 1966. 256p. (Borzoi books on Latin America)
$1.95
 A well-chosen collection of 19 essays which analyze foreign investment in
Latin America during the last century and a half from the private-enterprise,
nationalist, economic as well as Marxist points of view. Includes a bibliog-
raphy.

71.
Bianchi, Los. CHILE IN PICTURES. Rev. ed. New York, Sterling Pub. Co.,
1966. 64p. illus., maps. $1.00
 The land, history, government, people, and economy of Chile are introduced in this illustrated volume.

72.
Bierck, Harold A. ed., LATIN AMERICAN CIVILIZATION: READINGS AND ESSAYS.
Boston, Allyn and Bacon, 1967. 438p. $4.95
 An attempt to present the student with readings and essays in Latin
American history that take him beyond the obvious and introduce him to
new views respecting a variety of economic, social and political problems.
The 33 selections range from the "colonial foundations" to "the contem-
porary scene." [Charles Fleener]

73.
Bingham, Hiram. LOST CITY OF THE INCAS: THE STORY OF MACHU PICCHU AND ITS
BUILDERS. New York, Atheneum, 1963. 240p. illus. $2.65
 First published in 1948, this is a popularized restatement of Bingham's
work on Machu Picchu and the neighboring sites in 1911-1915 with excellent
illustrations. The book contains no new archaeological material and the old
data have not been brought up to date.

74.
Blacker, Irwin R., ed. THE PORTABLE HAKLUYT'S VOYAGES. New York, Viking,
 1967. 522p. $1.85
 Letters, reports, official correspondence, diaries, logs and other first-
hand accounts constitute Hakluyt's Voyages. Richard Hakluyt's 1,700,000 word
compendium is basically an anthology of materials written by eminent
Elizabethans. The editor has chosen 49 selections. The editor's able introduction places the original work in historical perspective.

75.
Blair, Calvin P., Richard P. Schaedel and James H. Street. RESPONSIBILITIES
OF THE FOREIGN SCHOLAR TO THE LOCAL SCHOLARLY COMMUNITY: STUDIES OF U.S. RE-
SEARCH IN GUATEMALA, CHILE, AND PARAGUAY. New York, Education and World
Affairs, 1969. 112p. tables. $2.50
 Three scholars report on the nature and state of social science research
in Guatemala, Chile and Paraguay. Richard N. Adams, in the introduction,
outlines a set of recommendations that suggest the responsibilities of the
individual investigator to the community of scholarship. An essential work
for the students of the three nations surveyed. [Charles Fleener]

76.
Blakemore, Harold. LATIN AMERICA. New York, Oxford University Press, 1966. 128p. illus., maps. $1.40
An introductory survey that describes the geographic, social and historic characteristics of Latin America in terms of "the challenge of change." Includes a bibliography.

77.
Blanksten, George I. ARGENTINA AND CHILE. Consultant ed. Lindley J. Stiles. Boston, Ginn, 1969. 122p. illus. maps, ports. $1.60
A brief study of these two important countries of South America, contrasting the two societies and cultures.

78.
Bock, Philip K., ed. PEASANTS IN THE MODERN WORLD. Albuquerque, University of New Mexico Press, 1969. 173p. $2.45
Three of the essays included here deal exclusively with Hispanic topics. Eva and Robert Hunt explore the diverse use of rural Mexican courts by Indians and Mestizos. Charles Erasmus addresses himself to the effects of land and agrarian reform in Mexico, Venezuela and Bolivia. Edward Dozier provides an overview of the changes wrought in Mexican-American culture by the disappearance of the traditional village structure. [Charles Fleener]

79.
Boland, Charles Michael. THEY ALL DISCOVERED AMERICA. Maps and drawings by the author. New York, Pocket books, 1963. 430., illus., maps $0.75
First published in 1961, this is a popular and fictionalized account about the people who discovered America before Columbus.

80.
Bolívar, Simón. ESCRITOS POLITICOS. Philadelphia, Center for Curriculum Development, 1970. n.p. $1.20
Political writings of the South American hero of independence, Simón Bolívar.

81.
Bolton, Herbert Eugene. CORONADO, KNIGHT OF PUEBLOS AND PLAINS. Drawings by Margaret Fearnside. Albuquerque, University of New Mexico Press, 1964. 494p. illus. $3.45
First published in 1949, this is a reconstruction of the Coronado expedition of 1540, showing the hardships endured by the explorers and the discoveries they made.

82.
------------------------. THE PADRE ON HORSEBACK: A SKETCH OF EUSEBIO FRANCISCO KINO, S. J., APOSTLE TO THE PIMAS. Chicago, Loyola University Press, 1963. 91p. (The American reprint series) $2.25
Recounts the life and forty expeditions of Eusebio Kino, Jesuit apostle to the Indians of New Spain's northwest frontier. John F. Bannon provides a knowledgeable introduction to this edition. The monograph was first published in 1932.

83.
------------------------. WIDER HORIZONS OF AMERICAN HISTORY. Notre Dame, Ind., Notre Dame University Press, 1967. 191p. $2.25
Contains four of Professor Bolton's most widely discussed essays: "The epic of greater America," his tentative panoramic synthesis of Western hemisphere history; "Defensive Spanish expansion and the significance of the borderlands" which sketches the meeting of two civilizations in the Southwest; "The mission as a frontier institution" which interprets the mission as an economic and socio-political institution, as well as a religious one; and "The Black robes of New Spain," which evaluates the work of the French and Spanish Jesuits in North America.

84.
Boorstein, Edward. THE ECONOMIC TRANSFORMATION OF CUBA: A FIRST-HAND
ACCOUNT. New York, Monthly Review Press, 1969. 303p. tables. $3.45
    The author worked from 1960 to 1963 in the top planning agencies of revo-
lutionary Cuba. Here he discusses the problems of running a socialist
economy. The author's close association with Che Guevara gave him an inside
view of the Castro regime.

85.
Borges, Jorge Luis. BORGES: SUS MEJORES PÁGINAS. Edited by Miguel Enguídanos.
Englewood Cliffs, N.J., Prentice-Hall 1970. 250p. port. $3.95
    The editor has selected essays, short stories, and poems by the great
Argentine author.

86.
----------, and Richard Burgin. CONVERSATIONS WITH JORGE LUIS BORGES. New
York, Avon, 1970. 144p. $1.65
    Burgin is a young graduate student who interviewed the Argentine writer and
philosopher with a tape recorder. The dialogue is warm, witty, and revealing
of the writer and his art.

87.
----------. DREAMTIGERS. Translated by Mildred Vinson Boyer and Harold
Morland. Pref. by Victor Lange. Introd. by Miguel Enguídanos. New York,
Dutton, 1970. 260p. $1.75
    The confrontation of the writer's inner life with reality is the theme of
this fascinating book containing Borges' poems, stories, and sketches. The
original Spanish edition is entitled El Hacedor.

88.
----------, et al. DUTTON REVIEW NO. 1. New York, Dutton, 1970. 357p.
$2.75
    This is an uneven selection of modern world poetry, essays, and short
stories, the best of which is Borges' "The Intruder."

89.
----------. FICCIONES. Edited by Anthony Kerrigan. New York, Grove Press,
1962. 174p. $2.45
    Includes Tlön, Uqbar, Orbis Tertius, El jardin de los senderos que se
bifurcan, La muerte y la brújula, and other stories.

90.
----------. LABYRINTHS: SELECTED STORIES AND OTHER WRITINGS. Translated and
edited by Donald A. Yates and James E. Irby. Pref. by André Maurois. New
York, New Directions, 1964. 260p. $1.95
    Contains stories, sketches, and richly inquisitive essays by a powerful
thinker endowed with a subtle sense of humor. Maurois' preface skillfully
analyzes Borges' literary world.

91.
----------. OTHER INQUISITIONS: 1937-1952. Translated by Ruth L. C. Simms.
Introd. by James E. Irby. New York, Washington Square Press, 1966. 205p.
$0.90
    The first English translation of Otras inquisiciones (1952), a collection
of graceful and outstanding essays. These essays analyze leading literary
figures such as Cervantes, Coleridge, Whitman, Hawthorne, and Shaw, and probe
the paradoxes and contradictions in their writings and actions.

92.
----------. OTHER INQUISITIONS: 1937-1952. Translated by Ruth L. C. Simms.
New York, Simon and Schuster, 1971. 205p. $1.95
    These outstanding essays range in time and place from Omar Khayyám to
Joseph Conrad. Also see review above.

11

93.
----------. A PERSONAL ANTHOLOGY. Translated by Anthony Kerrigan.
New York, Grove Press, 1969. 210p. $1.95
   Antología personal (1961) contains the author's own choice of his
favorite stories, essays, poetry, and parables. Included are the following
short stories: The aleph, Death and the compass, Funes, the memorious, and
A new refutation of time. These stories by Borges have no match in Spanish-
American literature.

94.
Bourne, Edward Gaylord. SPAIN IN AMERICA, 1450-1580. New York, Barnes and
Noble, 1962. 366p. $2.25
   Published originally in 1904, this is an excellent source for the early
colonial period. A detailed index and bibliography have been added to this
edition. Readers who wish to extend their acquaintance with the literature
of this topic should examine the section edited by Howard F. Cline and C. E.
Nowell in the American Historical Association's Guide to Historical
literature (New York, Macmillan, 1961).

95.
Bourne, Richard. POLITICAL LEADERS OF LATIN AMERICA. Baltimore, Penguin,
1969. 306p. $1.65
   Analyzes the careers and personalities of Che Guevara, Alfredo Stroessner,
Eduardo Frei, Eva Perón, Juscelino Kubitschek and Carlos Lacerda, all of
whom have played major roles in shaping contemporary Latin American History.

96.
Boxer, Charles R. THE GOLDEN AGE OF BRAZIL: 1695-1750. Berkeley, University of California Press, 1962. 443p. illus. $2.45
   This is a highly literate and useful presentation of Brazil's most interesting colonial decades. While not comprehensive, it is a thorough work
by a well-known Brazilianist. Included are appendixes on economic, social,
and political materials.

97.
Boyd, Maurice. TARASCAN MYTHS AND LEGENDS. Fort Worth, Texas Christian
University Press, 1969. 82p. illus. maps   (Texas Christian University
monographs in history and culture, 4) $3.50
   This imaginative history starts with the pre-Columbian period when the
Tarascans of western Mexico were building a powerful empire. At this time
myths and legends appeared. The Spanish conquest provided a source for new
legends, many of them based on the Tarascans' hatred of the Aztecs and
Spaniards. The legends recorded provide a useful source of oral history.
Tarascan design motifs illustrate the legends.

98.
Brand, Donald Dilworth. MEXICO: LAND OF SUNSHINE & SHADOW. Princeton, N.J.,
Van Nostrand, 1966. 159p. 5 maps $1.75

99.
Brand, W. IMPRESSIONS OF HAITI. New York, Humanities Press, 1968. 77p.
maps $2.75
   The author was member of an OAS mission to Haiti concerned with demography in 1962. This essay is primarily concerned with his major interest,
Haiti's population, its size, distribution and economic activity. The
author also discusses the state of Haitian education, housing and other
social topics. [Charles Fleener]

100.
Brandi, Karl. THE EMPEROR CHARLES V; THE GROWTH AND DESTINY OF A MAN AND
OF A WORLD EMPIRE. Translated by C. V. Wedgewood. New York, Humanities
Press, 1968. 655p. $3.75
   This excellent biography of Charles V stresses his role as emperor,
rather than as king of Spain. Unfortunately for the scholar, the annota-
tions and bibliography of the original German edition are not included here.

101.
Brau, Maria. ISLAND IN THE CROSSROADS; THE HISTORY OF PUERTO RICO. Illus.
by Herbert Steinberg. New York, Doubleday, 1968. 116p. illus. map $1.45
A general history of Puerto Rico with attractive illustrations.

102.
Brayer, Herbert O. PUEBLO INDIAN LAND GRANTS OF THE RIO ABAJO NEW MEXICO.
Albuquerque, University of New Mexico Press, 1969. 135p. map $1.00
Examines Spanish land grants of the Rio Abajo area of New Mexico.

102A.
Brebner, John Bartlet. THE EXPLORERS OF NORTH AMERICA, 1492-1806. New York,
World Pub. Co., 1964. 431p. maps $2.95
Mexico dominates the first chapters as the author draws together as a
related whole the explorations which revealed the general character of the
North American continent.

103.
Brill, William H. MILITARY INTERVENTION IN BOLIVIA: THE OVERTHROW OF PAZ
ESTENSSORO AND THE MNR. Washington, Institute for the Comparative Study of
Political Systems, 1967. 68p. $2.00
A survey of the military coup which overthrew President Paz Estenssoro in
1964. The information itself is factual, but the analysis is too brief for
the specialist. Intended for the generalist.

104.
Brisk, William J. THE DILEMMA OF A MINISTATE: ANGUILLA. Chapel Hill, University of North Carolina Press, 1969. 93p. tables $2.00
Anguilla, in the British West Indies, is three miles wide and 16 miles
long with a population of 5,500. Its thrust for independence is examined
in this thorough study.

105.
Brooks, Rhoda, and Earle Brooks. THE BARRIOS OF MANTA; A PERSONAL ACCOUNT
OF THE PEACE CORPS IN ECUADOR. New York, New American Library, 1967. 280p.
illus. $0.75
This is an interesting account by a returned Peace Corps volunteer from
Ecuador. Manta is a small Ecuadorean fishing village and this warm ac-
count is full of the humor, frustrations, victories, and defeats of Peace
Corps life.

106.
Brotherston, Gordon, and Mario Vargas Llosa, eds. SEVEN STORIES FROM
SPANISH-AMERICA. New York, Pergamon Press, 1968. 98p. $2.50
The most influential young writers have been included in this anthology,
among them: Gabriel García Márquez Julio Cortázar, Juan Rulfo, Mario
Benedetti, Alejo Carpentier, and others. Excellent introductions precede
each story.

107.
--------------------, ed. SPANISH-AMERICAN MODERNISTA POETS; A CRITICAL
ANTHOLOGY. Selected, with an introd. by Gordon Brotherston. New York,
Pergamon Press, 1968. 171p. $3.00
Modernismo initiated at the end of the 19th century the contemporary
period in Spanish-American literature, superseding romanticism. The editor
has included the most representative modernist poets.

108.
Brower, Kenneth, ed. GALÁPAGOS; THE FLOW OF WILDERNESS. New York,
Ballantine, 1971. 2v. illus. map $3.95 each
The text includes excerpts from Charles Darwin, Herman Melville, and
others. It also analyzes what the islands mean to the world's ecosystems
and to the natural sciences. Beautiful illustrations enhance the text.

109.
Brunnschweiler, Tamara. CURRENT PERIODICALS: A SELECT BIBLIOGRAPHY IN THE
AREA OF LATIN AMERICAN STUDIES. East Lansing, Michigan State University
Press, 1968. 100p. $2.00
This bibliography is based on the Michigan State University Library
holdings. Preference was accorded to serial titles in agriculture, science,
technology, and the applied sciences. Included are 740 unannotated entries,
as well as an index classifying materials by countries.

110.
Brushwood, John S. MEXICO IN ITS NOVEL: A NATION'S SEARCH FOR IDENTITY.
Austin, University of Texas Press, 1970. 292p. $2.45
The author analyzes Mexican reality as seen through the nation's novels.
He presents the Mexican novel as a cultural and historical phenomenon.

111.
Bullock, Alice. LIVING LEGENDS OF THE SANTA FE COUNTRY. Denver, Colo.,
Green Mountain Press, 1970. 144p. illus., map. $2.45
The author outlines the history of folktales originating from Indian and
Spanish-American cultures. 104 photos and one map supplement the text.

112.
Bullrich, Francisco. NEW DIRECTIONS IN LATIN AMERICAN ARCHITECTURE.
New York, Braziller, 1969. 128p. illus. $2.95
A succinct study of new trends in Latin American architecture by a well-
known Argentine architect. He points out and describes the dynamic
architectural milieu in Brazil, Mexico, and Argentina. Handsome black and
white photographs enhance the text.

113.
Burland, Cottie Arthur. GODS OF MEXICO. New York, Putnam, 1967. 219p.
illus. maps. $1.85
Describes the principal archaeological sites which had been used for
worship.

114.
Burma, John H., comp. MEXICAN-AMERICANS IN THE UNITED STATES. New York,
Schenkman, 1970. 450p. $4.95
Offers a detailed coverage of the social, political, and behavioral
patterns of Mexican-Americans. Several articles deal with the relations
of Mexican-Americans with other minority groups.

115.
Burnett, Ben G., _and_ Moisés Poblete Troncoso. RISE OF THE LATIN AMERICAN
LABOR MOVEMENT. New York, Bookman Associates, 1960. 179p. $1.75
This is a valuable study of labor movements in Latin America.

116.
Burns, E. Bradford, _ed._ A DOCUMENTARY HISTORY OF BRAZIL. New York, Knopf,
1966. 398p. $2.95
This is a useful collection of basic documents, sometimes marred by
simplistic introductions. The documents on Dom Pedro II's "abdication" may
astound many readers. Includes a bibliography.

117.
--------------------. NATIONALISM IN BRAZIL: A HISTORICAL SURVEY. New York,
Praeger, 1968. 158p. $1.95
Defines the concept of nationalism and explains the formation of "19th
century defensive nationalism." There is a good chapter on the bases of
contemporary nationalism, another one entitled "Getúlio Vargas and economic
nationalism," and a discussion of the impact that literary figures have had
on Brazilian nationalism.

118
Burr, Richard N. BY REASON OR FORCE. CHILE AND THE BALANCING OF POWER IN
SOUTH AMERICA, 1830-1905. Berkeley, University of California Press, 1967.
322p. map $3.50
Studies Chile's growth from disorder to authority in the international
affairs of 19th century South America. The author explores Chilean foreign
policy with regard to her powerful neighbors and explains her shift from a
non-interventionist role to that of an aggressive regulator of the balance
of power in her continental sphere. Winner of the 1965 Bolton Prize.
[Charles Fleener]

119.
Busey, James L. LATIN AMERICAN POLITICAL INSTITUTIONS AND PROCESSES.
New York, Random House, 1964. 184p. $2.95
This is a succinct study of Latin American political institutions.

120.
--------------. NOTES ON COSTA RICAN DEMOCRACY. Boulder, University of
Colorado Press, 1967. 84p. map $2.50
After a careful analysis of the political features of Costa Rican democ-
racy, Professor Busey examines the economic conditions of the country.

121.
Bushnell, David. EDUARDO SANTOS AND THE GOOD NEIGHBOR; 1938-1942.
Gainesville, University of Florida Press, 1967. 128p. tables $3.75
Studies in depth Colombian-U.S. relations during the administration of
Eduardo Santos. It is largely a discussion of political, military, and
economic contacts at the governmental level.

122.
--------------. LIBERATOR: SIMON BOLIVAR. New York, Knopf, 1970. 218p.
map, port. $2.75
The author presents a stimulating and well-researched study about Bolivar.

123.
Bushnell, Geoffrey H. S. ANCIENT ARTS OF THE AMERICA. New York, Praeger,
1965. 287p. illus., maps $3.95
This is a thorough outline of pre-Columbian art. Includes a good bibliography. A basic source for art and ethnohistory.

124.
----------------------. THE FIRST AMERICANS: THE PRE-COLUMBIAN CIVILIZA-
TIONS. New York, McGraw-Hill, 1968. 144p. illus. $2.95
This handsome volume on the pre-Columbian civilizations of America
describes the significant stages of the beginning, growth, and apex of the
different cultures. Beautiful illustrations enhance the text.

125.
----------------------. PERU. Rev. ed. New York, Praeger, 1963. 246p.
illus., maps. $3.45
The author intended this excellent summary of Peruvian archaeology for
the general reader.

126.
Butterfield, Marvin E. JERÓNIMO DE AGUILAR, CONQUISTADOR. University,
University of Alabama Press, 1969. 54p. $2.00
The author presents a brief biography of one of the Conquistadors who
accompanied Hernán Cortés in the Conquest of Mexico. He served as one
element in the interpreting and intelligence team composed by Doña Marina,
Cortés, and Jerónimo.

127.
Caballero Calderón, Eduardo. EL CRISTO DE ESPALDAS. Edited by Roberto C.
Esquenazi-Mayo. New York, Macmillan, 1967. 153p. $2.50
   The Colombian novelist Caballero Calderón wrote this work in 1952 about
a recently ordained young priest who began to work in a small town parish
lost in the Andes. In less than five days he was aware of all the infamy,
ugliness, injustice, and violence that the people suffered.

128.
California, University. Los Angeles. DEMOCRATIC REVOLUTION IN THE WEST
INDIES. Edited by W. Bell. Cambridge, Mass., Schenkman Pub. Co., 1969.
284p. $3.95
   This is an incisive study of democratic movements in the West Indies.

129.
California (State). Association for Supervision and Curriculum Development.
A STUDY OF MEXICO AND CENTRAL AMERICA. Menlo Park, Calif., Pacific Coast
Publishers, 1965. 108p. illus. $2.00
   This source book presents basic information for the development of units
concerned with Mexico and Central America. It is intended for teachers of
social studies. [Charles Fleener]

130.
Calvert, Peter. LATIN AMERICA: INTERNAL CONFLICT AND INTERNATIONAL PEACE.
New York, St. Martin's Press, 1969. 231p. maps. $2.95
   Presents a chronological outline of the political and diplomatic history
of Latin America in this century. [Charles Fleener]

131.
Campa, Arthur Leon. BIBLIOGRAPHY OF SPANISH FOLKLORE IN NEW MEXICO.
Alburquerque, University of New Mexico Press, 1930, 28p. $1.00
   A very useful and interesting bibliography of the rich Spanish folklore
in New Mexico.

132.
Campos, G. G. CAMILO TORRES, LE CURÉ GUERILLERO. Port Washington, N.Y.,
Paris Publications, 1970. 302p. $4.30
   A sympathetic book about the Colombian priest and guerrilla fighter.

133.
Cancian, Frank. ECONOMICS AND PRESTIGE IN A MAYA COMMUNITY; THE RELIGIOUS
CARGO SYSTEM IN ZINACANTAN. Stanford, Calif., Stanford University Press, 1969.
238p. illus. maps $2.95
   This is a penetrating study of the religious hierarchy of an Indian
municipio in the Highland Maya area of Southern Mexico. The "cargo system"
provides one of the keys to the understanding of the social, religious and
economic systems of these Indian communities. Includes a selective bibliography.

134.
Canton, Wilberto L. NOSOTROS SOMOS DIOS: PIEZA EN DOS ACTOS. Edited by
Samuel Trifilo, and Louis Soto-Ruiz, New York, Harper & Row, 1966. 158p.
$3.25
   An annotated version of this outstanding contemporary Mexican play-
wright's drama.

135.
Carter, E. Dale, ed, ANTOLOGÍA DEL REALISMO MÁGICO. New York, Odyssey
Press, 1970. 256p. $2.50
   This college text contains stories written by Argentine, Mexican, and
Cuban authors.

136.
------------, Jr. and Joe Bas, eds. CUENTOS ARGENTINOS DE MISTERIO.
New York, Appleton-Century-Crofts, 1968. 112p. $1.95
   This is a textbook edition of Argentine mystery stories. It includes
stories by Silvina Ocampo, Manuel Peyrou, W.I. Eisen, Rodolfo J. Walsh,
Enrique Anderson-Imbert, and Jorge Luis Borges. The authors are all con-
temporary and the stories have all been published recently.

137.
Carter, William E. AYMARA COMMUNITIES AND THE BOLIVIAN AGRARIAN REFORM.
Gainesville, University of Florida Press, 1964. 90p. $2.00
   This is an interesting study of Bolivia's agrarian reform program as it
affects the Aymara Indians. The family and social structure of the Aymara
communities receives special emphasis, and is contrasted with that of the
landed estates. It is a very useful analysis with a good bibliography.

138.
------------. NEW LANDS AND OLD TRADITIONS: KEKCHI CULTIVATORS IN THE
GUATEMALAN LOWLANDS. Gainesville, University of Florida Press, 1969. 149p.
illus., map $3.75
   This is a study of agricultural practices in the Guatemalan lowlands.

139.
Castañeda, Carlos. THE TEACHINGS OF DON JUAN: A YAQUI WAY OF KNOWLEDGE.
New York, Ballantine Books, 1969. 195p. $0.95
   An account and analysis of the author's apprenticeship to a Yaqui
Sorcerer in Arizona and Sonora in 1961-65. Interesting points are the
rigorous discipline involved in the preparation and use of hallucinogenic
plants and the extraordinary force and leadership displayed by Don Juan
as a guide and teacher. Castañeda explains the cohesion and logic of the
Yaquis' world view.

140.
Castedo, Leopoldo. A HISTORY OF LATIN AMERICAN ART AND ARCHITECTURE FROM
PRE-COLUMBIAN TIMES TO THE PRESENT. New York, Praeger, 1969. 330p. illus.,
maps $4.95
   This well-researched volume traces over 3,000 years of Latin American art
and architecture, emphasizing the fusion of Indian, African, and European
elements which eventually formed a very unique style. Many illustrations,
some in color, enhance the text.

141.
Castells Capurro, Enrique. GAUCHOS: PRENDAS Y COSTUMBRES. Introd. by
Serafín García. New York, George Wittenborn, 1960. 2p. 26 plates (part
col.) $6.00
   This is an attractively illustrated book about the gauchos' clothing and
their life style.

142.
Castro, Josué de. THE BLACK BOOK OF HUNGER. Boston, Beacon Press, 1967.
161p. illus. $1.95
   Studies poverty in Brazil.

143.
------------. DEATH IN THE NORTHEAST: POVERTY AND REVOLUTION IN THE
NORTHEAST OF BRAZIL. New York, Random House, 1965. 247p. $1.95
   The problem of land use and land ownership is the focus of a short and quite
powerful book. Dr. Castro, a leading Brazilian man of public affairs, does
not pretend to be objective; as a nordestino he has a specific view to state.
the original appeared as Sete palmos de terra e um caixão (1965). [HLAS 29:
6413]

144.
-----------------., et al. LATIN AMERICAN RADICALISM: A DOCUMENTARY REPORT
ON THE LEFT AND NATIONAL MOVEMENTS. New York, Random House, 1970. 656p.
illus. $2.45
    Essays by prominent thinkers about the various radical movements in Latin
America.

145.
Castro Ruz, Fidel. CASTRO SPEAKS ON UNEMPLOYMENT. New York, Pioneer
Publications, 1967. 30p. $0.25

146.
-----------------. FIDEL CASTRO DENOUNCES BUREAUCRACY AND SECTARIANISM:
Speech of March 26, 1962. Pref. By H. Ring. New York, Pioneer Publishers,
1967. $0.50

147.
-----------------. FIDEL CASTRO SPEAKS. Edited by Martin Kenner and James
Petras. New York, Grove Press, 1970. 299p. $1.45
    The editors have arranged Castro's speeches in a topical rather than a
chronological sequence. They concentrate on the 1966-1968 period when
Castro was increasingly concerned with armed struggle, revolution, and the
vision of a communist society organized without the need for money. Some
1959 speeches are included.

148.
-----------------. FIDEL CASTRO'S TRIBUTE TO CHE GUEVARA. New York,
Pioneer Publishers, 1969. 31p. $0.25
    This is the text of Fidel Castro's speech eulogizing his old friend and
co-revolutionary.

149.
-----------------. HISTORY WILL ABSOLVE ME. Introd. by K. S. Karol.
New York, Grossman, 1968. 109p. map. $1.50
    On October 16, 1953, Fidel Castro delivered this speech in "self-defense
and explanation" for his involvement in the July 26, 1953 attack on the
Moncada Barracks of Santiago, Cuba. He presents a fiery indictment of
Batista's regime and outlines a program for reforms in Cuba.

150.
-----------------. A NEW STAGE IN THE ADVANCE OF CUBAN SOCIALISM. New York,
Pioneer Publishers, 1968. 48p. $0.50
    An official Cuban translation of a speech delivered by Castro on April
19, 1968, commemorating the seventh anniversary of the Bay of Pigs (Playa
Giron) invasion. [Charles Fleener]

151.
-----------------. NEW STAGE IN THE ADVANCE OF CUBAN SOCIALISM. Speech of
April 19, 1968. New York, Pioneer Publishers, 1969. 34p. $0.50

152.
-----------------. REFORM OR REVOLUTION. New York, Pioneer Publishers, 1970.
31p. $0.35

153.
-----------------. THE REVOLUTION MUST BE A SCHOOL OF UNFETTERED THOUGHT.
New York, Pioneer Publishers, 1963. $0.25.
    Text of a speech given at the University of Havana, March 13, 1962, by
Fidel Castro.

154.
-----------------. SECOND DECLARATION OF HAVANA. New York. Pioneer Publishers, 1962. 33p. $0.35
    A speech given on February 4, 1962, in reply to the Punta del Este
decision to exclude the Castro regime from the OAS.

155.
----------------. THOSE WHO ARE NOT REVOLUTIONARY FIGHTERS CANNOT BE CALLED
COMMUNISTS. New York, Pioneer Publishers, 1968. 72p. $0.75
    This is a speech delivered by Castro at the University of Havana, March
13, 1967. Among his targets are the conventional Communist parties of Latin
America and, the "evolutionary" policies of the Soviet Union.[Charles Fleener]

156.
Catlin, Stanton Loomis, and Terence Grieder. THE ART OF LATIN AMERICA SINCE
INDEPENDENCE. New York, October House, 1965. 246p. illus. $8.50
    The authors present an attractively illustrated history of Latin American
art since Independence.

157.
Cesaire, Aimée. THE TRAGEDY OF KING CHRISTOPHE. Translated by Ralph Manheim.
New York, Grove Press, 1970. 96p. $1.95
    Aimée Cesaire, the celebrated black poet from Martinique, presents here
the epic of independence of a colony and a psychological profile of Henri
Christophe, the ex-slave and cook, who at the beginning of the 19th century
became king of Haiti.

158.
Chase, Gilbert. A GUIDE TO THE MUSIC OF LATIN AMERICA. 2d ed. rev. and enl.
A joint publication of the Pan American Union and the Library of Congress.
Washington, Pan American Union, 1962. 411p. $1.50
    This is a useful bibliography first published in 1945 as Guide to Latin
American music. This edition has been enlarged and brought up to date.

159.
Chevalier, François. LAND AND SOCIETY IN COLONIAL MEXICO: THE GREAT HACIENDA.
Edited by Lesley Bird Simpson. Translated by Alvin Eustis. Berkeley,
University of California Press, 1970. 334p. map. $2.65
    The central theme of this important work, which first appeared in 1952 as
La formation des grands domains au Méxique, is the evolution of a landed
aristocracy at a time when little progress was made in any other aspect of
colonial life. Editing has deleted voluminous footnotes.

160.
Chommie, John C. eds. et al. EL DERECHO DE LOS ESTADOS UNIDOS: New York,
Oceana Publications, 1963. 3v. $15.00
    This is a compendium of U.S. law intended for Spanish speakers.

161.
Cleaves, Peter S. DEVELOPMENTAL PROCESSES IN CHILEAN LOCAL GOVERNMENT.
Berkeley, University of California, Institute of International Studies, 1969.
63p.
    This monograph studies the relationship between national and local govern-
ment in Chile. The reform objectives of the Christian Democratic administration of President Eduardo Frei are also analyzed.

162.
Cline, Howard Francis. MEXICO: REVOLUTION TO EVOLUTION, 1940-1960. New York,
Oxford University Press, 1963. 374p. $1.95
    Published in 1962, this work describes the character, strength, and
structure of the Mexican labor movement. It points out that the labor movement is a product of the Revolution and is deeply interwoven with its goals.
As a co-partner in the Revolution, the labor movement must necessarily accept
limitations upon its claims for increased benefits with the government acting
as final arbiter between labor and management. Contains an excellent bibliography.

163.
———————————————————. THE UNITED STATES AND MEXICO. Rev. and enl. ed.
New York, Atheneum, 1963. 484p. maps. (Atheneum paperbacks, 40) $2.45
    An especially important book on Mexico since 1910. The author stresses
the need to study Mexico from the point of view of the population, region-
alism, and industrialization rather than the traditional national political
interpretation. The chapters on the Revolution and the period since 1934
are outstanding. Originally published in 1953, this edition includes a new
preface, and epilogue entitled "A decade of developments, 1952-1962," and
an updated bibliography.

164.
Clissold, Stephen. LATIN AMERICA: A CULTURAL OUTLINE. New York, Harper
and Row, 1966. 160p. $1.60
    This is an interpretation of the literature and thought of Latin
America from the colonial period to the present. Includes a bibliography.

165.
Coe, Michael D. THE MAYA. New York, Praeger, 1966. 252p. illus. maps.
$3.95
    An excellent survey of Maya civilization with emphasis on the
achievements of the classic period. The rise, development, and fall of
Maya culture is integrated with a description of Mayan life and thought.
Excellent plates and drawings illustrate the volume.

166.
———————————————. MEXICO. New York, Praeger, 1966. 245p. illus., maps,
tables. $3.45
    Concise, well illustrated general account of pre-Hispanic culture
history of central Mexico. Contains considerable material on late pre-
Hispanic and Contact culture of the area, derived from standard primary
and secondary sources. The hard-cover edition was published in 1962.
Includes a bibliography.

167.
Cohen, John Michael, ed. THE FOUR VOYAGES OF CHRISTOPHER COLUMBUS.
Baltimore, Penguin Books, 1969. 320p. maps. $1.75
    The subtitle aptly describes this volume: "Being his own log-book,
letters and dispatches with connecting narrative drawn from the life
of the Admiral by his son Hernando Colon and other contemporary
historians."

168.
———————————————————, ed. LATIN AMERICAN WRITING TODAY. Baltimore, Penguin
Books, 1967. 267p. $1.25
    A varied selection of the most outstanding contemporary literary figures
of Latin America such as Jorge Luis Borges, Alejo Carpentier, Gabriela
Mistral, Julio Cortázar, Carlos Fuentes, Juan Rulfo, Gabriel García
Márquez, Pablo Neruda, and others, The selection shows a vigorous,
independent, and imaginative literature.

169.
———————————————————, ed. WRITERS IN THE NEW CUBA. Harmondsworth, England,
Penguin Books, 1967. 191p. $1.25
    This anthology includes 14 short stories, a short play, and 11 poems,
written by Cubans between 1959 and 1965. The editor has visited Cuba in
1965 and has taken part in awarding a literary prize of the Casa de las
Américas. He is quite familiar with contemporary Cuban literature.

170.
Cohn, Arthur. THE COLLECTOR'S TWENTIETH-CENTURY MUSIC IN THE WESTERN
HEMISPHERE. Philadelphia, Lippincott, 1961. 256p. $1.95
    This is a survey of contemporary music in the Americas, although a
large part deals with the United States, the works of Carlos Chávez,
Alberto Ginastera, Silvestre Revueltas, and Heitor Vill-Lobos are also in-
cluded. Lists long-playing records of the composers' music.

171.
Cole, Hubert, CHRISTOPHE, KING OF HAITI. New York, Viking Press, 1969.
308p. illus. maps. $2.45
   A sympathetic study of the New World's first crowned King, Henry I of
Haiti. The bloody wars of liberation, out of which rose an independent
French-speaking black nation, serve as the backdrop for this well-researched
book.

172.
Coleman, Alexander, ed. CINCO MAESTROS: CUENTOS MODERNOS DE HISPANOAMERICA.
New York, Harcourt, Brace, & World. 1969. 318p. ports. $4.50
   Includes short stories by Jorge Luis Borges, Julio Cortázar, Juan Rulfo,
José Donoso, and Gabriel García Márquez.

173.
--------------------. OTHER VOICES: A STUDY OF THE LATE POETRY OF LUIS
CERNUDA. Chapel Hill, University of North Carolina Press, 1969. 185p.
(Studies in the romance languages and literatures, 81) $3.50
   The author studies the post- 1936 poetry of Luis Cernuda. The poet's
approach is "the suppression of the subjective in the poetry, and the con-
comitant elaboration of objective, 'dramatic' voices which define the
trajectory between the first and third persons, the lyric and the dramatic."
Includes a bibliography.

174.
Coleman, William J. LATIN-AMERICAN CATHOLICISM. A SELF EVALUATION.
Maryknoll, N.Y., Maryknoll Publications, 1958. 105p. $1.00
   In 1953 an Interamerican Catholic Action Week was held in Chimbote,
Peru, attended by representatives of most of the Catholic Action organi-
zations of Latin America. The meeting produced a self-critique of Latin
American Catholicism. In this volume Father Coleman attempts to acquaint
North American Catholics with the state of the Church in the Southern
hemisphere.

175.
Colford, William E., ed. CLASSIC TALES FROM SPANISH AMERICA. Woodbury,
N.Y., Barron's Educational Series, 1962. 210p. $1.50
   A collection of 21 Spanish-American short stories in English trans-
lation, by Manuel Rojas, Ricardo Palma, Rubén Darío, Amado Nervo, Leopoldo
Lugones, and others. Each story is preceded by an individual commentary
on the author and his work.

176.
Collier, John. INDIANS OF THE AMERICAS. Abridged ed. New York, New
American Library, 1968. 191p. (Mentor, MP-496) $0.75
   The author spent twelve years as Commissioner of Indian Affairs for the
U.S. Government. The history of the treatment of the American Indian is
reviewed and a policy is outlined which is based on wide experience and a
wealth of facts. The first half of the book deals with Indians of Latin
America.

177.
Collver, O. Andrew. BIRTH RATES IN LATIN AMERICA. NEW ESTIMATES OF
HISTORICAL TRENDS AND FLUCTUATIONS. Introd. by K. Davis. Berkeley,
University of California Press, 1969. 187p. illus. $2.50
   This is a very useful study of demographic trends in Latin America
viewed from a historical perspective.

178.
Colonnese, Louis M., ed. HUMAN RIGHTS AND THE LIBERATION OF MAN IN THE
AMERICAS. Notre Dame, Ind., University of Notre Dame Press, 1970. 278p.
illus. $3.95
   The 21 papers included in this volume were presented at the 6th annual
Catholic Inter-American Cooperation Program (CICOP) Conference held in
New York, January, 1969. The contributors range from Helder Pessoa Cámara,
Archbishop of Recife, and Cardinal Dearden of Detroit, to Robert J.
Alexander, and Victor Alba.

179.
Columbus, Christopher. FOUR VOYAGES TO THE NEW WORLD: LETTERS AND
SELECTED DOCUMENTS. Translated and edited by R.H. Major; bilingual ed.
Introd. by John E. Fagg. New York, Corinth Books, 1961. 240p. (The
American experience series, AE5) $1.75
    Originally published under the title Select letters of Christopher
Columbus, with other original documents relating to his four voyages to the
New World (1847), this edition contains seven documents in English trans-
lation and in the original Spanish and Latin. New introduction by John E.
Fagg.

180.
Concheff, B., ed. PAN-AMERICANA: A PAGEANT OF THE AMERICAS. Skokie, Ill.,
National Textbook, Corp., 1969. 120p. $2.00 5 or more ea. $1.60
    Descriptive essays on the countries of the Americas and their social
customs.

181.
Considine, John J. ed. THE RELIGIOUS DIMENSION IN THE NEW LATIN AMERICA.,
Notre Dame, Ind., Fides, 1966. 238p. $2.95
    The articles are divided into three sections, "contemporary religious
challenges," "activation of religious personnel," and "the new pastoral
apostolate." Clerics, both North and Latin Americans, delivered sixteen
of the eighteen papers herein reproduced. Lady Barbara Ward, however, is
probably the best known contributor; her essay is entitled: "Have and
Have-nots-the Spiritual Factor."

182.
------------------. ed. SOCIAL REVOLUTION IN THE NEW LATIN AMERICA; A
CATHOLIC APPRAISAL. Notre Dame, Ind., Fides, 1965. 245p. $2.95
    Nearly half of the 18 papers deal with social problems confronting the
Catholic Church in Latin America. Dictatorship, Christian Democrary,
capitalism and social movements are among the topics treated.
[Charles Fleener]

183.
Contreras de Darío, Rafaela. SHORT STORIES. Collected, with an introd.,
by Evelyn Uhrhan Irving. Coral Gables, Fla., University of Florida Press,
1965. 41p. $2.00
    A collection of short stories by Rubén Darío's first wife, daughter of
a distinguished Salvadorean (Álvaro Contreras). She was married to Darío
from 1891 until she died in 1893. She is better known under her literary
pseudonym Stella, and was probably the great love in Darío's tormented
life. Includes a bibliography.

184.
Converse, Hyla Stuntz, comp. RAISE A SIGNAL: GOD'S ACTION AND THE CHURCH'S
TASK IN LATIN AMERICA TODAY. New York, Friendship Press, 1961. 126p.
$1.75
    This is a survey of progress made by several Protestant denominations
in Latin America.

184A
Cooper, John M. ANALYTICAL AND CRITICAL BIBLIOGRAPHY OF THE TRIBES OF
TIERRA DEL FUEGO AND ADJACENT TERRITORY. New York, Humanities Press, 1967.
233p. maps. $8.00
    This monograph is intended to be "a practical or working guide to the
sources of Fuegian and Chonoan anthropology." The author has gathered,
analyzed, and evaluated the written sources available as of 1916. The work
is divided into three parts: The Introduction, the Bibliography of Authors,
and the Bibliography of Subjects.

185.
Cortázar, Julio. BLOW-UP AND OTHER STORIES. Translated by Paul Blackburn,
New York, Macmillan, 1967. 248p. $1.50
   Contains well-known short stories by one of Argentina's most gifted
writers.

186.
----------. HOPSCOTCH. Translated by Gregory Rabassa. New York, New
American Library, 1969. 564p. $0.95
   English translation of Rayuela (1963), an important and unusual novel
which describes in minute detail the aimless wanderings of a brilliant but
troubled man who enters into a series of tortured and bizarre relationships
with a fascinating group of people in Paris and Buenos Aires. The writer
uses a multiple point of view, presenting his protagonist in both the first
and the third person.

187.
Cortés, Hernando. CONQUEST: DISPATCHES OF CORTÉS FROM THE NEW WORLD. Introd.
and commentaires by Irwin R. Blacker. Texts edited by Harry M. Rosen. New
York, Grosset & Dunlap, 1962. 269p. illus., maps $1.95
   A handy abridged edition of the famous dispatches from Cortés to Charles
V concerning the conquest of Mexico and Guatemala. Intended for the general
reader.

188.
----------. FIVE LETTERS, 1519-1562; translated by J. Bayard Morris. New
York, Norton, 1962. 388p. (The Norton, library, N180). $1.95
   This translation was originally published in 1928. The five letters of
Cortés concern the conquest of Mexico, and contain excellent descriptions of
Mexico as seen by the conqueror.

189.
Cossa, Robert M. NUESTRO FIN DE SEMANA. Edited by Donald Yates, New York,
Macmillan, 1966. 92p. $1.95
   This is annotated version of a contemporary Argentine novel.

190.
Courlander, Harold, and Rémy Bastie. RELIGIONS AND POLITICS IN HAITI.
Washington, Institute for Cross-Cultural Research, 1966. 81p. illus. maps.
$2.95
   Includes two articles: "Voudoun in Haitian culture" by Harold Courlander,
and "Voudoun and politics in Haiti," by Rémy Bastien. They seek to explain
how folk religion influences and in turn in influenced by the body politic.
An important contribution. [Charles Fleener]

191.
Crawford, William Rex. A CENTURY OF LATIN AMERICAN THOUGHT. Rev. ed.
New York, Praeger, 1966. 322p. $2.50
   A selected group of essays on prominent Latin American thinkers from such
19th century figures as Sarmiento and Alberdi to some 20th century thinkers
such as Gálvez, Ingenieros, Freyer, Caso, Vasconcelos, and Mariátegui. It
was first published in 1944. Includes a bibliography.

192.
Cronon, Edmund David. JOSEPHUS DANIELS IN MEXICO. Madison, University of
Wisconsin Press, 1960. 369p. illus. $1.95
   Surveys the diplomatic mission of Josephus Daniels in Mexico (1934-41),
based on extensive use of manuscript materials including the Daniels
Roosevelt, and State Department papers in the United States, and on inter-
views, contemporary press, and published sources. Daniels is protrayed as
a consistent liberal and idealist, a warm friend of Mexican social reform.

193.
Cuban Economic Research Project. <u>University of Miami</u>. LABOR CONDITIONS
IN COMMUNIST CUBA. Translated by Raul M. Shelton. Coral Gables, Fla.,
1963. 149p. maps. $2.95
   This is a study of the worker's situation before and after the 1959
revolution, pointing out the radically altered role of the businessman vis-
á-vis the state. It comments also on the new regime's method of imposing a
Russian brand of communism upon the Cuban people and its political activities among other nations of the hemisphere.

194.
Cumberland, Charles C. THE MEANING OF THE MEXICAN REVOLUTION. Boston,
Heath, 1967. 110p. $2.25
   Treats the Mexican revolution and its effect on Mexico's economic and
political life.

195.
----------------------. MEXICO: THE STRUGGLE FOR MODERNITY. New York,
Oxford University Press, 1968. 304p. maps $2 50
   Describes the great changes occurring in Mexico between 1940-1960, the
period in which the country achieved lasting political stability and saw
phenomenal economic growth. These achievements were the result of the
great social revolution which destroyed the traditional social alignments,
ushered in agrarian reforms and saw the rise of the labor unions as a
political force.

196.
Cunha, Euclydes da. REBELLION IN THE BACKLANDS. OS SERTÕES. Translated
with an introduction by Samuel Putnam. Chicago, University of Chicago
Press, 1957. 536p. illus., maps. $2.95
   This English translation first appeared in 1944. It is commonly con-
ceded to be Brazil's greatest and best loved classic. Writing in the <u>New
York Times book review</u>, February 6, 1944, Erico Verissimo describes it as
an "...admirable translation, in itself a literary landmark, for it is more
difficult to translate da Cunha into English than to render into Portuguese,
for example, the rich and untamed prose of Thomas Wolfe..."

197.
Dame, Hartley F. LATIN AMERICA, 1970. Edited by P. E. Dostert and R. C.
Horst. Washington, Stryker-Post Publications, 1970. 89p. maps $1.75
   Briefly describes Latin America. After an essay on the general historical background, each of the 24 independent nations are studied in terms
of their history, culture, economy and future. An appendix contains statistics and other data.

198.
Darwin, Charles. VOYAGE OF THE BEAGLE. Annotated and with an introd. by
Leonard Engel. Garden City, N.Y., Doubleday, 1962. 524p. $1.45
   The original edition was entitled <u>Journal of researches into the geology
and natural history of the various countries visited by H.M.S. Beagle</u> (1839).
It is a very interesting account by the famous British scientist of his
voyage around much of the South American coast including Patagonia.

199.
Dauster, Frank N., <u>ed</u>. TEATRO HISPANOAMERICANO: TRES PIEZAS. New York,
Harcourt, Brace, and World, 1965. 272p. $2.95
   This annotated selection of Spanish-American plays includes <u>Rosalba y los
llaveros</u> by Emilio Carballido of Mexico, a delighful comedy; Francisco
Arrivi's <u>Vejigantes</u> (Puerto Rico) which is concerned with the problem of
racial conscience; and <u>Collacocha</u> by Enrique Solari Swayne (Peru) which
portrays the relationship between man and his natural surroundings.

200.
Davidson, Basil. THE AFRICAN SLAVE TRADE. PERCOLONIAL HISTORY, 1450-1850.
Boston, Little, Brown 1964. 311p. maps $2.45
   Primarily a history of Black Africa from 1450 to 1850, this book also
treats African-American contacts through the slave trade. (Originally
entitled Black Mother, 1961).

201.
Davis, David Brion. THE PROBLEM OF SLAVERY IN WESTERN CULTURE. Ithaca, N.Y.,
Cornell University Press, 1966. 505p. $2.95
   Winner of the 1967 Pulitzer Prize in nonfiction, this is an important contribution to intellectual and social history. It is mainly concerned with the
different ways in which men have responded to slavery and demonstrates that
the institution has always been a source of social and psychological tension.

202.
Davis, Harold Eugene. LATIN AMERICAN SOCIAL THOUGHT; DEVELOPMENT SINCE INDE-
PENDENCE WITH SELECTED READINGS. 2d ed. Washington, University Press of
Washington, 1967. 560p. $6.00
   Presents valuable biographical and bibliographical data on 38 men who
have influenced social thought in Latin America.

203.
------------. SOCIAL SCIENCE TRENDS IN LATIN AMERICA. Washington, University
Press of Washington, 1960. 136p. $2.50
   Professor Davis analyzes social science trends in Latin America through
the 1950's.

204.
Davis, Russell G. SCIENTIFIC, ENGINEERING AND TECHNICAL EDUCATION IN MEXICO.
Washington, Education and World Affairs, 1967. 39p. tables. $1.50
   Contains a survey of scientific and technical education in Mexican engi-
neering and technical schools up to 1964.

205.
Davison, R.B. WEST INDIAN MIGRANTS, SOCIAL AND ECONOMIC FACTS OF MIGRATION
FROM THE WEST INDIES. New York, Oxford University Press, 1962. 89p. tables.
$2.50
   Studies West Indian migration to Great Britain and the resulting dis-
locations suffered and advantages gained by the individuals and the states
involved. This publication of the Institute of Race Relations also includes
an excellent critical essay by Dr. A.D. Knox.

206.
Day, Arthur Grove. CORONADO'S QUEST: THE HISTORY-MAKING ADVENTURES OF THE
FIRST WHITE MAN TO INVADE THE SOUTHWEST. Berkeley, University of California
Press, 1966. 419p. $2.25
   A careful study of Corondo (ca. 1510-1554), the first explorer to reach
the present southwestern part of the United States. The book, semi-popular
in style, has a few debatable or clearly erroneous statements, but is based
on a thorough examination of all known evidence. Includes an extensive
bibliography.

207.
Debray, Regis. REVOLUTION IN THE REVOLUTION. Translated by Victoria Ortiz.
New York, Grove Press, 1967. 126p. $0.95
   Translation of Révolution dans la révolution: lutte armée et lutte
politique en Amérique Latine (1967), in which a young French philosopher
describes the Cuban Revolution as different from either the Russian or the
Chinese revolutions.

208.
De Fleur, Lois B. DELINQUENCY IN ARGENTINA; A STUDY OF CÓRDOBA'S YOUTH.
Pullman, Washington State University Press, 1971. 164p. illus. tables.
$4.00

A cross-cultural study of delinquency based on field work carried out in 1962. The conclusion reached is that the Argentine poor, responsible for a large percentage of delinquency, lack contact with major social institutions of their society, namely, stable families, schools, church, steady jobs.

210.
Delgado, Rafael. EL DESERTOR. Philadelphia, Chilton Books, 1970. 47p. illus. $1.80.
    This is a Spanish-language edition of a short story by the Mexican novelist Delgado (1853-1914).

211.
Delwart, Louis O. THE FUTURE OF LATIN AMERICAN EXPORTS TO THE UNITED STATES: 1965 and 1970. Washington, National Planning Association, 1960. 130p. tables. $2.00.
    A survey of expected developments in the economically vital field of exports.

212.
Denevi, Marco, and others. CEREMONIA SECRETA Y OTROS CUENTOS. Edited by Donald A. Yates. New York, Macmillan, 1965. 117p. $2.25
    This is an anthology of short stories which won prizes in the Life en español literary contest. Marco Denevi, Carlos Martinez Moreno, and Alfonso Echeverría Yáñez are among the authors included.

213.
--------------. ROSAURA A LAS DIEZ. Edited, with an introd. by Donald A. Yates. New York, Scribner's, 1964. 219p. illus. $2.95
    Published in 1955 as the winner of the first prize in the Guillermo Kraft literary competition, this was one of the most popular Latin American novels of the past decade. The setting is present-day Buenos Aires. Includes a vocabulary.

214.
Dewey, John JOHN DEWEY'S IMPRESSIONS OF SOVIET RUSSIA AND THE REVO-LUTIONARY WORLD: MEXICO, CHINA, TURKEY. Edited by W. W. Brickman, New York Teacher's College Press, 1964. 178p. $1.95
    Dewey studies the most important revolutions of the first part of the 20th century.

215.
Díaz del Castillo, Bernal. THE CONQUEST OF NEW SPAIN. Translated, with an introd. by John Michael Cohen. Baltimore Penguin Books, 1963. 412p. map $1.45
    This is an abridged edition of Díaz del Castillo's classic account. Mr. Cohen has omitted some repetitions, modernized punctuations, and abandoned the illogical chapter divisions of the original. This is an important addition to English versions of early works on Spanish America.

216.
------------------------. THE DISCOVERY AND CONQUEST OF MEXICO: 1517-1521. Edited from the only exact copy of the original manuscript....Translated, with an introd. and notes by A. P. Maudslay. Introd. by Irving A. Leonard. New York, Noonday Press, 1965. 478p. $2.95
    This is a re-edition of the 1956 abridged edition of Maudslay's English translation (1908-1916) based on Genaro García's Mexican edition (1904), of Díaz del Castillo's eyewitness account of the conquest of Mexico.

217.
Dibble, Charles E., ed. CODEX HALL: AN ANCIENT MEXICAN HIEROGLYPHIC PICTURE MANUSCRIPT. Illus. by L. H. Ewing. Albuquerque, University of New Mexico Press, 1947. 16p. illus. col. facsim. $5.00
    Includes a facsimile of Codex Hall, with excellent notes by Professor Dibble.

218.
Dibner, Bern. DARWIN OF THE BEAGLE. New York, Dover, 1970. 150p. $1.00
    Presents a short study of Darwin's voyage aboard the Beagle.

219.
Diederich, Bernard, and Al Burt. PAPA DOC: THE TRUTH ABOUT HAITI TODAY.
Foreword by Graham Greene. New York, McGraw Hill, 1971. 393p. $1.25
    In the words of British novelist Graham Greene "this is a very full
account of Duvalier's reign which will be indispensable to future
historians." It gives a good synopsis of Haitian history and then proceeds
with a thorough analysis of Dr. Duvalier's life and regime.

220.
Dinerstein, Herbert S. INTERVENTION AGAINST COMMUNISM. Baltimore, Johns
Hopkins University Press, 1967. 53p. $1.45
    In this study of U.S. intervention against communism the author
considers the Soviet Union, Greece, Vietnam, Cuba and the Dominican
Republic. His major conclusion is that, with the exception of Greece,
intervention against communism has tended not to inhibit the spread of
communism but to increase it, largely because these interventions have
been perceived as directed primarily against national aspirations rather
than against communism.

221.
Dix, Robert Heller. COLOMBIA: THE POLITICAL DIMENSIONS OF CHANGE. New
Haven, Conn., Yale University Press, 1967. 452p. maps. $3.45
    A professor Yale expands his doctoral dissertation to what is by far
the best work on Colombian government. The emphasis is political, and the
period covered, is for the most part, contemporary. [HLAS 31:7497]

222.
Donoso, José, and William Henkin, eds. THE TRI-QUARTERLY ANTHOLOGY OF
CONTEMPORARY LATIN AMERICAN LITERATURE. New York, Dutton, 1969. 496p.
illus. $3.95
    Poetry, fiction, and critical essays are presented in this collection of
Latin American literature. More than 75 contributors are included and
special anthologies of Cuban, Peruvian, Argentine, Paraguayan, Mexican, and
Chilean poetry survey national trends. The artwork, dispersed throughout
the book, is also Latin American.

223.
Dooley, L. M. THAT MOTHERLY MOTHER OF GUADALUPE. Boston, Daughters of
St. Paul, 1962. 74p. illus., map. $1.00
    Father Dooley has written a brief devotional account of the apparitions
of the patroness of Mexico, the Lady of Guadalupe, to Juan Diego in 1531.
Hymns and prayers to Mary are included.

224.
Dorn, Edward, and Gordon Brotherston, eds. OUR WORD: GUERRILLA POEMS FROM
LATIN AMERICA. New York, Grossman, 1968. 58p. illus. 2.95
    Includes two dozen poems by revolutionary poets from Peru, Guatemala, and
Nicaragua. Argentina is represented by Che Guevara's "Song to Fidel." This
is a bilingual edition, the poems and the introduction appear in both English
and Spanish.

225.
Downey, Joseph T. THE CRUISE OF THE PORTSMOUTH, 1845-1847. A SAILOR'S
VIEW OF THE NAVAL CONQUEST OF CALIFORNIA. Edited by Howard Lamar. New
Haven, Yale University Press, 1969. 246p. illus. $1.75
    A lower-deck account of a naval cruise around South America and the ship's
involvement in the Mexican-American War. The witty and irrepressible yeoman's
journal presents a lively and uninhibited account of the seizure of San
Francisco and the battles of La Mesa and San Gabriel. [Charles Fleener]

226.
Dozer, Donald Marquand, ed. THE MONROE DOCTRINE; ITS MODERN SIGNIFICANCE.
New York, Knopf, 1968. 208p. $2.50
   The editor's excellent introduction traces the historical evolution of
the Monroe Doctrine. The 26 selections which include articles, editorials,
and official policy statements, illustrate the interpretations of the
Doctrine.

227.
Draper, Theodore. CASTROISM: THEORY AND PRACTICE. New York, Praeger, 1965.
263p. $2.50
   This is a summation and bringing up to date of the author's conclusions
on the topic, attempting to provide answers to two basic questions: what is
the nature of the Castro regime; and, what is its relation to other
Communist governments? The book includes bibliographical footnotes.

228.
-----------------. CASTRO'S REVOLUTION; MYTHS AND REALITIES. New York,
Praeger, 1962. 218p. $1.95
   This is an authoritative and well written study of Castroism; however,
it is somewhat short on historical perspectives.

229.
Dreyer, F. C. CATOLICISMO ROMANO A LA LUZ DE LAS ESCRITURAS. Chicago,
Moody, 1960. 256p. $0.85
   Roman Catholicism in the light of the scriptures. Is presented in a
Spanish version.

230.
Driver, Harold Edson, ed. THE AMERICAS ON THE EVE OF DISCOVERY. Englewood
Cliffs, N. J., Prentice-Hall, 1964. 179p. map (Global history series,
S-93) $1.95
   Various authors describe the most representative aboriginal tribes in
pre-Columbian America from Alaska to Tierra del Fuego. A good description
of the different types of cultures in the Western hemisphere.

231.
Duffey, Frank M. THE EARLY CUADRO DE COSTUMBRES IN COLOMBIA. Chapel Hill,
University of North Carolina Press, 1956. 116p. (Studies in the Romance
Languages and Literatures, 26) $2.50
   This work studies the development of the cuadro de costumbres in Colombia
during the 19th century by examining sketches written by 15 different authors.

231A.
Dulles, Foster Rhea. THE IMPERIAL YEARS. New York, Apollo, 1966. 340p.
$2.25
   Studies the 1885-1908 period emphasizing U.S. emergence as a great power.
Latin America appears importantly in the narrative as the U.S. expands its
influence in the Caribbean. [Charles Fleener]

232.
Duncan, W. Raymond, and James Nelson Goodsell, eds. QUEST FOR CHANGE IN
LATIN AMERICA; SOURCES FOR A TWENTIETH-CENTURY ANALYSIS. New York, Oxford
University Press, 1970. $2.95
   The editors have selected writings, speeches, and documents of prominent
Latin American leaders of the 20th century which reflect divergent approaches
to social and economic change. The leaders range from José Martí of the
turn of the century to Fidel Castro, Eduardo Frei, Rómulo Bentancourt, and
Che Guevara.

233.
Duncan, W. Raymond, _ed_. SOVIET POLICY IN DEVELOPING COUNTRIES. Waltham,
Mass., Ginn-Blaisdell, 1971. 350p. $3.95.
The readings included here review sensitive trouble zones in developing
countries and analyze Soviet relationships with the Third World.

234.
Dunne, John Gregory. DELANO; THE STORY OF THE CALIFORNIA GRAPE STRIKE.
New York, Farrar, Straus, and Giroux, 1967. 176p. illus. $1.95
Presents a report on the first year of the _huelga_. In a dispassionate
manner the author examines the strike's impact on the community; analyzes
the actions of both labor and employers and describes the atmosphere that
permeates the battlefront at Delano. A popular account.

235.
Durand, René L. F. LA NÉGRITUDE DANS L'OEUVRE POÉTIQUE DE RUBÉN DARÍO.
Dakar, Centre de Hautes Études Afro-Ibéro-Américaines de l'Université de
Dakar, 1970. 38p. $1.00.
This is an excellent monograph analyzing Negro elements in the poetry of
the most celebrated Latin American poet of the first half of the 20th
century.

235A
Earle, Peter G., ed. VOCES HISPANOAMERICANAS. Under the general
editorship of Robert G. Mead. New York, Harcourt, Brace, and World, 1966.
303p. $3.95.
Included in this reader are poems, short stories, and essays by such
diverse Spanish-American authors as José Martí, José Enrique Rodó,
Ezequiel Martinez Estrada, Octavio Paz, Rubén Darío, Jorge Luis Borges,
Julio Cortázar, and others.

236.
Easby, Elizabeth Kennedy, and John F. Scott. BEFORE COTRÉS: SCULPTURE OF
MIDDLE AMERICA. Introd. by Dudley T. Easby, Jr. New York, Metropolitan
Museum of Art, 1970. Distributed by the New York Graphic Art Society.
324p. illus. $6.95.
This impressive and extensively annotated catalog reproduces 308 works
in stone, pottery, and metal, including loans from European and American
collections. It also contains very useful "Relative chronology of Middle
America." This work is a good outline to study the cultures of Middle
America.

237.
Ebel, Roland H. POLITICAL MODERNIZATION IN THREE GUATEMALAN INDIAN
COMMUNITIES. New Orleans, Middle American Research Institute, Tulane
University, 1969. 75p. illus., tables, map. $2.00
To understand the social, political and economic modernization of
Guatemala one must study changes in the community's political system.
The author has investigated three municipios of western Guatemala.
[Charles Fleener]

238.
Eister, Allan W. THE UNITED STATES AND THE A.B.C. POWERS. 1889-1906.
Dallas, University Press in Dallas. 92p. $1.50
Surveys the diplomatic and commercial relations between the U.S. and
Argentina, Brazil, and Chile from 1816 to 1906. He concentrates on the
years indicated in the title. [Charles Fleener]

239.
Eiteman, David K. STOCK EXCHANGES IN LATIN AMERICA. Ann Arbor, University
of Michigan Press, 1966. 83p. illus. $3.00
Examines the operations and structure stock exchanges in Latin America.

240.
Ekholm, Gordon, F., ed. MAYA SCULPTURE IN WOOD. New York, Museum of
Primitive Art, 1964. 12p. illus. $1.50.
   Contains attractive illustrations of unusual Maya wood sculptures.

241.
Elder, Jacob D. SONG GAMES FROM TRINIDAD AND TOBAGO. Austin, Published
for the American Folklore Society by the Texas University Press, 1962. 119p.
$2.00
   This handsome volume includes popular and many less well-known song
games of Trinidadian folklore.

242.
Ellis, Howard S. THE APPLICABILITY OF CERTAIN THEORIES OF ECONOMIC DEVELOP-
MENT TO BRAZIL. Madison, Latin American Center, University of Wisconsin,
1968. 33p. $1.50
   Surveys theories of development that are related primarily to labor,
capital, foreign trade, economic planning. These theories are analyzed
in terms of the Brazilian case. [Charles Fleener]

243.
Ellis, John Tracy ed. DOCUMENTS OF AMERICAN CATHOLIC HISTORY. Chicago,
Regnery, 1967. 2v. (ii, 702p.) $2.25
   Vol. 1 deals with the Catholic Church in the Spanish colonies up to the
Second plenary Council of Baltimore.

244.
Embree, Edwin R. INDIANS OF THE AMERICAS. New York, Macmillan, 1970.
270p. $1.50
   The author sees the Americas as a great pageant of diverse peoples.

245.
Emmerich, André. ART BEFORE COLUMBUS: THE ART OF ANCIENT MEXICO FROM THE
ARCHAIC VILLAGES OF THE SECOND MILLENIUM B.C. TO THE SPLENDORS OF THE AZTECS.
Photography by Lee Boltin. New York, Simon and Schuster, 1963. 256p.
illus., plates. $4.95
   This succinct discussion of the pre-classic, great classic, and historic
periods of Middle American art, is relevant for the student as well as
the collector of pre-Columbian artifacts. The photographs by Lee Boltin
are excellent.

246.
Enciso, Jorge. DESIGN MOTIFS OF ANCIENT MEXICO. New York Dover, 1959.
192p. illus. $2.50
   The author has assembled a catalog of designs from ancient Mexico,
categorized and with provenience but lacking any interpretation.

247.
Engber, Marjorie, comp. CARIBBEAN FICTION AND POETRY. New York, Center
for Inter-American Relations, 1970. 86p. $1.25
   Includes 427 entries by Caribbean authors published in the U.S. and
Great Britain since 1900 until the end of 1969. English translations of
French, Spanish, and Dutch works have also been included.

248.
Englekirk, John E. ed. AN ANTHOLOGY OF SPANISH AMERICAN LITERATURE. 2d. ed.,
by John E. Englekirk and others, New York, Appleton-Century-Crofts, 1968. 2v.
$4.50
   This is a companion volume to the 3d ed. of Outline history of Spanish
American literature. This anthology offers a good sampling of contemporary
writers, including novelists and playwrights. Each selection is preceded by
an introductory paragraph which evaluates the author and places him within
literary trends.

249.
---------------. and others, eds., AN OUTLINE HISTORY OF SPANISH
AMERICAN LITERATURE. 3d ed. New York, Appleton-Century-Crofts, 1965.
252p. maps $3.65
Outlines the development of Spanish-American literature. The following
periods are covered:from Discovery to Independence; from Independence to
the Mexican Revolution; and the twentieth century. Each topic inlcudes
bibliographies.

250.
Engel, Frederic. A PRECERAMIC SETTLEMENT ON THE CENTRAL COAST OF PERU:
ASIA, UNIT 1. Philadelphia, American Philosophical Society, 1963. 139p.
Illus., tables, maps $4.50
One hundred kilometers south of Lima on the Omas River near the Indian
community called Asia the author, in 1957, visited some mounds that were to
be flooded for agricultural purposes. Engle's entire work during 1958 was
devoted to a single small mound which he calls Unit 1. He sifted the major
part of the refuse before water inundated the site and destroyed everything.
He discovered 52 funeral or cache pits and thus was able to contribute this
monograph on life in a perceramic Peruvian settlement. [Charles Fleener]

251.
English, Peter. PANAMA AND THE CANAL ZONE IN PICTURES. New York, Sterling,
1969. 64p. illus., map $1.00
The pictures dominate this brief introduction to the isthmus and its
canal. The text presents a basic survey of the land, history, government,
people, and economy of Panama and the Canal Zone.

252.
Eoff, Sherman Hinkle, and Paul C. King. eds. SPANISH-AMERICAN SHORT STORIES.
New York, Macmillan, 1964. 204p. illus. $2.95
A useful collection of short stories by contemporary Spanish-American
authors which have been adapted for the intermediate Spanish level. Jesús
Millán, Horacio Quiroga, and Juan Pablo Echagüe are among the authors
included.

253.
Espinosa, Aurelio Macedonio. CONCHITA ARGUELLO: HISTORIA Y NOVELA
CALIFORNIANA. New York, Macmillan, 1966. 71p. $1.50
The setting is an 18th century Spanish-American colonial town. The
simple and charming story concerns the daughter of the Presidio commander
of San Francisco and Count Rézanov, a dashing Russian adventurer who
visited California. The novel is based on notes made by Rézanov.

254.
Esquemeling, John. THE BUCANEERS OF AMERICA. Introd. by P.G. Adams.
New York, Dover, 1967. 506p. illus., maps $3.00
The original edition of 1893 was subtitled "A true account of the most
remarkable assaults committed of late years upon the coast of the West
Indies...containing also Basil Rengrose's account of the dangerous voyage
and bold assaults of Capt. Bartholomew Sharp."

255.
Evans, F. C. A FIRST GEOGRAPHY OF TRINIDAD AND TOBAGO. New York,
Cambridge University Press, 1968. 56p. illus., maps $2.00
Surveys the geography, population, and economy of Trinidad and Tobago
for the secondary school student.

256.
Ewing, Ethel. LATIN AMERICAN SOCIETY. 2d ed. Chicago, Rand McNally,
1963. 78p. illus., maps. $1.40
Latin American history is outlined here from Columbus to Castro for the
high school student.

257.
Facts on File, Inc., New York. CUBA, THE U.S., AND RUSSIA, 1960-1963; A
JOURNALISTIC NARRATIVE OF EVENTS IN CUBA AND OF CUBAN RELATIONS WITH THE
U.S. AND THE SOVIET UNION. Compiled by the editors of Facts on File.
New York, 1964. 138p. illus., maps $2.45
    The material in this work appeared in News Year for 1960-63.

258.
Fagan, Stuart I. CENTRAL AMERICAN ECONOMIC INTEGRATION: THE POLITICS OF
UNEQUAL BENEFITS. Berkeley, University of California International Center,
1971. 81p. $1.95
    Analyzes the problems facing the Central American Common Market. The
member countries' unequal productivity and economic development present
certain difficulties, as does occasional rivalry and nationalism.

259.
Fagan, Richard D. CUBA: THE POLITICAL CONTENT OF ADULT EDUCATION.
Stanford, Calif., The Hoover Institution on War, Revolution, and Peace,
1964. 77p. $1.50
    Fidel Castro declared that 1961 would be the "year of education." More
than a million Cubans participated as either teachers or students. The
author explains that the first purpose of this movement was "skill
training," but that "civic training" was also an important element of the
program. [Charles Fleener]

260.
Fagg, John Edwin. CUBA, HAITI, AND THE DOMINICAN REPUBLIC. Englewood
Cliffs, N.J., Prentice-Hall, 1965. 181p. illus., maps $1.95
    This is an excellent survey, half of which is devoted to Cuba. The
extensive critical bibliography enhances the value of the text.

261.
Farabee, William Curtis. THE CENTRAL ARAWAKS. New York, Humanities Press,
1967. 299p. illus., maps $9.75
    The material included in this study of Arawak tribes of Northern Brazil
and Southern British Guiana was collected during the first year of field
work by the University of Pennsylvania Museum's South American Expedition,
1913-1916. The somatic data and much of the ethnological and linguistic
material presented are based on personal observation. [Charles Fleener]

262.
----------------------------. THE CENTRAL CARIBS. New York, Humanities Press,
1967. 299p. illus., maps $10.50
    More than a dozen Carib tribes of Southern British Guiana and Northern
Brazil were studied by the University of Pennsylvania Museum's South
American Expedition, 1913-1916. This monograph presents detailed and
scientific account of the language, culture, and somatic characteristics
of these isolated Amerindians. [Charles Fleener]

263.
Faron, Louis C. THE MAPUCHE INDIANS OF CHILE. New York, Holt, Rinehart,
and Winston, 1968. 113p. illus., tables   (Case Studies in Cultural
Anthropology) $1.95
    A case study of a culture that has managed to retain significant
traditional characteristics despite centuries of contact and conquest.
The conflict between forces for change and those for stability is analyzed.
Includes a bibliography. [Charles Fleener]

264.
----------------. MAPUCHE SOCIAL STRUCTURE. Urbana, University of Illinois
Press, 1961. 247p. illus., tables $4.95
    A thorough analysis of Mapuche social relationships, including an
analysis of the Mapuche's belief in supernatural forces. Includes a bibliography.

265.
Fehr, Howard Franklin, ed. MATHEMATICAL EDUCATION IN THE AMERICAS. New York, Columbia University, Teachers College, 1962. 180p. $1.50
   Studies how mathematics is taught in the Western hemisphere.

266.
Fergusson, Erna. DANCING GODS: INDIAN CEREMONIALS OF NEW MEXICO & ARIZONA. Albuquerque, University of New Mexico Press, 1957. 276p. illus. $2.45
   Describes native dances and rites in Arizona and New Mexico with handsome illustrations and extensive text.

267.
--------------. MEXICAN COOKBOOK. Illus. by Valentín Vidurreta. Garden City, N.Y., Doubleday, 1961. 119p. illus. $0.95
   First published in 1934, this book contains the Mexican dishes in common use when the province of New Mexico was a part of Mexico. It points out the subtlety and delicacy in the use of spices and how the ingredients have to be well balanced and blended to form an authentic Mexican meal.

268.
Fergusson, Erna. MEXICAN COOKBOOK. Albuquerque, University of New Mexico Press 1945. 118p. illus.(part. col.) $1.65
   See above.

269.
Fergusson, Harvey. RIO GRANDE. Illus. by C. Whitman, New York, Apollo Publications 1955. 296p. $1.95
   Traces the story of the conquest of the Rio Grande valley from pre-Columbian days up to the early 20th century. The narration focuses on individual histories which symbolize the area's development. [Charles Fleener]

270.
Fernández, Justino. A GUIDE TO MEXICAN ART. FROM ITS BEGINNINGS TO THE PRESENT. Translated by Joshua C. Taylor. Chicago, University of Chicago Press, 1969. 398p. illus. $3.95
   This survey of   than 20 centuries of art provides a critical introduction to a great artistic heritage and serves as guide to the masterpiices of the Mexican tradition. The 183 illustrations depict ceramics, sculptures, murals, buildings and engravings.

271.
Fernández de Oviedo, Gonzalo. DE LA NATURAL HISTORIA DE LAS INDIAS. Chapel Hill, University of North Carolina Press, 1970. 250p. illus. $5.00
   An early, eye-witness description of the Caribbean and Middle America, first published in 1526. This is a valuable historical document for the conquest period.

272.
Fillol, Tomás Robert. SOCIAL FACTORS IN ECONOMIC DEVELOPMENT: THE ARGENTINE CASE. Cambridge, Massachusetts Institute of Technology Press, 1961. 118p. tables $2.50
   Presents a thorough study of diverse social problems which influence Argentine economic development.

273.
Fitzgerald, Gerald E. ed. THE CONSTITUTIONS OF LATIN AMERICA. Chicago, Regnery, 1968. 242p. $2.95
   Six Latin American constitutions have been chosen as representative of the varieties of Latin American constitutionalism. Introductions by the author compare political reality with constitutional appearance, and place the documents in their cultural and historical context. The constitutions of Chile, Colombia, Costa Rica, El Salvador, Mexico, and Venezuela are included.

274.
Flandreau, Charles Macomb. VIVA MEXICO. Edited with an introd. by C.
Harvey Gardiner. Urbana, University of Illinois Press, 1964. 302p. $1.95
    First published in 1908, this is a delightful description of rural Mexico
under Díaz by an American humorist.

275.
Fleener, Charles J., and Harry Cargas, eds. RELIGIOUS AND CULTURAL FACTORS
IN LATIN AMERICA. St. Louis, Office of International Programs, Saint Louis
University, 1970. 180p. $3.95
    Includes nine articles delivered at the 1968 meeting of the Midwest
Association for Latin American Studies at Saint Louis University. The
papers range from the broad view of Roger Vekemans' comments of "The
Uniqueness of Latin America" to Richard Millett's detailed study of
"Catholic-Protestant Relations in Costa Rica in the Twentieth Century."

276.
Fluharty, Vernon Lee. DANCE OF THE MILLIONS: MILITARY RULE AND THE SOCIAL
REVOLUTION IN COLOMBIA, 1930-1956. Pittsburgh, Pittsburgh University Press,
1966. 336p. maps $2.95
    This is a scholarly interpretation of recent Colombian history. The
author analyzes the underlying cause of the "Bogotazo" riots of 1948 and
the military coup of General Gustavo Rojas Pinilla in 1953. The original
edition was published in 1957.

277.
Forbes, Jack D., ed. THE INDIAN IN AMERICA'S PAST. Englewood Cliffs, N.J.,
Prentice-Hall, 1964. 182p. $1.95
    Includes a collection of documents concerning the Indian in the United
States. Some 10 percent of the quotations are from Spanish or Mexican
sources.

278.
Ford, Norman D. ALL OF MEXICO AND GUATEMALA AT LOW COST. Rev. ed. New
York, Harian, 1967. 175p. illus. $2.50
    Fiesta lands (1965) is reprinted here with new illustrations.

279.
--------------. FABULOUS MEXICO: WHERE EVERYTHING COSTS LESS. 9th ed.
New York, Crown Publishers, 1963. 82p. 1.50
    A guide for the economy-minded tourist. Thorough financial information
about banks, real estate, and investment.

280.
Fore, William F. SOUTH AMERICANS ALL. New York, Friendship Press, 1970.
111p. $1.75
    Discusses religion in South America.

281.
Foscue, Edwin J. TAXCO: MEXICO'S SILVER CITY. Dallas, Texas, Southern
Methodist University Press, 1960. 34p. illus. $1.50
    This is an attractive and knowledgeable introduction and guide to the
geography and history of Taxco, Mexico, "a resort town out of the colonial
past." The author is a geographer at Southern Methodist University. The
book was first published in 1947.

282.
Foster, David William. THE MYTH OF PARAGUAY IN THE FICTION OF AUGUSTO ROA
BASTOS. Chapel Hill, University of North Carolina Press, 1969. 88p. (North
Carolina University, Studies in the romance languages and literature) $3.50
    Roa Bastos is considered the most important figure in contemporary Para-
guayan literature. Foster analyzes El trueno entre las hojas (1953) and
Hijo de hombre (1959), both of which capture the spirit of Paraguayan social
history and create a prophetic vision of mankind struggling towards self-
liberation and a sensitive human fraternity.

283.
Foster, George McClelland. TZINTZUNTZAN: MEXICAN PEASANTS IN A CHANGING
WORLD. Boston, Little, Brown, 1967. 372p. $4.25
    An incisive monographic study about Mexican peasants and their adapta-
tion to a rapidly changing social and economic environment.

284.
Franco, Jean, ed. HORACIO QUIROGA: CUENTOS ESCOGIDOS. New York, Pergamon
Press, 1965. 293p. $3.00
    A textbook edition of stories by Horacio Quiroga of Uruguay, the great
narrator of abnormal themes for whom nature became a literary topic.

285.
----------. THE MODERN CULTURE OF LATIN AMERICA: SOCITEY AND THE ARTIST.
Baltimore, Penguin, 1970. 339p. illus. $2.95
    The author covers a large number of specialized topics concerning the
contemporary Latin American artist and his relationship to his environment.
She points out that the Latin American writer, artists, and intellectual
reflects his society and in many instances acts as its social conscience.

286.
Frank, Andre Gunder. CAPITALISM AND UNDERDEVELOPMENT IN LATIN AMERICA:
HISTORICAL STUDIES OF CHILE AND BRAZIL. Rev. and enl. ed. New York,
Monthly Review Press, 1969. 343p. 3.45
    This economic history studies underdevelopment and agriculture in Brazil
and Chile; the "Indian problem;" and foreign investment in Latin America, as
well as economic and social inequalities.

287.
Frank, Waldo David. CUBA: PROPHETIC ISLAND. New York, Marzani, 1962. 191p.
$1.95
    A sympathetic portrait of the revolution which attempts to place events
in historical perspective. History has proved that many hopes have gone
unfulfilled.

288.
Freidel, Frank Burt. THE NEGRO AND THE PUERTO RICAN IN AMERICAN HISTORY.
Boston, Heath, 1964. 27p. $0.60
    A short interpretation of black and Puerto Rican contributions to the
economic and social life of the U.S.

289.
Freyre, Gilberto. THE MASTERS AND THE SLAVES: A STUDY IN THE DEVELOPMENT
OF BRAZILIAN CIVILIZATION. 2d ed. Translated by Samuel Putnam. New York,
Knopf, 1964. 432p. (Borzoi books on Latin America) $2.95
    This is an abridged version of Samuel Putnam's 1948 English translation
of Casa grande e senzala (1933), which is an outstanding work of social
history on colonial Brazil. It examines Portuguese, Indian, and black contributions to Brazilian culture, interpersonal relations, and life on the
great plantations of the North.

290.
----------------. NEW WORLD IN THE TROPICS: THE CULTURE OF MODERN BRAZIL.
New York, Random House, 1963. 286p. $1.95
    This is an expanded version of the author's Brazil: an interpretation
(1945). It is an excellent study of Brazilian society and culture by a
leading social historian of Brazil.

291.
----------. RACIAL FACTORS IN CONTEMPORARY POLITICS. New York, Fernhill,
1966. 32p. $1.00
    A Brazilian historian analyzes race relations and its impact on politics.

292.
Friedmann, John. VENEZUELA FROM DOCTRINE TO DIALOGUE. Syracuse, N.Y.,
University of Syracuse Press, 1969. 87p. $2.95
   Venezuela's national planning organization, the Oficina Central de
Coordinación y Planificación (CORDIPLAN), is the subject of this study.
Recognized as the outstanding example of democratic planning, CORDIPLAN is
also one of the most effective economic organizations in Latin America.

293.
Fuentes, Carlos. ADAMI. New York, Wittenborn, 1970. 251p. illus. $2.50
   English translation of Líneas para Adami which Fuentes wrote about the
work of his artist friend Valerio Adami.

294.
---------------. THE DEATH OF ARTEMIO CRUZ. Translated by Sam Hileman.
New York, Noonday Press, 1966. 306p. $1.95
   This panoramic novel about the life and death of a rich and powerful
landowner, covers the last half century of Mexican history. The original
title is La muerte de Artemio Cruz (1962).

295.
---------------. GOOD CONSCIENCE. New York, Noonday Press, 1961. 148p.
$1.95
   The original Spanish edition, Las buenas conciencias was published in
1959. It describes the life of a bourgeois Catholic family in Guanajuato
around the time when Porfirio Díaz was president of Mexico. The plot
concerns an adolescent's rebellion and his intellectual friendship with an
Indian.

296.
---------------, Paul Johnson, and others. WHITHER LATIN AMERICA? New
York, Monthly Review Press, 1963. 144p. $1.75
   A collection of articles published in Monthly Review, July 17, 1963,
by Carlos Fuentes, Francisco Julião, Paul Johnson and others. It touches
on many subjects concerning Latin America with dire predictions for the
future.

297.
Furtado, Celso. DEVELOPMENT AND UNDERDEVELOPMENT. Translated by Ricardo
W. de Aguiar and Eric Drysdale. Berkeley, University of California Press,
1967. 181p. tables $1.75
   In an attempt to criticize and revise more traditional methods of economic
interpretation, this study seeks to explain the process of growth, and the
cause of underdevelopment, all within an historical context. Translation
of Desenvolvimento e subdesenvolvimento (1961).

298.
---------------. ECONOMIC GROWTH OF BRAZIL: SURVEY FROM COLONIAL TO MODERN
TIMES. Translated by Ricardo W. de Aguiar and Eric Charles Drysdale.
Berkeley, University of California Press, 1963. 285p. $2.45
   This is a translation of Formação econômica do Brasil (1959), in which a
well-known Brazilian economist sketches his country's economic history and
analyzes the many factors that have affected its development. Includes a
section on the problems of inflation and coffee.

299.
---------------. OBSTACLES TO DEVELOPMENT IN LATIN AMERICA. Translated by
Charles Ecker. Garden City, N.Y., Doubleday, 1970. 204p. $1.45
   Emphasizes external factors which tend to aggravate and perpetuate underdevelopment in Latin America. He also discusses underdevelopment and
its relation to industrial capitalism. The author is one of the best known
economists of Latin America.

300.
Gabbert, Jack B., ed. AMERICAN FOREIGN POLICY AND REVOLUTIONARY CHANGE.
Olympia, Washington State University Press, 1968. 56p. $2.00
    Studies briefly U.S. policy switches to contemporary revolutionary
changes.

301.
Galarza, Ernesto. MERCHANTS OF LABOR: THE MEXICAN BRACERO STORY. Santa
Barbara, Calif., McNally and Loftin, 1964. 284p. illus., tables $2.95
    Describes in detail the managed migration of Mexican farm workers to
California from 1942 to 1960. It is an important social document relating
to U.S. and Mexican agriculture.

302.
---------------, Herman Gallegos, and Julian Samora. MEXICAN-AMERICANS IN
THE SOUTHWEST. Santa Barbara, Calif., McNally and Loftin, 1969. 90p. illus.
tables $2.50
    The result of a two-year survey, this study assesses the current economic,
political, and educational status of the Mexican-Americans in the Southwest.

303.
---------------. ZOO-RISA. Santa Barbara Calif., McNally, 1968. 48p.
illus. $1.25
    A humorous book in Spanish about people and animals by a prominent
Chicano scholar.

304.
Galeano, Eduardo. GUATEMALA: OCCUPIED COUNTRY. Translated by Cedric Bel-
frage. New York, Monthly Review Press, 1969. 159p. map $2.25
    English translation of Guatemala: país ocupado (1967), presenting the
point of view of the Guatemalan guerrilla fighters and states that they
have settled for a long-term revolution rather than for immediate gains.
Relies on some old clichés, but the book is well written and should be read
to understand the strife and violence of contemporary Guatemala.

305.
Gallegos, Rómulo. DOÑA BARBARA. Edited by Lowell Dunham. New York,
Appleton-Century- Croft, 1962. 280p. $2.65
    When it appeared in 1929, this work was hailed as one of the best novels
of South America. Gallegos describes the tremendous power and beauty of the
Venezuelan landscape. He is a master of spontaneous and authentic dialogue.
His character, Doña Barbara, is a skillful study as the ruthless devourer of
men.

306.
Gallenkamp, Charles. MAYA: THE RIDDLE AND REDISCOVERY OF A LOST CIVIL-
IZATION. Illus. John Skolle. New York, Pyramid Books, 1962. 240p.
illus. $0.75
    Originally published in 1959, this is a popularly written, somewhat
superficial volume on the ancient Maya, emphasizing the romantic aspects of
Maya exploration.

307.
Gálvez, Manuel. LAS DOS VIDAS DEL POBRE NAPLEÓN. Edited by Myron I.
Lichtblau. New York, Scribner, 1963. 278p. $3.95
    First published in 1954, this is a novel with autonomous characters by
the gifted Argentine writer who was awarded the National Prize for Literature in 1932.

308.
García Robles, Alfonso. THE DENUCLEARIZATION OF LATIN AMERICA. Translated by Marjory Urquidi. Washington, Carnegie Endowment, 1967. 167p. $1.95
Contains eleven speeches delivered by García Robles, Mexico's Under-Secretary for Foreign Affairs, at various inter-national meetings related to the denuclerization of Latin America. Also included are official documents on the subject.

309.
Garcilaso de la Vega, El Inca. THE INCAS. Translated by María Jolas. Edited by Alain Gheerbrant. New York, Avon Books, 1961. 447p. $1.00
This edition of the classic Royal commentaries of the Inca was translated by María Jolas from the annotated French edition.
narrative runs from the origins of the Incas to Atahualpa's death. Contemporary illustrations are included.

310.
Garrett, M. Truett, Sr. GUIDE TO RETIREMENT IN MEXICO. Brownsville, Texas, Gary Press, 1963. 183p. $3.95
Presents a guide to retirement in Mexico. It points out many useful hints for the shopper and the traveler.

311.
Gasparini, Graziano. ARQUITECTURA COLONIAL EN VENEZUELA. New York, Wittenborn, 1965. 379p. illus. $30.00
Describes colonial architecture in Venezuela. The text is enhanced by attractive illustrations and photographs.

312.
--------------------. CASA COLONIAL VENEZOLANA. New York, Wittenborn, 1962. 187p. illus. $7.50
Studies Venezuelan colonial architecture and interior decoration. It is an exhaustive and attractively illustrated volume.

313.
Gastmann, Albert L. THE POLITICS OF SURINAM AND THE NETHERLANDS ANTILLES. Rio Piedras, Institute of Caribbean Studies, University of Puerto Rico, 1968. 185p. $4.00.
A scholarly survey of the political and constitutional questions that currently face the Netherlands Caribbean. [Charles Fleener]

314.
Geiger, Theodore. CONFLICTED RELATIONSHIP: THE WEST AND THE TRANSFORMATION OF ASIA, AFRICA & LATIN AMERICA. New York, McGraw-Hill, 1967. 303p.
Surveys Western attitudes towards what is known as the "third world."

315.
Genovese, Eugene, and Laura Foner, eds. SLAVERY IN THE NEW WORLD. Englewood Cliffs, N.J., Prentice-Hall, 1970. 268p. $3.95
The first part deals with general views on slavery in the New World. It includes articles by Frank Tannenbaum, Sidney Mintz, Marvin Harris, etc. The second part covers comparative viewpoints by Herbert S. Klein, Eugene Genovese, among others. The third part raises issues in the debate over differences among slave societies in the New World.

316.
Gerald, Rex E. SPANISH PRESIDIOS OF THE LATE EIGHTEENTH CENTURY IN NORTHERN NEW SPAIN. Albuquerque, Museum of New Mexico Press, 1968. 60p. illus. tables, maps $2.95
Studies the location and design of a number of presidios established by Hugo O'Connor, commander-inspector of the military forces of the frontier provinces of New Spain from 1773 to 1775. [Charles Fleener]

317.
Gerassi, John. THE GREAT FEAR IN LATIN AMERICA. New rev. ed. New York, Collier Books, 1965. 478p. tables $1.50
A new and revised edition of The great fear (1964). The first part of the book contains a country by country report on political, social, and economic trends, while the second part examines major problems in U.S.-Latin American policy. The author advocates some radical changes of U.S. hemishperic policy. The tables and the bibliography have been brought up to date.

318.
Gerber, Stanford N., ed. THE FAMILY IN THE CARIBBEAN: PROCEEDINGS OF THE FIRST CONFERENCE ON THE FAMILY IN THE CARIBBEAN. Rio Piedras, Institute of Caribbean Studies, University of Puerto Rico, 1968. 147p. $3.00
Contains papers presented at the first conference on the Family in the Caribbean (March 21-23), St. Thomas, Virgin Islands. The objective of the conference was to present "the widest possible range of topics," from the anthropological sociological, economic, and psychological viewpoints.

319.
Gibson, Charles, ed. THE BLACK LEGEND; ANTI-SPANISH ATTITUDES IN THE OLD WORLD AND THE NEW. New York, Knopf, 1971. 222p. $4.50
The "Black Legend" considered Spaniards guilty of excesses and cruelties in the American conquests and was essentially anti-Hispanic propaganda. The editors assembled different views of Spain by historical figures of the 16th through the 19th centuries, such as Willian of Orange, Oliver Cromwell, Bartolomé de las Casas, Julián Juderías, Ramón Menéndez Pidal, and others.

320.
--------------. SPAIN IN AMERICA. New York, Harper and Row, 1967. 239p. maps, plates (New American nation, TB-3077) $2.45
This excellent study is an over-all summary of colonial Spanish-American history. It covers the conquest, the encomienda, church and state relations, social stratification, and the problem of empire. There is a special chapter on the Spanish borderlands of North America.

321.
--------------, ed. THE SPANISH TRADITION IN AMERICA. New York, Harper and Row, 1968. 257p. $2.45
Contains documentary selections extending from the late 15th century when Spain conquered part of the New World, to the beginnings of the 19th century when most of Spanish America overthrew Spanish rule. The documents are very well chosen and will provide the student with a glimpse of contemporary documents, treaties, laws, and accounts by conquistadors and other important political figures.

322.
Gil, Federico. THE POLITICAL SYSTEM OF CHILE. Boston, Houghton, Mifflin, 1966. 323p. $3.25
This is an excellent analysis of the Chilean political scene, the best example of a multiparty system in Latin America. It is an indispensable tool for the student of contemporary Latin America. A good selective bibliography is included.

323.
Girard, Rafael. INDIENS DE L'AMAZONE PERUVIENNE. Port Washington, N.Y., Paris Publications, 1970. 321p. illus. $4.80
Surveys Indian tribes in the Amazon region of Peru.

324.
--------------. POPOL-VUH: HISTOIRE CULTURELLE DES MAYA-QUICHÉS. Port Washington, N.Y., Paris Publications 1952. 351p. illus. $4.25
Analyzes the Mayas sacred book, the Popol-Vuh.

325.
Gittler, J.B. UNDERSTANDING MINORITY GROUPS. New York, Wiley, 1970.
289p. $2.45
   Studies minority groups and their integration into the mainstream of
social and economic life.

326.
Glade, William P. LATIN AMERICAN ECONOMIC DEVELOPMENT. Princeton, N.J.,
Van Nostrand, 1967. 510p. $2.95
   This is a thoughtful analysis of Latin American economic development.

327.
----------. and Charles W. Anderson. THE POLITICAL ECONOMY OF MEXICO: TWO
STUDIES. Madison, University of Wisconsin Press, 1969. 242p. $2.45
   By analyzing political situations as they affect credit institutions,
Anderson offers a good study of mechanisms operating in the development of
a national economy. Glade devotes his study to the clarification of the
economic, political, and social factors affecting development and the
changes that have taken place since the Revolution of 1910.

328.
Glazer, Nathan and Daniel Patrick Moynihan. BEYOND THE MELTING POT: THE
NEGROES, PUERTO RICANS, JEWS, ITALIAN AND IRISH OF NEW YORK CITY. Cam-
bridge, Massachusetts Institute of Technology Press, 1970. 363p. map
$1.95
   This is an examination of cultural patterns assumed by diverse ethnic
groups in the U.S.

329.
Goldbaum, D. TOWNS OF BAJA CALIFORNIA. Translated by W. B. Hendricks.
Glendale, Calif., La Siesta, 1970. 210p. illus. $2.75
   Attractively describes Baja California and its towns.

330.
Goldman, Irving. CUBEO: INDIANS OF THE NORTHWEST AMAZON. Urbana, University of Illinois Press, 1969. 305p. illus., maps $5.95
   Based on ten months of field work in 1938-40, it describes a Tucanoan-
speaking, relatively unacculturated tribe of the Uapés River near the
Brazilian border. This ethnographic classic is valuable because the Cubeo
sociocultural system was recorded before appreciable disorganization, due
to contact, had significantly altered its aboriginal ways. Enhanced by
illustrations and a bibliography.

331.
Goldrich, Daniel. SONS OF THE ESTABLISHMENT: ELITE YOUGH IN PANAMA AND
COSTA RICA. Chicago, Rand-McNally, 1966. 139p. tables, maps $3.95
   An interesting parallel study of the young men who will dominate the
political establishments of their respective nations and their views about
the existing systems.

332.
Gómara, Francisco López de. CORTÉS: THE LIFE OF THE CONQUEROR OF MEXICO,
by his secretary Francisco López de Gómara. Translated and edited by
Lesley Bird Simpson. Berkeley, University of California Press, 1966.
425p. $2.45
   Translation of Istoria de la conquista de México, the second part of
Gómara's Historia general de las Indias, (1578), this book is a vivid
personal narration of the exploits of Hernán Cortés, essentially a
biography which also describes the conquest of Mexico.

333.
Gómez, Rosendo Adolfo. GOVERNMENT OF POLITICS IN LATIN AMERICA. Rev. ed.
New York, Random House, 1963. 128p. (Studies in political science, PS-32)
$1.95
   A short, general, but very useful introduction to the subject, intended
for textbook use. Its brevity prevents it from being more than a
suggestion of themes, although the work is base on an intelligent and well-
defined pattern. [HLAS 24:3421]

334.
González, Antonio J. TRATADO MODERNO DE ECONOMÍA GENERAL Cincinnati, South-
Western Publishing Company, 1969. 494p. illus. $7.00
   This is a Spanish-language book on economics.

335.
González, Justo L. THE DEVELOPMENT OF CHRISTIANITY IN THE LATIN CARIBBEAN.
Grand Rapids, Mich., W. B. Eerdmans Pub. Co., 1969. 136p. $2.65
   A historian and professor at the Union Evangelical Seminary of Puerto Rico
describes the development of Christianity in the Latin Caribbean from the
period of the conquest to the present. He deals with Spanish and French
missions, the establishment of the Catholic Church, and with other aspects
of Christianity under progressively changing social and political
circumstances.

336.
González, Luis J. and G. A. Sánchez Salazar. THE GREAT REBEL: CHE GUEVARA
IN BOLIVIA. New York, Grove Press, 1969. 254p. illus., maps, ports.
$1.45
   Presents an interesting account of Che Guevara's trying period in Boliva.

337.
González, Nancie L. THE SPANISH-AMERICANS OF NEW MEXICO: A HERITAGE OF
PRIDE. Rev. ed. Albuquerque, University of New Mexico Press, 1969. 246p.
illus., map, tables $3.95
   Traces the history of the Hispanos of New Mexico from 1598 to the present,
describing the mounting tensions between their traditional culture and the
aggressive Anglo society that surrounds it, with particular emphasis on the
problems of urbanization. This edition includes a concluding chapter on
the recent growth of political activism.

338.
González Peña, Carlos. HISTORY OF MEXICAN LITERATURE. 3d. ed. Translated
by Gusta Barfield Nance and Florence Johnson Dunstan. Dallas, Southern
Methodist University Press, 1968. 540p. $3.45
   This is the most authoritative single volume in its field. It provides
a clear interpretation of Mexican literature to English-speaking readers.
The translators have retained the author's style. Previous Mexican
editions have been brought up-to-date by the addition of appendixes.

339.
Goodman, Marian. MISSIONS OF CALIFORNIA. Redwood City, Calif., Redwood
City Tribune, 1962. 47p. illus. $1.50
   This book presents brief histories of 21 California missions founded
between 1769 and 1823.

340.
Goodman, Morris F. COMPARATIVE STUDY OF CREOLE FRENCH DIALECTS. New York,
Humanities Press, 1964. 143p. map $8.25
   This is a very thorough comparative study of several French creole
dialects in the Caribbean.

341.
Gordon, Wendell C. THE POLITICAL ECONOMY OF LATIN AMERICA. New York,
Columbia University Press, 1965. 401p. tables $2.95
   This is a substantially rewritten version of The economy of Latin America
(1950). The new title is more appropriate since major emphasis has been
given to institutional factors utilizing the theoretical framework of Veblen
and Ayres. A brief selective bibliography is included as an appendix.

342.
Goslinga, Cornelius Christian. VENEZUELAN PAINTING IN THE NINETEENTH
CENTURY. New York, Wittenborn, 1967. 128p. illus. $6.75
   Surveys Venezuelan painting in the 19th century. It points out the
different scale, and contains biographic information on some of the artists.

342A.
   Graff, Henry Franklin. AMERICAN IMPERIALISM AND THE PHILIPPINE IN-
SURRECTION. Boston, Little, Brown, 1969. 172p. $2.95
   Studies U.S. policy at the time of the Philippine Insurrection.

343.
Graham, Lawrence. POLITICS IN A MEXICAN COMMUNITY. Gainesville, University
of Florida Press, 1968. 73p. (University of Florida monographs. Social
sciences, 35) $2.00
   Examines the politics of a Mexican city in the central highland plateau.
He has chosen a municipality of 125,000 inhabitants in order to study the
general style of local politics, the tensions between external and internal
political groups and leaders, and the degree of pluralism or elitism to be
found in the city. Culturally, the municipality is predominantly Spanish-
American and its value system is shaped by conservative Roman Catholicism.

344.
Graham, Richard. A CENTURY OF BRAZILIAN HISTORY SINCE 1865: ISSUES AND
PROBLEMS. New York, Knopf, 1969. 233p. $2.75
   An excellent study of Brazilian history, in which the author points out
the social, economic, and cultural factors which influenced its political
history.

345.
Grauer, Ben. HOW BERNAL DIAZ'S TRUE HISTORY WAS REBORN. New York,
Between-Hours Press, 1960. 32p. illus. $5.00
   This is an unusual account of a collector's successful attempt to
original Bernal Díaz del Castillo manuscript of his True history of the
conquest of New Spain restored. Mr. Grauer reproduced this volume on his
own press. The narrative is very interesting.

346.
Greco, El. EL GRECO. Edited by J.F. Matthews. New York, Harry N. Abrams,
1969. 90p. illus. $0.95
   An attractively illutstrated book dealing with the work of El Greco.

347.
Green, Gilbert. REVOLUTION. CUBAN STYLE. New York, International Pub. Co.,
1970. 125p. $1.25
   The author describes his recent visit to Cuba and outlines his impressions
on the role of incentives, the goal of the sugar harvest, and the transformation of man under the socialist system.

348.
Greene, Graham. ANOTHER MEXICO. New York, Viking Press, 1964. 279p.
$1.45
   First published in 1934, this is the English novelist's personal im-
pression of a small part of Mexico and its religious problem in 1938

349.
-----------------. THE POWER AND THE GLORY. New York, Viking Press, 1965.
280p. (Compass books) $1.65
    Greene has written a powerful novel about a Catholic priest caught in
the Mexican Revolution. It has high literary quality with good descriptions
of the Mexican people and countryside.

350.
-----------------. THE POWER AND THE GLORY. New York, Bantam Books. $0.95
    See previous comment.

351.
Greene, Theodore P., ed. AMERICAN IMPERIALISM IN 1898. Boston, Heath,
1955. 105p. $2.25
    Papers by Samuel F. Bemis, Charles A. Beard, Richard Hofstadter, and
others, analyze the background of the Spanish-American War, as well as
other issues arising out the conflict.

352.
Greenleaf, Richard E., ed. THE ROMAN CATHOLIC CHURCH IN COLONIAL LATIN
AMERICA. Edited with an introd. by Richard E. Greenleaf. New York, Knopf,
1971. 272p. $4.50
    Includes essays on a broad range of Catholic Church activities in colonial
Latin America in an effort to present a balanced picture. Church history is
one of the most difficult aspects of Latin American colonial history. The
essays were prepared by the most prominent colonialists.

353.
Gregg, Andrew K. DRUMS OF YESTERDAY: THE FORTS OF NEW MEXICO. Santa Fe,
Press of the Territorian, 1968. 40p. illus. $1.50
    Describes and illustrates old forts of New Mexico, many of them hailing
from the Spanish colonial period.

354.
Griffen, William B. CULTURAL CHANGE AND SHIFTING POPULATIONS IN CENTRAL
NORTHERN MEXICO. Phoenix, University of Arizona Press, 1969. 196p. maps
$6.00
    Studies demographic and cultural changes in the central notrhern area of
Mexico.

355.
Grove, David C. THE OLMEC PAINTINGS OF OXTOTITLÁN CAVE, GUERRERO, MEXICO.
Washington, Dumbarton Oaks, 1970. 36p. illus., plate (Studies in pre-
Columbian art and archaeology, 6) $2.50
    An attractive survey of the paintings of the Oxtotitlán Cave with ex-
cellent illustrations and a handsome color plate.

356.
Guevara, Ernesto. CHE: SELECTED WORKS OF ERNESTO GUEVARA. Edited with an
introd. by Rolando E. Bonachea and Nelson P. Valdés. Cambridge, Massachusetts Institute of Technology Press, 1970. 512p. $3.95
    This is the best and most complete selection of Che's essays, speeches,
interviews, and letters for the years 1958 through 1967.   editors chose
those that most clearly illustrate Guevara's development as a political
thinker.

357.
-----------------. CHE GUEVARA SPEAKS. Edited by G. Lavan and J. Hansen.
New York, Grove Press, 1967. 159p. $0.95
    Includes a brief selection of writings by Che Guevara.

358.
----------. THE COMPLETE BOLIVIAN DIARIES OF CHE GUEVARA AND OTHER
CAPTURED DOCUMENTS. Edited by James Daniel. New York, Stein, and Day,
1969. 330p. illus., maps $2.95
   The editor's 70 page introduction serves as a useful guide to Guevara's
diary of the Bolivian campaign that ended with the leader's assassination
in October, 1967. Three additional diaries offer a counterpoint to
Guevara. [Charles Fleener]

359.
-----------------. EPISODES OF THE REVOLUTIONARY WAR. Introd. by J. S.
Allen, New York, International Publishers, 1968. 144p. illus., maps
$1.65
   English translation of Pasajes de la guerra revolucionaria. (1963).
Guevara describes how his small band of followers was transformed into a
Rebel Army, starting with the first battle of December 1956 in which Che
was wounded and then covers the eight months during which the army took
shape in Sierra Maestra.

360.
-----------------. GUERRILLA WARFARE. New York, Random House 1969. 387p.
$1.65
   Guevara gives his views on guerrilla warfare and on how to organize the
populations for the revolution.

361.
-----------------. ON VIETNAM & WORLD REVOLUTION. New York, Pioneer
Publishers 1967. $0.25
   A small booklet analyzing world revolution and the war in Vietnam.

362.
-----------------. REMINISCENCES OF THE CUBAN REVOLUTIONARY WAR. Translated by Victoria Ortiz, New York, Grove Press, 1968. 287p. illus., maps
$1.25
   Personal reminiscences of attacks, battles, and skirmishes in which the
author participated in his effort to overthrow President Fulgencio Batista.
The memoirs were written several years later, based on hasty notes taken on
the battlefield. An important book, written by one of the most influential
revolutionaries of Latin America.

363.
-----------------. SOCIALISM & MAN. New York, Pioneer Publishers, 1965.
18p. $0.35
   In this pamphlet Guevara expounds his theory about man in a socialist
system.

364.
----------. VENCEREMOS: THE SPEECHES AND WRITINGS OF CHE GUEVARA. Edited
annotated, and introduced by John Gerassi. New York, Simon and Schuster,
1969. 442p. $2.95
   Includes selected writings of Guevara. The editor neglects to inform
the reader when he leaves out parts of the text. This is one of the least
satisfactory of the many books of Guevara writings which have appeared
since his death.

365.
Güiraldes, Ricardo. DON SEGUNDO SOMBRA. Edited by Angela B. Dellepiane.
Englewood Cliffs, N.J., Prentice-Hall, 1971. 265p. port. $4.95
   This classic from Argentina was first published in 1926. Don Segundo is
a shadow, an idea, emerging from an Argentina that is passing. Scenes of
country life are knitted into poetic prose about regional customs and folk
tales.

366.
------------------. DON SEGUNDO SOMBRA, SHADOWS ON THE PAMPAS. Translated by Harriet de Onís. New York, New American Library, 1966. 222p. illus. $0.75

This is an excellent English translation of the Argentine classic about gaucho life.

367.
Gunther, John. INSIDE SOUTH AMERICA. New York Pocket Books, 1970. 386p. $1.25

A general book on Latin America, aimed at the lay reader.

368.
Guzmán, Martín Luis. EL ÁGUILA Y LA SERPIENTE. Edited by E. R. Moore. New York, Norton, 1969. $2.50

This novel was first published in 1928. It is a collection of episodes drawn from Guzmán's own experiences during the Mexican Revolution. The style is vigorous and colorful.

368A.
Hageman, Alice, and Philip Wheaton, eds. REVOLUTION AND RELIGION IN CUBA. New York, Association Press, 1971. 357p. $2.00

This volume was prepared under the sponsorship of the Movimiento Estudiantil Cristiano, a member of the World Council of Churches. Contributors include Sergio Arce, Germán Renés, and the statements by various Cuban religious leaders.

369.
Haigh, Roger M. MARTIN GUEMES: TYRANT OR TOOL? A STUDY OF THE SOURCES OF POWER OF AN ARGENTINE CAUDILLO. Fort Worth, Texas Christian University Press, 1968. 88p. $3.50

Studies the powerful provincial caudillo of Argentina, who with his gauchos of Salta made an invaluable contribution to the cause of Independence by holding off the Royalists in 1915. The intricate patterns of the ruling provincial oligarchy to which Güemes was related are analyzed deftly. When Güemes opposed the establishment he was destroyed.

370.
Hall, Barbara J. MEXICO IN PICTURES. Rev. ed. New York, Sterling Pub. Co., 1967. 64p. illus., maps $1.00

This is a popular survey of Mexico's history, the land, the people, and the government. The text contains statistical data as well as numerous pictures in black and white.

371.
Halmos, Paul, ed. LATIN-AMERICAN SOCIOLOGICAL STUDIES. New York, Humanities Press, 1967. 179p. $5.25

Contains essays on Latin America ranging from K. H. Silvert's "The Politics of Social and Economic Change in Latin America," and Stanislav L. Andreski's "Genealogy of Public Vices in Latin America" to Luis Bossano's essay on "Pertinent Facts Concerning Latin America." Charles Wagley provides the introduction.

372.
Hamilton, Daniel Lee, and Ned Carey Fahs, eds. CONTOS DO BRASIL. New York, Appleton-Century-Crofts, 1965. 332p. $3.95

Includes short stories by prominent Brazilian authors such as Machado de Assis, Monteiro Lobato, Mario de Andrade, and others, written in various levels of language ranging from the classical style of Machado de Assis to the colloquial idiom of Mario de Andrade.

373.
Hammel, Eugene A. POWER IN ICA: THE STRUCTURAL HISTORY OF A PERUVIAN
COMMUNITY. Boston, Little, Brown, 1969. 142p. illus., maps (Latin
American case study, 1) $2.25
     An abridged version of Wealth, authority, and prestige in the Ica Valley,
which describes agriculture, industry, trade, and transportation as these
have influenced the distribution of power in the valley. Modern families
are used to illustrate the values and organization patterns found in five
social classes.

374.
----------. WEALTH, AUTHORITY, AND PRESTIGE IN THE ICA VALLEY, PERU.
Albuquerque, University of New Mexico Press, 1962. 110p. maps, plates
$2.00
     A thorough case study of the distribution of power in the Ica Valley from
the socio-economic viewpoint. The author also examines social mobility
and cultural change as related to wealth, authority, and prestige.

375.
Hamill, Hugh M., Jr., ed. DICTATORSHIP IN SPANISH AMERICA. New York, Knopf,
1965. 242p. $2.50
     The editor has selected papers by prominent U.S. and Latin American
historians which trace the development of caudillismo and personalismo
through the 19th century to such contemporary figures as Trujillo and Juan
and Eva Perón. Includes a bibliography.

376.
Hanke, Lewis U. ARISTOTLE AND THE AMERICAN INDIANS: A STUDY IN RACE
PREJUDICE IN THE MODERN WORLD. Bloomington, Indiana University Press, 1970.
164p. illus. $1.95
     This is an account of the debates between Juan Ginés de Sepúlveda and
Bartolomé de las Casas held in Valladolid 1550-1551. Sepúlveda based his
defense of Cortés' method of conquest on the doctrine propounded by
Aristotle in Politics, that some men are born to slavery, and on Aquinas'
grounds for a just war. Las Casas declared these arguments to be in direct
contradition to the Gospels, to the laws of the Church and to his personal
knowledge of the Indians. The debate continues to this day. [Charles
Fleener]

377.
---------------. DO THE AMERICAS HAVE A COMMON HISTORY? A CRITIQUE OF THE
BOLTON THEORY. New York, Knopf, 1964. 269p. $2.75
     Professor Hanke compiles and analyzes a wealth of material which brings
to life this most fascinating debate on the unity of the Western hemisphere.
It includes a bibliography.

378.
----------., ed. HISTORY OF LATIN AMERICAN CIVILIZATION: SOURCES AND
INTERPRETATIONS V. 1 THE COLONIAL EXPERIENCE. Boston, Little Brown,
1967. 553p. $4.95
     This is a selection of writings covering such topics as the New World's
Influence on the Old; Favorable Assessments of the 16th century; The
Spanish Justification for Conquest; Relations Between Indians and Spaniards;
Population Statistics and History; Urban Life, The Inquisition; Science
and Medicine.

379.
---------------., ed. HISTORY OF LATIN AMERICAN CIVILIZATION. SOURCES AND
INTERPRETATIONS. V. 2, THE MODERN AGE. Boston Little, Brown, 1968. 55p.
$4.95
     Includes writings on the following topics among others; The Revolution
Occurred in Spanish America between 1810 and 1830; Juan Manuel de Rosas;
Negro Slavery in Brazil; The Chilean Revolution of 1891; Porfirio Díaz's
Mexico; Historical Destiny in Spanish America; and Imperialism, Inter-
vention and Communism in the Caribbean.

380.
---------------., ed. MEXICO AND THE CARIBBEAN. 2d. ed. Princeton, N.J.,
Van Nostrand, 1967. 192p. $1.95
     Consists of a general historical introduction comprising about half the
book. Over 30 readings are appended, some consisting of documents, others
of secondary sources.

381.
---------------., ed. SOUTH AMERICA. 2d. ed. Princeton, N.J., Van Nostrand,
1967. 191p. $1.95
     This handy volume sets forth the nature of the fundamental problems of
South America. The editor presents a long historical introduction and then
adds a large number of readings dealing with different problems.

382.
---------------. READINGS ON LATIN AMERICAN HISTORY: SELECTED ARTICLES FROM
THE HISPANIC AMERICAN HISTORICAL REVIEW. New York, Crowell, 1966. 2 v.
$3.95
     Volume 1 covers the colonial period from the time of contact to 1810,
and volume 2 brings the readings up to the present. The authors include
Lyle N. McAlister, Woodrow Borah, Robert Potash, Stanley R. Ross, Richard M.
Morse, and many others.

383.
---------------. THE SPANISH STRUGGLE FOR JUSTICE IN THE CONQUEST OF
AMERICA. Boston, Little, Brown, 1967. 217p. illus. $2.95
     First published in 1949, this is a definitive study of the Spaniards
who fought for justice in the colonies. The study centers around Bartolomé
de las Casas, a strong advocate of the application of Christian ethics to
the administration of the Spanish empire. It includes bibliographical
appendixes.

384.
Hansen, Roger D. CENTRAL AMERICA: REGIONAL INTEGRATION AND ECONOMIC DEVELOP-
MENT. Washington, National Planning Association, 1967. 106p. tables
$2.50
     A succinct account of the problems facing the Central American Common
Market. This regional economic community is the most succesful to date in
Latin America, although it is still too early to predict the total impact
it will have on social, economic, and political developments in Central
America.

385.
Hanson Earl Parker. PUERTO RICO: ALLY FOR PROGRESS. Princeton, N.J., Van
Nostrand, 1962. 136p. (Searchlight books, 7) $1.45
     The author describes the developments which have taken place in Puerto
Rico during the past few years, and suggests that the relationship between
the United States and Puerto Rico is an example of what the Alliance for
Progress can accomplish, although it is not any sense an exact model for the
Alliance.

386.
Harding, Timothy F. THE UNIVERSITY, POLITICS, AND DEVELOPMENT IN CONTEM-
PORARY LATIN AMERICA. Riverside, University of California, Latin American
Research Program, 1968. 32p. $1.00
     Maintains that there exists a gap between the Latin American university's
self-image of innovation and freedom of action and its behavior which
reflects the elitist social structure which it perpetuates. The university
in Latin America is "bound by its antecedent" and it rarely promotes social
change.

387.
Hardoy, Jorge Enrique. URBAN PLANNING IN PRE-COLUMBIAN AMERICA. New York,
G. Braziller, 1968. 128p. illus., maps $2.95
Surveys the process of urbanization in pre-Columbian America. Attractive
photographs, plans, and drawings illustrate the text, which analyzes the
forms and designs of urban areas in Central Mexico and South America.
[Charles Fleener]

388.
Hardoy, Jorge Enrique and Richard P. Schaedel, eds. THE URBANIZATION
PROCESS IN AMERICA FROM ITS ORIGINS TO THE PRESENT DAY. Buenos Aires,
Editorial del Instituto Torcuato Di Tella, 1969. 364p. illus., maps,
tables $2.50
These papers were originally presented at the 37th International
Conference of Americanists, Mar del Plata, 1966. The 24 articles appear
in their original language; half are in English. The articles include
Charles Gibson's "Spanish-Indian Institutions and Colonial Urbanism in
New Spain;" Richard Morse's "Cities and Society in XIX Century Latin
America: Brazil;" Richard P. Schaedel's "On the Definition of Civilization:
Urban City and Town in Prehistoric America;" and George Kubler's "The Colonial
Plan of Cholula." [Charles Fleener]

389.
Haring, Clarence H. EMPIRE IN BRAZIL: A NEW WORLD EXPERIMENT WITH MONARCHY.
New York, Norton, 1968. 182p. maps $1.75
This is a reissue of the same title published in 1958. It is a general
survey, and the first in English, of the Brazilian monarchy. Useful for
college courses, this book represents an able interpretation of the Brazilian
empire.

390.
————————————. THE SPANISH EMPIRE IN AMERICA. New York, Walker, 1966.
154p. illus., maps $3.95
This is a thorough and amply documented history of the colonial period
with emphasis on political and economic administration. Originally published
in 1947, it is an indispensable volume for the student of Spanish colonial
institutions, and the politics of empire in Spain. Includes a bibliography.

391.
Harss, Luis and Barbara Dohmann. INTO THE MAINSTREAM: CONVERSATIONS WITH
LATIN AMERICAN WRITERS. New York, Harper and Row, 1969. 385p. $2.95
These essays cover the literary styles of the following Latin American
writers: Alejo Carpentier, Miguel Ángel Asturias, Jorge Luis Borges, João
Guimarães Rosa, Juan Carlos Onetti, Julio Cortázar, Carlos Fuentes, Juan
Rulfo, Gabriel García Márquez, and Mario Vargas Llosa.

392.
Harris, Marvin. PATTERNS OF RACE IN THE AMERICAS. New York, Walker, 1964.
154p. illus., maps $ 2.45
Discusses the different patterns of race relations in Latin America and
the United States. The author maintains that the evolution of manpower
exploitation in several parts of the New World is the main determinant of
race relations. He effectively attacks the notion of benign slavery in
Brazil. Includes a bibliography.

393.
Hart, Betty Turner. CONQUISTADOR, INCA PRINCESS, AND CITY FATHERS: THE
AMPUERO FAMILY OF LIMA, PERU IN THE SIXTEENTH CENTURY. Miami, Miami
University Press, 1968. 30p. (University of Miami Hispanic American
studies, 18) $1.00
The author has written an interesting monograph about a conquistador and
his aristocratic heirs in 16th century Lima.

394.
Hartz, Louis. THE FOUNDING OF NEW SOCIETIES: STUDIES IN THE HISTORY OF THE
UNITED STATES, LATIN AMERICA, SOUTH AFRICA, CANADA AND AUSTRALIA. New York,
Harcourt, Brace and World, 1964. 336p. $2.45
    In the first part of this work Professor Hartz develops a theory on the
development of new societies. In the second part five case studies are
reviewed. Richard M. Morse presents a provocative view of "The Heritage of
Latin America." [Charles Fleener]

395.
Haselden, Kyle. DEATH OF MYTH: NEW LOCUS FOR SPANISH AMERICAN FAITH. New
York, Friendship Press, 1964. 175p. $1.75
    The author maintains that Latin Americans are as intellectually receptive
towards Protestantism as they are towards Catholicism.

396.
Hartzfeld, Helmut Anthony. CRITICAL BIBLIOGRAPHY OF THE NEW STYLISTICS
APPLIED TO THE ROMANCE LITERATURES, 1900-1966. Berkeley, University of
California Press, 1968. 2v. $7.00
    Volume one covers the 1900-1952 period while volume 2 deals with 1953-
1966. This is a very important work.

397.
Havighurst, Robert J., and J. Roberto Moreira. SOCIETY AND EDUCATION IN
BRAZIL. Pittsburgh, University of Pittsburgh Press. 1965. 263p. illus.
maps $2.50
    The authors analyze Brazilian education within the social and cultural
context of the country.

398.
Hayner, Norman S. NEW PATTERNS IN OLD MEXICO: A STUDY OF TOWN AND METROPOLIS.
New Haven, Conn., College and University Press, 1966. 316p. illus., tables.
$2.45
    The author emphasizes selected social institutions in Mexico during the
dynamic 1941-1961 period, by comparing the Spanish-Indian Town of Oaxaca
with Mexico City.

399.
Hegen, Edmund Eduard. HIGHWAYS INTO THE UPPER AMAZON BASIN: PIONEER LANDS
IN SOUTHERN COLOMBIA, EDUADOR, AND NORTHERN PERU. Gainesville, University
of Florida Press, 1966. 168p. illus., maps, tables $3.75
    A study of the role of roads, rivers, and runways in penetrating the vast
tropical lowlands of Colombia, Ecuador, and Peru. These nations have
developed considerably and Bogotá, Quito, and Lima have become dynamic foci
from which elements of material and non-material culture are radiating.

400.
Helfritz, Hans. MEXICAN CITIES OF THE GODS: AN ARCHAEOLOGICAL GUIDE. New
York, Praeger, 1970. 180p. illus., maps $3.50
    Describes pre-Hispanic religious monuments of the Plateau, Gulf Coast,
and Southern areas of Mexico. Attractive black and white illustrations
enhance the text. The author has added information on archaeological
details and also on travel.

401.
Heller, Celia Stopnicka. MEXICAN-AMERICAN YOUTH: FORGOTTEN YOUTH AT THE
CROSSROADS. New York, Random House, 1966. 113p. tables $2.25
    Studies trends among Mexican American youth suggesting that they do not
constitute an exception to the characteristic historical pattern of minority
ethnic groups in the United States.

402.
Helm, J. SPANISH-SPEAKING PEOPLE IN THE UNITED STATES. Seattle, University
of Washington Press, 1971. 369p. $4.00
Surveys the Spanish-speaking population in the U.S. in a methodic and
thorough monograph. Includes a bibliography.

403.
Hemingway, Ernest. THE OLD MAN AND THE SEA, New York, Scribner, 1961. 195p.
illus. $1.20
This is a text book edition of what many critics consider Hemingway's
best work, the struggle of an old Cuban fisherman to catch a large fish.
The setting is Cuba and the descriptions of the sea are hauntingly beautiful.

404.
Henríquez Ureña, Pedro. A CONCISE HISTORY OF LATIN AMERICAN CULTURE.
Translated and with a supplementary chapter by Gilbert Chase. New York,
Praeger, 1966. 224p. $2.50
An English translation of Historia de la cultura en la America hispánica
(1947), by one of Latin America's foremost literary historians. It describes
the origin and development of Latin American culture, encompassing literature,
music, the plastic arts, physical science, political science, philosophy,
education, and journalism. The study traces Latin American cultural identity
from the interaction of the Indian and Spanish cultures to European and
North American influences.

405.
Hernández, Luis F. FORGOTTEN AMERICANS. Introd. by Robert H. Finch. 56p.
Washington, B'nai B'rith, 1969. 56p. $0.75
A resource unit for teachers concerning the Mexican-American with relevant sections on background, acculturation, values, the family unit,
education, and, Chicano power. It includes a bibliography of recommended
readings, a brief survey of Mexican history and culture with a chronological outline, and a bibliography. [Charles Fleener]

406.
Hernández Alvarez, José. RETURN MIGRATION TO PUERTO RICO. Berkeley,
Institute of International Studies, University of California, 1967. 153p.
tables, maps $2.00
One-quarter of Puerto Rico's inhabitants have migrated to the United
States. In recent years the island has industrialized and urbanized rapidly,
thus attracting back many of its migrants. This phenomenon is analyzed here
in terms of the geographic mobility, family structure, fertility and
economic impact of the returning migrants. [Charles Fleener]

407.
Henry, Jules. JUNGLE PEOPLE: A KAINGÁNG TRIBE OF THE HIGHLANDS OF BRAZIL.
New York, Random House, 1964. 215p. illus. $1.95
This classic work by a noted anthropologist was first published in 1941.
It is an excellent study on the Kaingáng Indians of Brazil. It includes
informative appendixes and a bibliography.

408.
Herschel, Manuel T. SPANISH-SPEAKING CHILDREN OF THE SOUTHWEST: THEIR
EDUCATION AND THE PUBLIC WELFARE. Austin, University of Texas Press, 1970.
222p. $2.50
The author examines educational training centers and indicates that
special instruction must be designed and implemented to overcome language
barriers and cultural gaps.

409.
Heyerdahl, Thor. KON-TIKI, THE GREATEST SEA VENTURE OF OUR TIME. Translated
by F. M. Lyon. New York, Pocket Books, 1962. 240p. $0.75
This is a reissue of the English translation published in 1950. Kon-Tiki
is the famous Nordic craft which sailed from Peru to the South Sea Islands.

410.
Heyerdahl, Thor. KON-TIKI. New York, Random House, 1965. 281p. illus.
$2.95
    The famous Norwegian explorer describes his epic voyage with five companions
on a raft built of balsa wood to prove that the Peruvian Indians traveled to
Polynesia carried by ocean currents.

411.
----------------. KON-TIKI. Edited by H. Shefter and others. New York,
Washington Square Press, 1966. 261p. illus. $0.75
    See above.

412.
Hildebrand, John Raymond. ECONOMIC DEVELOPMENT: A LATIN AMERICAN EMPHASIS.
Austin, Texas Pemberton Press, 1969. 153p. illus., tables $3.95
    The author attempts to define the "critical issues and values relevant to a
foundation that will support dynamic societies oriented toward change and
development." He also examines specific developmental problems related
to agriculture and a Latin American common market. [Charles Fleener]

413.
Hill, Clifford S. WEST INDIAN MIGRANTS AND THE LONDON CHURCHES. New York,
Oxford University Press, 1963. 89p. (Institute of Race Relations series)
$1.95
    The author examines the participation of West Indian immigrants in the
religious life of London and argues that more could and should be done to
draw them into the community life of the churches. Rev. Hill includes information on West Indian family and religious customs and a commentary on the
1961 population census of Britain as it affects West Indians. [Charles
Fleener]

414.
Hirschman, Albert O., ed. LATIN AMERICAN ISSUES: ESSAYS AND COMMENTS. New
York, Twentieth Century Fund, 1961. 201p. $1.45
    A series of essays by Víctor Alba, Lincoln Gordon, David Felix, Joseph
Grunwald, Raymond Mikesell, Victor L. Urquidi, and Thomas F. Carroll, on
political ideology, inter-American relations, economic problems,and land
reform. An essay by the editor presents a critical analysis of current
economic trends.

415.
--------------------. THE STRATEGY OF ECONOMIC DEVELOPMENT. New Haven, Conn.,
Yale University Press, 1961. 217p. $1.95
    This general theoretical analysis of economic development is of special
interest. The author's concepts were inspired by his experience in Colombia
and other Latin American countries. He takes issue with the traditional
concept of "balanced development" and puts considerable emphasis on com-
plementary and "linkeage" effects which some industries show to a higher
degree than others. [HLAS 23:1671]

416.
Hodder, B.W. ECONOMIC DEVELOPMENT IN THE TROPICS. New York, New York,
Barnes and Noble, 1968. 258p. tables $3.00
    In an inter-disciplinary manner the author examines the major problems
of development confronting tropical countries today. Venezuela and Trinidad
and Tobago are used as case studies in a work that basically transcends the
Latin American region. [Charles Fleener]

417.
Holiday Editors. TRAVEL GUIDE TO MEXICO. Rev. ed. New York, Random House,
1966. 278p. illus. $1.65

418.
----------. TRAVEL GUIDE TO THE CARIBBEAN AND THE BAHAMAS. Rev. ed.
New York, Random House, 1966. 258p. illus. $1.65

419.
Holmberg, Allan R. NOMADS OF THE LONG BOW: THE SIRIONO OF EASTERN BOLIVIA.
New York, Doubleday, 1950. 104p. $1.95
An important study on the Siriono Indians by a noted anthropologist.
Includes a bibliography.

420.
Hopkins, Jack W. THE GOVERNMENT EXECUTIVE OF MODERN PERU. Gainesville,
University of Florida Press, 1967. 141p. map, tables $1.95
This case study examines the senior civil servants of the Peruvian government. The origins, family education, and attitudes are investigated empirically. An introductory study of the role and nature of the Latin American
government executive has been added. [Charles Fleener]

421.
Hopper, Janice H., ed. INDIANS OF BRAZIL IN THE TWENTIETH CENTURY. Edited
and translated by Janice H. Hopper. Washington, Institute for Cross-Cultural
Research, 1967. 246p. illus. maps $6.95
This work provides the most complete and accurate source of information
now available in English on indigenous Brazilian tribes. It includes one
original contribution by Dale W. Kietzman, and three translated items by
Darcy Ribeiro, Eduardo Galvão, and Herbert Baldus. The book also includes an
up-to-date tribal catalogue, a glossary of Brazilian terms of the interior,
a critical report on ethnological research completed between 1953 and 1960,
and a select bibliography. The translations are very good.

422.
Hopson, William L., and L. O'Conner. MEXICO AFTER DARK. New York, Macfadden,
1969. 193p. $0.75

423.
Horgan, Paul. THE CENTURIES OF SANTA FE. New York, Dutton, 1960. 363p.
illus. $1.75
This is a well-written history of Santa Fe under Spanish rule (1610-1821),
under Mexico (1821-1846), and as part of the United States. It points out the
long Hispanic tradition of this old capital of Spain in America. Includes a
selective bibliography.

424.
-------------. CONQUISTADOS IN NORTH AMERICAN HISTORY. Greenwich, Conn.,
Fawcett Publications, 1965. 240p. $0.95
Popular treatment of the Spanish conquerors in what is today Mexico and
the United States. This interesting narrative includes a brief
bibliography.

425.
Horowitz, Irving Louis. ANARCHISTS. New York, Dell, 1964. 640p. $0.95
An able student of radical movements analyzes anarchism and many of its
leading figures.

426.
----------------------, ed. CUBAN COMMUNISM. New York, Aldine Pub. Co.,
1970. 143p. $2.45
These essays originally appeared in the April 1969 issue of Trans-action.
The essays are entitled "Cuban Communism;" Revolution: For Internal Con-
sumption only;" "Student Power in Action;" "The Revolutionary Offensive;"
"The Moral Economy of a Revolutionary Society;" and "Cuba Revolution without
a Blueprint."

427.
------------------------, Josué de Castro and John Gerassi, eds. LATIN
AMERICAN RADICALISM: A DOCUMENTARY REPORT ON LEFT AND NATIONALIST MOVEMENTS.
New York, Vintage Books, 1969. 646p. $2.45
This documentary reader includes contributions from several distinguished
economists such as Raul Prebisch and Celso Furtado, political leaders such
as Eduardo Frei, Che Guevara and Fidel Castro, influential thinkers such as
Hélio Jaguaribe and Gino Germani. The essays attempt to explain the role of
the Latin American left.

428.
------------------------, ed. MASSES IN LATIN AMERICA. New York, Oxford
University Press, 1970. 608p. tables $3.95
The essays included here seek to define social sectors, interest groups,
and ethnic and national elements existing in Latin America, to place them
in historical perspective and to show empirically how they exert pressures.

429.
--------------------------. THE RISE AND FALL OF PROJECT CAMELOT: STUDIES
IN THE RELATIONSHIP BETWEEN SOCIAL SCIENCE AND PRACTICAL POLITICS. Cambridge,
Massachusetts Institute of Technology Press, 1967. 385p. tables $3.95
Includes articles and papers representing the viewpoints of social
scientists and statesmen who were involved in Project Camelot, "a study whose
objective is to determine the feasibility of developing a general social
systems model which would make it possible to predict and influence
politically significant aspects of social change in the developing countries
of the world." The major point at issue is the extent to which the academic
community should assist in governmental studies and comment upon matters relevant to military science and technology. [Charles Fleener]

430.
Howell, Roger, ed. PRESCOTT: THE CONQUEST OF MEXICO AND THE CONQUEST OF PERU.
New York, Washington Square Press, 1966. 406p. $1.45
Abridged versions of Prescott's two classic histories.

431.
Huberman, Leo and Paul M. Sweezy. eds. REGIS DEBRAY AND THE LATIN AMERICAN
REVOLUTION: A COLLECTION OF ESSAYS. New York, Monthly Review Press, 1969.
147p. $1.95
These essays review Régis Debray's 1967 book Revolution in the revolution?
Most of the commentators are critical of Debray's severe judgment handed
down against all the existing political parties in a letter from his Bolivian
jail cell. It appears here as the last entry. [Charles Fleener]

432.
Hudson, William Henry. GREEN MANSIONS. Introd. by N. R. Teitel. New York,
Airmont, 1970. 254p. $0.50
The introduction analyzes Hudson's life and work.

433.
------------------------. GREEN MANSIONS. New York, AMSCO Music Book Pub. Co.,
1965. $0.85
A haunting novel revealing a passionate love of nature by the famous
Anglo-Argentine naturalist and writer. By sheer glow of beauty it is a
prose poem in a South American jungle setting.

434.
------------------------. GREEN MANSIONS. New York, Bantam Books, 1963. 269p.
$0.60
See above comment.

435.
------------------------. GREEN MANSIONS. New York, Dell, 1968. 256p. $0.60
Another edition of this perennial favorite about the South American jungle.

436.
Huebener, Theodore. ASI ES PUERTO RICO! New York, Holt, Rinehart, and
Winston, 1960. 122p. $3.80
    Textbook edition intended for Spanish courses.

437.
Hulet, Claude L., comp. LATIN AMERICAN POETRY IN ENGLISH TRANSLATION: A
BIBLIOGRAPHY. Washington, Pan American Union, 1965. 192p (PAU 860-E-7157;
Basic bibliographies, 2) $0.75
    This is a very useful bibliography of anthologies, books and individual
poems by Latin Americans which have been translated into English.

438.
----------------------. LATIN AMERICAN PROSE IN ENGLISH TRANSLATION: A
BIBLIOGRAPHY. Washington, Pan American Union, 1964. 191p. (PAU-E-6939;
Basic bibliographies, 1) $0.75
    The first in the Basic bibliographies series of the Pan American Union,
this work attempts to cover all English translations of Latin American
novels, short stories, and literary articles published through August 1,
1962. A useful reference tool.

439.
Humphreys, Robert Arthur, and John Lynch, eds. THE ORIGINS OF THE LATIN
AMERICAN REVOLUTION, 1808-1826. Edited with an introd. by R. A. Humpreys
and John Lynch. New York, Knopf, 1965. 308p. (Borzoi books on Latin
America) $2.50
    A collection of scholarly papers on such topics as the enlightenment in
Spanish America, the exiled Jesuits, the role of Britain, France, and the
United States, and the decline of the Spanish empore. It includes a
bibliography.

440.
Hunter, Frederick James, ed. A GUIDE TO THEATRE AND DRAMA COLLECTION AT THE
UNIVERSITY OF TEXAS PRESS. Austin, University of Texas Press, 1967. 84p.
illus. $2.00
    This is a welcome guide to the University of Texas Library's outstanding
collection of theatrical works.

441.
Huxley Francis. AFFABLE SAVAGES: AN ANTHROPOLOGIST AMONG THE URUBU INDIANS
OF BRAZIL. New York, Putnam, 1966. 285p. maps $1.75
    First published in 1956, this is an anthropological study of the Urubu
Indians in the State of Maranhão, Brazil.

442.
Hyidtefeldt, A. TEOTL AND IXIPTLATLI: SOME CENTRAL CONCEPTIONS IN ANCIENT
MEXICAN RELIGION. New York, Humanities Press, 1970. Price not set
    This is a thorough study of pre-Columbian religions of Mesoamerica.

443.
Im Thurn, Everard F. AMONG THE INDIANS OF GUIANA. New York, Dover Publications, 1967. 445p. illus., maps $3.00
    Originally published in 1883, this work presents the first extensive
observations of the culture of the Indians of the forest and remote
interior Savannah country of present day Guyana. This edition is an
unabridged version of the first one.

444.
Ingram, L. S. MORMONISMO INVESTIGADO. Chicago, Moody Press, 1970. 94p.
$0.35
    This is a basic explanation of Mormonism to a Spanish-speaking audience.

445.
Inman, Samuel Guy. INTER-AMERICAN CONFERENCES, 1826-1954; HISTORY AND
PROBLEMS. Edited by Harold Eugene Davis. Washington, University Press
of Washington, 1966. 282p. $5.00
    The author traces the development of the inter-American system through
the hemispheric conferences. This is a very valuable survey for the
student of international relations.

446.
Instituto Internacional de Literatura Iberoamericana. AN OUTLINE HISTORY
OF SPANISH AMERICAN LITERATURE. 3d. ed. John E. Englekirk, editor.
New York, Appleton-Century-Crofts, 1965. 252p. maps $3.45
    This revised edition published in 1941, is a continuous outline of the
development of Spanish-American literature arranged into three periods:
from discovery to Independence; from Independence to the Mexican Revolution;
from the Mexican Revolution to the present. Each topic has references to
the leading handbooks and works of criticism, and sound reevaluations of
the writers. An excellent compilation which will be very useful in
literature courses.

447.
International Bank for Reconstruction and Development. ECONOMIC DEVELOP-
MENT OF NICARAGUA. Baltimore, Johns Hopkins University Press 1970. 57p.
tables $1.00
    Outlines briefly the principal aspects of economic development in
Nicaragua.

448.
International Music Council. FOLK SONGS OF THE AMERICAS. Edited by A. L.
Lloyd and Isabel Aretz de Ramón y Rivera. New York, Oak Publications, 1970.
285p. $2.95
    This is a polyglot edition of the most popular fold songs of the
hemisphere. It includes the music and words of 150 folk songs. Those in
Spanish and French Creole are accompanied by English translations.

449.
ISLE OF ENCHANTMENT: STORIES AND PEOPLE OF PUERTO RICO. St. Louis, Mo.,
Bethany Press, 1970. 96p. $1.95
    Puerto Rico is depicted in eight stories that portray the simple dignity
and untarnished grace of the people.

450.
Jackson, D. Bruce. CASTRO, THE KREMLIN, AND COMMUNISM IN LATIN AMERICA.
Baltimore, Johns Hopkins Press, 1969. 163p. (Studies in international
affairs series,9) $2.45
    Surveys Soviet-Cuban relations from 1964 to 1967, concentrating on
Cuban radicalism, Castro's feud with Mao Tse-Tung, the 1965 Dominican
crisis, the 1966 Tricontinental Conference, the withdrawal of the
Venezuelan Communist Party from guerrilla warfare, and the replacement of
Che Guevara by Régis Debray as chief Cuban ideologist.

451.
Jacobs, Charles R., and Babette M. Jacobs. MEXICO TRAVEL DIGEST. 3d. rev.
ed. Los Angeles, Paul, Richmond, and Co., 1969. 169p. illus. $2.50

452.
--. SOUTH AMERICA TRAVEL DIGEST.
6th ed. Los Angeles, Paul, Richmond, and Co., 1970. 159p. illus. $3.50
    The authors present and attractive and informative guide to travel
throughout South America.

453.
Jacobs, Wilbur R., John W. Caughey, and Joe B. Frantz. TURNER, BOLTON, AND WEBB: THREE HISTORIANS OF THE AMERICAN FRONTIER. Seattle, University of Washington, Press 1965. 113p. illus. $1.95
Of the three historians presented in this work, Bolton studies chiefly the Spanish borderlands and Spain's influence in North America. Turner and Webb deal with the cultural clash between Anglo-American and Spanish-Mexican traditions on the American frontier. Includes a bibliography.

454.
Jahn, Ernst A. PAN AMERICAN HIGHWAY GUIDE. New York, Compsco Pub. Co., 1969. 421p. illus., maps $4.95
The author has compiled current information on train, bus, and freighter fares and schedules of both the popular and remote areas of Mexico, Central, and South America.

455.
James, Cyril Lionel Robert. BLACK JACOBINS: TOUSSAINT L'OUVERTURE AND THE SAN DOMINGO REVOLUTION. 2d ed. rev. New York, Random House, 1963. 426p. map $1.95
First published in 1938, this book traces the career of Toussaint l'Ouverture and the history of the San Domingo Revolution. The appendix entitled "From Toussaint l'Ouverture to Fidel Castro" deals with Haiti and the West Indian quest for national identify during the last century and a half. Includes a bibliography.

456.
James, Daniel. CHE GUEVARA. New York, Stein and Day, 1970. 256p. $3.95
The author has assembled a thorough biography of Ernesto (Che) Guevara.

457.
James, Rebecca Salisbury. CAMPOSANTOS; A PHOTOGRAPHIC ESSAY. Photographs by Dorothy Benrimo. Austin, University of Texas Press, 1966. 75p. (chiefly illus.) $4.00
A beautiful photographic essay about New Mexico crosses and other folk art, accompanied by a historical essay.

458.
James, Thomas. THREE YEARS AMONG THE INDIANS AND MEXICANS. Philadelphia, Lippincott, 1962. 173p. illus. $1.25
This is an abridged version of the original 1846 edition of the author's experiences as a fur trader among the Comanches and Mexicans along the Santa Fe trail, 1809-1810, and 1821-1824. It also discusses U.S. expansion into Mexico.

459.
Jekyll, Walter, ed. JAMAICAN SONG AND STORY; ANNANCY STORIES, DIGGING TUNES, RING TUNES, AND DANCING. New York, Dover, 1966. 288p. $2.50
51 stories and 145 songs collected by the editor are presented with their music. This volume is an unabridged reproduction of the 1907 edition which includes an introduction by Alice Werner describing the connection of African folklore with Jamaican stories. Three new essays appraise the contemporary relevance of these stories and the importance of Jekyll's book. [Charles Fleener]

460.
Jesús, Carolina María de. CHILD OF THE DARK: THE DIARY OF CAROLINA MARIA DE JESUS. Translated from the Portuguese by David St. Clair. New York, New American Library, 1969. 159p. $0.75
English translation of the award-winning Brazilian novel Quarto de de despejo: diário de uma favelada (1960) written by a woman who was unemployed, uneducated, and burdened with three illegitimate children. A moving account of life in a São Paulo slum as it could be described only by one who has lived there many years.

461.
Jiménez, E. and C. Puncel. JUEGOS MENIQUES. Illus. by G.T.Martinez.
Glendale, Calif., Bowmar, 1970. 269p. $2.25
  Describes popular games of Latin America.

462.
----------------------------. VERSITOS PARA CHIQUITINES. Glendale, Calif.,
Bowmar, 1970. 254p. $2.25
  Contains poems for children in Spanish.

463.
Johnson, Harvey L., ed. CONTEMPORARY LATIN AMERICA. Houston, Texas,
University of Houston, Office of International Affairs, 1969. 69p. $2.00
  This volume contains 11 papers that were presented at the University
of Houston's Third Annual conference on Latin America, April, 1969. The
subjects range from Gloria Shatto's study of the San Blas Indians to Germán
Arciniegas' reflections on "Nuestra América en los libros." [Charles
Fleener]

464.
----------. ed. CONTINUITY AND CHANGE IN LATIN AMERICA. Stanford, Calif.,
Stanford, University Press, 1967. 282p. $2195
  Nine papers prepared for a conference held at Scottsdale, Arizona, in
1963. The authors are academic specialists in the several disciplines of
the social sciences and humanities. Although the central theme is of
change and continuity, each has its political connotations. This is a
distinguished collection, worthy of attention. [HLAS 27:3038b]

465.
----------. THE MILITARY AND SOCIETY IN LATIN AMERICA. Stanford, Calif.,
Stanford University Press, 1964. 308p. $2.95
  A good interpretation of military and civilian relations in the
Latin American republics during the 19th and 20th centuries. The chapter
on Brazil is especially good. The Cuban military under Castro is also
covered.

466.
----------------. POLITICAL CHANGE IN LATIN AMERICA: THE EMERGENCE OF THE
MIDDLE SECTORS. Stanford, Calif., Stanford University Press, 1961. 272p.
$2.95
  First published in 1958 this work this work argues that political change
occurs when the "middle sectors" (not middle classes of society become
aware of their interests and demand appropriate political power. Five
countries are covered: Argentina, Brazil, Chile, Mexico, and Uruguay.
Originally published in 1958.

467.
----------------. ed. THE ROLE OF THE MILITARY IN UNDER-DEVELOPED COUNTRIES.
Princeton, N.J., Princeton University Press, 1962. 426p. $2.95
  Presents the papers read at a 1959 RAND Corporation conference designed
to provide a forum for the exchange of information and ideas on militarism.
The editor, Edwin Lieuwen, and Victor Alba present views on different
aspects of the military in Latin America. [Charles Fleener]

468.
----------------. SIMON BOLIVAR AND SPANISH AMERICAN INDEPENDENCE; 1783-
1830, by John J. Johnson with the collaboration of Doris M. Ladd.
Princeton, N.J., Van Nostrand, 1968. 223p. $1.95
  A factual biography of Simón Bolívar, the most influential figure in
the Latin American independence movement. Bolívar was in favor of strong
government as the only workable system to ward off anarchy. He also
wanted a large federated state for South America. Includes a bibliography.

469.
Johnson, Kenneth F. ARGENTINA'S MOSAIC OF DISCORD, 1966-1968. Washington, Institute for the Comparative Study of Political Systems, 1969. 61p. $2.00

Surveys Argentine politics from the Onganía Revolution of 1966 through 1968, emphasizing the different ideologies from the Marxist and socialist sectors to the Peronist factions, including the liberal and conservative groups.

470.
----------. THE GUATEMALAN PRESIDENTIAL ELECTION OF MARCH 6, 1966: AN ANALYSIS. Washington, Institute for the Comparative Study of Political Systems, 1967. 25p. $1.00

Includes a succinct background outline of Guatemalan political life as well as a description of the 1966 election which was orderly and democratic.

471.
Jones, Fayette Alexander. OLD MINES AND GHOST CAMPS OF NEW MEXICO. Edited by E. E. Bartholomew. 2d. ed. Fort Davis, Texas, Frontier Book Co., 1964. 92p. illus. $4.00

The original title was New Mexico mines and minerals. It is a thorough analysis of New Mexico mining.

472.
Jones Julie. THE ART OF EMPIRE: THE INCA OF PERU. New York, Museum of Primitive Art, Distributed by the New York Graphic Arts Society, 1964. 56p. illus., map $3.95

This is a beautifully illustrated guide to the art of the Inca empire, reproducing art works in gold, silver, and also textiles.

473.
----------. A BIBLIOGRAPHY OF OLMEC SCULPTURE. NO. 2. New York, Museum of Primitive Art, Distributed by the New York Graphic Arts Society, 1969. 31p. illus. $0.75

This useful bibliography of Olmec sculpture is a welcome addition for the collector's and the student's library of pre-Columbian art.

474.
----------. SCULPTURE FROM PERU. New York, Museum of Primitive Art, Distributed by the New York Graphic Arts Society, 1963. 8p. illus. $0.75

A catalog of an exhibit of Peruvian sculptures which bridges several periods.

475.
Jones, Tom Bard, and others. A BIBLIOGRAPHY OF SOUTH AMERICAN ECONOMIC AFFAIRS: ARTICLES IN 19th CENTURY PERIODICALS. Minneapolis, University of Minnesota Press, 1955. 146p. $5.50

476.
Joralemon, Peter David. A STUDY OF OLMEC ICONOGRAPHY. Washington, Dumbarton Oaks, 1971. 40p. illus. (Studies in pre-Columbian art and archaeology, 7) $2.50

Comprises and analytical study of diverse elements of Olmec sculpture. It is attractively illustrated.

477.
Kahl, Joseph Alan. COMPARATIVE PRESPECTIVES OF STRATIFICATION: MEXICO, GREAT BRITAIN, JAPAN. Boston, Little Brown, 1968. 235p. illus. $3.95

Compares levels of economic development and social stratification in three countries at different stages of industrialization.

479.
Kan Michael. ANCIENT SCULPTURE OF WEST MEXICO. Los Angeles, Los Angeles
Count Museum of Art, 1971. 116p. illus. $2.45
 The text is enhanced by 74 illustrations depicting clay sculptures from
the graves and tombs of Nayarit, Jalisco, and Colima.

480.
Kantor, Harry, IDEOLOGY AND PROGRAM OF THE PERUVIAN APRISTA PARTY. Rev.
ed. Washington, Savile Book Store, 1966. 175p. $4.95
 An authoritative analysis of Aprismo, its development, policies, and
programs. The first edition appeared in 1952, and a Spanish translation
entitled Ideología y programa del movimiento Aprista was published in 1955.
The present edition has been brought up to date with an epilogue which
continues the history of the movement up to 1965.

481.
----------. LATIN AMERICAN POLITICAL PARTIES: A BIBLIOGRAPHY. Gainesville,
University of Florida Press, 1968. 113p. $2.50
 A specialized bibliography of the most important political parties of
Latin America. More than 2,200 items are included. This will be a very
useful guide to researchers in the field.

482.
Karner, Frances P. THE SEPHARDICS OF CURAÇAO: A SHORT STUDY OF SOCIO-
CULTURE PATTERNS IN FLUX. New York, Humanities Press, 1971. 94p. $3.50
 Studies the social accultruation of the Sephardic Jews in Curaçao. It
is an incisive and thoughtful contribution, with a very good foreword by
Harry Hoetink, leading sociologist in Caribbean studies.

483.
Kaufman, Robert R. THE CHILEAN POLITICAL RIGHT AND AGRARIAN REFORM:
RESISTANCE AND MODERATION. Washington, Institute for the Comparative Study
of Political Systems, 1967. 48p. tables $2.00
 Argues that the rightist political groups in Chile have shown a dis-
position toward bargaining and compromises on the issue of agrarian reform
and that this basic attitude in an important factor in understanding the
stability of the Chilean political system. [Charles Fleener]

484.
Keen Benjamin A., ed. AMERICANS ALL: THE STORY OF OUR LATIN AMERICAN
NEIGHBORS. New York, Dell, 1966. 254p. $0.50
 A simplified history of Latin America from conquest to the present. It
includes a chapter on the history of United States relations with Latin
America.

485.
----------. READING IN LATIN AMERICAN CIVILIZATION; 1492 TO THE PRESENT.
2d. ed. Boston, Houghton, Mifflin, 1963. 477p. tables $2.25
 This is a balanced collection of translations, with helpful introductory
materials.. These are chiefly source materials, stressing creeds, ideals,
often juxtaposing rivil or clashing contemporary views.

486.
Kelemen, Pál. ART OF THE AMERICAS: ANCIENT AND HISPANIC, WITH A COM-
PARATIVE CHAPTER ON THE PHILIPPINES. New York, Crowell, 1970. 402p.
illus. $4.95
 The archaeological sections on ancient American art includes new data
gathered at new sites. This is a valuable book showing the transition of
pre-Hispanic to colonial art, pointing out trends, and including a section
on colonial art in the Philippines. The text is enhanced by 338 well-chosen
black and white photographs.

487.
----------. BAROQUE AND ROCOCO IN LATIN AMERICA. **Rev. ed.** New York,
Dover Publications, 1967. 2 v. illus. $3.00
   Originally published in 1951, this handsome work contains a comprehen-
sive picture of colonial art in Latin America. Of special interest is the
method of presenting the work in iconographic groups, so that a given theme
may be seen as interpreted in different countries throughout the New World.
This is a major contribution to the history of art in Latin America.

488.
----------. MEDIEVAL AMERICAN ART: MASTERPIECES OF THE NEW WORLD BEFORE
COLUMBUS. Rev. ed. New York, Dover Publications, 1970. 2 v. illus.
$3.75
   One of the foremost authorities on American art proves that the great
art period of pre-Columbian America coincides in time and quality with
those of medieval Asia and Europe. The text describes the art history
of native Americans from the U.S. Southwest through the Andean regions.
Almost 1,000 photographs illustrate outstanding art and architectural works.

489.
Kendrick, Edith Johnston. REGIONAL DANCES OF MEXICO. Illus. by Rose
Remund. Lincolnwood, Ill., National Textbooks, 1963. 58p. maps $1.00
   Descriptions of folk music and dances from various regions of Mexico.
The author aims to provide programs for Spanish classes. [Charles Fleener]

490.
Kennedy, Robert F. THIRTEEN DAYS. Introd. by Robert S. McNamara and
Harold MacMillian. New York, Norton, 1970. 224p. illus. $0.95
   The principal protagonist of the momentous confrontation between the
U.S. and the Soviet Union over the Cuban missiles presents his memoirs
about those fateful days. An important document.

491.
Kenner, Martin, <u>and</u> James Petras, <u>eds</u>. FIDEL CASTRO SPEAKS. New York,
Grove Press, 1969. 332p. $1.45
   The editors have selected a broad topical selection of speeches by
Fidel Castro.

492.
Kenworthy, Leonard S. STUDYING SOUTH AMERICA IN ELEMENTARY AND SECONDARY
SCHOOLS. Rev. ed. New York, Columbia University Teachers College, 1967.
54p. $1.95
   Contains a curriculum for elementary and secondary school teachers who
are presenting units on South America. Also included are lists of a wide
variety of teaching aids on the subject, such as film strips, booklets, etc.
[Charles Fleener]

493.
Kepple, Ella Huff. FUN AND FESTIVAL FROM LATIN AMERICA. New York, Friend-
ship Press, 1961. 48p. $0.95
   Describes a variety of celebrations and <u>fiestas</u> in Latin America.

494.
Kidder, Alfred Vincent. THE ARTIFACTS OF UAXACTUN, GUATEMALA. Washington,
Carnegie Institution of Washington, 1947. 76p. illus. $2.15
   Contains full descriptions of all the artifacts of stone, bone, shell,
clay, and perishable material from the site. The areal and temporal dis-
tributions of many of the now important forms are traced in detail and
their implications discussed, making it an extremely valuable contribution
to Mesoamerican archaeology.

495.
----------. INTRODUCTION TO THE STUDY OF SOUTHWESTERN
ARCHAEOLOGY. Introd. by Irving Rouse. New Haven, Conn., Yale University
Press, 1962. 377p. illus. $2.95
   Describes archaeological sites and materials in the Southwest.

496.
King, Mary Elizabeth. ANCIENT PERUVIAN TEXTILES FROM THE COLLECTION OF
THE TEXTILE MUSEUM, WASHINGTON, D.C. New York, Museum of Primitive Art,
distributed by the New York Graphic Arts Society, 1965. 45p. chiefly
illus. map $3.75
   Presents items from Washington's Textile Museum. The illustrations are
excellent.

497.
Kingsbury, Robert C., and Ronald M. Schneider. AN ATLAS OF LATIN AMERICAN
AFFAIRS. New York, Praeger, 1965. 136p. maps $1.95
   60 excellent maps by Kingsbury, and accompanying text by Schneider,
present a sound picture of the historical background and the contemporary
political, economic, and social reality of Latin America.

498.
Kinsbruner, Jay. DIEGO PORTALES: INTERPRETATIVE ESSAYS ON THE MAN AND
TIMES. The Hague, Martinus Nijhoff, 1967. 102p. $4.00
   This work's central feature is the Chilean constitution of 1833. It is
framed by essays on Diego Portales, the dictator who controlled Chile from
1829 to 1837. The author imaginatively questions the conventional wisdom
of historians who have dealt with this period and suggests some new
interpretations of the man and his age. [Charles Fleener]

499.
Korngold, Ralph. CITIZEN TOUSSAINT. New York, Hill and Wang, 1965. 338p.
$2.25
   Biography of the Haitian slave who became the leader of his country's
independence movement which was first published in 1944. It is a balanced
study, part personal biography and part a general history for the struggle
for independence from France. [Charles Fleener]

500.
Kraft, Walter C. CODICES VINDOBONENSES HISPANICI. Corvallis, Oregon State
University Press, 1957. 64p. illus. $1.00
   Presents facsimile reproductions from and commentaries about the Vienna
codices.

501.
Kramer, P., and Robert E. McNicoll, eds. LATIN AMERICAN PANORAMA. New
York, Putnam, 1971. 321p. illus. $2.75

502.
Kriesbert, Martin, ed. PUBLIC ADMINISTRATION IN DEVELOPING COUNTRIES.
Washington, Brookings Institution, 1965. 168p. $2.95
   Despite the general title, Latin America is the focus of this collection
of papers delivered at a 1963 conference in Bogotá. The articles analyze
factors affecting public administration in developing countries; the
organization of government for development; establishment of a civil service;
and education, training, and research in public administration.

503.
La Barre, Weston. THE PEYOTE CULT. Rev. ed. New York, Schocken Books.
1969. 260p. illus. $2.45
   This scholarly anthropological study was first published in 1938. The
author has added a new preface, as well as a survey of recent studies
about the Amerindian ritual based on the peyote plant. Contains a bibliograpy
bibliography.

504.
Lamb, Ruth Stanton. LATIN AMERICA: SITES AND INSIGHTS. Claremont, Calif.,
Creative Press, 1963. 67p. $4.00
   Vignettes about people, places, and ideas in Latin America from Conquest
to the present. Includes a brief bibliography.

505.
Lambert, Jacques. LATIN AMERICA: SOCIAL STRUCTURE AND POLITICAL INSTITU-
TIONS. Translated by Helen Katel. Berkeley, University of California
Press, 1967. 413p. $3.25
    Analyzes Latin American political institutions in relation to the
different social structures.

506.
Landy, David. TROPICAL CHILDHOOD: CULTURAL TRANSMISSION AND LEARNING IN
A PUERTO RICAN VILLAGE. New York, Harper and Row, 1965. 291p. tables
$1.95
    First published in 1959, this is essentially a study of the socializa-
tion process among lower class families in a sugar cane area of eastern
Puerto Rico. Two chapters which describe culture and society in Valle
Caña add to the scope and interest of the work, as does a chapter on
marriage and family.

507.
Langley, Lester D. THE CUBAN POLICY OF THE UNITED STATES: A BRIEF HISTORY.
New York, Wiley, 1968. 203p. maps $2.95
    A brief historical outline of the Cuban policy of the U.S. from the
early part of the 19th century to the Cuban missile crisis of 1962. Points
out the self-interest and idealism that has characterized U.S. policy
towards Cuba, and maintains that Cuba has always played an important part
in U.S. foreign policy.

508.
------------------. THE U.S., CUBA, AND THE COLD WAR: AMERICAN FAILURE OR
COMMUNIST CONSPIRACY. Boston, Heath, 1971. 285p. $1.25
    Analyzes U.S.-Cuban relations during the aftermath of the 1962 missile
crisis.

509.
Lanning, Edward P. PERU BEFORE THE INCAS. Englewood Cliffs, N.J., Prentice-
Hall, 1967. 216p. illus., tables $2.95
    A survey of Peruvian prehistory beginning about 12,000 years ago. The
author divides Peruvian cultural history into preceramic and ceramic stages
and then further into periods. This work is a major contribution to the
study of Andean prehistory updating with new research reports the works
Andean culture history by Bennett and Bird, and Ancient civilizations of
Peru by Mason. Includes a bibliography.

510.
Lara-Braud, Jorge. OUR CLAIM ON THE FUTURE: A CONTROVERSIAL COLLECTION FROM
LATIN AMERICA. Illus. by K. Tureck. New York, Friendship Press, 1971.
135p. $1.95
    Studies protestantism in Latin America.

511.
------------------, trans. SOCIAL JUSTICE AND THE LATIN CHURCHES. Richmond,
Va., John Knox Press, 1969. 137p. $2.95
    Contains papers presented at the Latin American Conference on Church
and Society which met in El Tabo, Chile, in January 1966. They conclude
that the hope for justice in Latin America lies in self-determination and
that this cannot be achieved without a radical transformation of society

512.
Larson, Magali Sarfatti, and Arlene Eisen Bergman. SOCIAL STRATIFICATION
IN PERU. Berkeley, University of California Press, 1970. 341p. $2.50
    According to the authors, this monograph attempts to present an image
of the structure of social stratification in Peru. They also outline processes that may represent important conditions in the evolution or stagnation of the Peruvian social system. [Charles Fleener]

513.
Lawrence, David Herbert. MORNINGS IN MEXICO AND ETRUSCAN PLACES. New York, Viking, 1965. 214p. $1.25
Written by a towering figure in English literature, this work contains penetrating glimpses and beautiful imagery of Mexico in the 1920's.

514.
------------------------. THE PLUMED SERPENT: QUETZALCOATL. Introd. by William York Tindall. New York, Random House, 1955. 487p. $1.95
A splendid novel set in Mexico and New Mexico, full of symbols and superb descriptions of dancing Indians and other indigenous spectacles.

515.
Leal, Luis. AMADO NERVO: SUS MEJORES CUENTOS. Boston, Houghton, Mifflin, 1969. 241p. $2.75
Includes the Mexican poet and novelist's best known short stories.

516.
----------. MEXICO: CIVILIZACIONES Y CULTURAS. Boston, Houghton, Mifflin, 1955. 205p. illus. $4.50
Outlines the rich mosaic of Mexican culture and civilization, tracing it back to the ancient pre-Columbian cultures.

517.
Lehman, Leona. LATIN AMERICAN DANCES. Bridgeport, Conn., Associated Bookseller, 1968. 95p. $1.00
Explains and describes a variety of Latin American folk dances.

518.
Leiden, Carl, and Karl M. Schmitt. THE POLITICS OF VIOLENCE: REVOLUTION THE MODERN WORLD. Englewood Cliffs, N.J., Prentice Hall, 1968. 244p. $2.95
Explores the meaning of revolution in the 20th century and seeks the connection between violence and the contemporary political process. Cuba and Mexico (along with Egypt and Turkey) are analyzed to ascertain the preconditions of revolution, the role of ideology, the developmental stages, and the relationship of violence to revolutionary action. [Charles Fleener]

519.
Leiserson, Alcira. NOTES ON THE PROCESS OF INDUSTRIALIZATION IN ARGENTINA, CHILE, AND PERU. Berkeley, University of California, Institute of International Studies, 1966. 99p. tables. $1.75
Reviews the economic development of Argentina, Chile, and Peru from the point of view of industrialization. It outlines the contribution of immigrants and foreign capital to industrialization.

520.
León-Portilla, Miguel. BROKEN SPEARS: THE AZTEC ACCOUNT OF THE CONQUEST OF MEXICO. Translated by Angel María Garibay and Lysander Kemp. Boston, Beacon Press, 1966. 168p. illus., map. $1.95
Put together from native accounts, this is largely the story of the defeat, and the subsequent chaos, and grief of the fallen Aztecs, written by men who wanted to remind Spain of her debt to them. The introduction summarizes the Aztec way of life, and the situation surrounding the conquest. It was first published in 1962.

521.
Leonard, Irving. BAROQUE TIMES IN OLD MEXICO: SEVENTEENTH-CENTURY PERSONS, PLACES, AND PRACTICES. Ann Arbor, University of Michigan Press, 1966. 260p. illus., maps. $1.95
Presents scenes, persons, and events of 17th century Mexico to show the Baroque characteristics of the period. Emphasis is on literary manifestations, but the Baroque is seen also as the pattern in which "the frustrated dynamism of Old and New Spain alike found its most enduring expression in life and thought." Chapters on Fray García Guerra, Francisco de Aguiar y Seijas, Sor Juana Inés de la Cruz, the Baroque society, and others. Includes a bibliography.

522.
Leonard, Olin E., _and_ Charles P. Loomis, _eds_. READINGS IN LATIN AMERICAN
SOCIAL ORGANIZATION AND INSTITUTIONS. East Lansing, Michigan State Uni-
versity Press, 1963. 320p. maps, tables. $5.00
   Contains 36 articles with a social science orientation designed to acq-
uaint students with Latin America.

523.
Levi-Strauss, Claude. TRISTES TROPIQUES: AN ANTHROPOLOGICAL STUDY OF
PRIMITIVE SOCIETIES IN BRAZIL. New York, Atheneum, 1964. 404p. $2.45
   This is a valuable anthropological study of primitive societies in
Brazil by a noted French scholar. Includes a bibliography.

524.
Levine, Suzanne Jill, _comp._ LATIN AMERICA; FICTION AND POETRY IN TRANS-
LATION. New York, Center for Inter-American Relations, 1971. 70p.
$1.25
   Includes books by authors from Spanish and Portuguese speaking countries
of the Americas through the end of 1961. This is a welcome addition to the
field of literature.

525.
Levinson, Jerome, _and_ Juan de Onís. THE ALLIANCE THAT LOST ITS WAY; A
CRITICAL REPORT ON THE ALLIANCE FOR PROGRESS. Chicago, Quadrangle
Books, 1970. 381p. $2.95
   This study was undertaken for the Twentieth Century Fund to report on
the causes of unrest in Latin America. The authors believe that "Latin
America is on the threshold of a new decade in which pressures for econo-
mic growth and social change will...test the political strength of the
inter-American relationship."

526.
Lewald, Herald Ernest. BUENOS AIRES: RETRATO DE UNA SOCIEDAD HISPÁNICA
A TRAVÉS DE SU LITERATURA. Boston, Houghton, Mifflin, 1968. 234p. illus.,
maps, ports. $3.95
   Illustrates Buenos Aires society through rich and varied literature.

527.
Lewis, Oscar. THE CHILDREN OF SÁNCHEZ; AUTOBIOGRAPHY OF A MEXICAN FAMILY.
New York, Random House, 1963. 499p. $2.95
   Taped interviews with members of a poor urban family in Mexico City give
a unique inside view of lower class family life. Dr. Lewis' work is an
important contribution to the study of social dynamics.

528.
------------. DEATH IN THE SANCHEZ FAMILY. New York, Random House, 1970.
160p. $1.65
   The author allows the members of the Sánchez family to tell their own
stories of how the poor die. This is the story of the death of Aunt
Guadalupe and of her funeral.

529.
------------. FIVE FAMILIES: MEXICAN STUDIES IN THE CULTURE OF POVERTY.
Foreword by Oliver LaFarge. New York, New American Library, 1959. 351p.
illus. $0.95
   The author presents one day in the life of five urban Mexican families.
It is a compellingly written, novel approach of considerable interest.

530.
------------. LIFE IN A MEXICAN VILLAGE: TEPOZTLÁN RESTUDIED. Illus. by
Alberto Beltrán. Urbana, University of Illinois Press, 1963. 512p. illus.
maps. $2.95
   A new study of the Mexican village where Robert Refield spent eight
months in 1926 and 1927, with special reference to methodological and
theoretical aspects of the study of social change.

531.
------------. PEDRO MARTINEZ; A MEXICAN PEASANT AND HIS FAMILY. New York,
Random House, 1964. 507p. illus. $2.95
   A detailed account of a Mexican peasant's life from birth (1889) to the
present. The book consists of taped materials, interviews, and conversations, as well as some projective data. This is the best available account of domestic relations in a Meso-american family. Data supplied by
the mother and one son are also included. [HLAS 29:1379]

532.
------------. TEPOZTLÁN; VILLAGE IN MEXICO. New York, Holt, Rinehart and
Winston, 1960. 104p. $1.95
   This is an abridged version of Lewis' Life in a Mexican village, a book
of broad scope about a single village.

533.
------------. LA VIDA: A PUERTO RICAN FAMILY IN THE CULTURE OF POVERTY:
SAN JUAN AND NEW YORK. New York, Random House, 1967. 669p. $2.95
   An important but controversial study utilizing the life history techniques developed by the author in his Mexican research. Methodological
refinements include intensification of the technique by which informants
and events are seen from multiple perspectives, the inclusion of observed
typical days in the life of the family, and the study of the family in
two urban settings: San Juan and New York. [HLAS 29: 1507]

534.
Leyburn, James Graham. THE HAITIAN PEOPLE. New Haven, Conn., Yale University Press, 1966. 342p. maps. $2.45
   A scholarly study of the development of Haitian culture and socio-
political structure since the wars of independence. The interweaving
of caste and class into every phase of Haitian life is explained, providing a basic clue to the use Haiti has made of her resources. This book
was first published in 1941. Includes bibliographies.

535.
Lieuwen, Edwin. ARMS AND POLITICS IN LATIN AMERICA. Rev. ed. New York,
Praeger, 1965. 351p. $2.50
   Published in 1961, this book has two distinct parts which deal with
both the past and present nature of Latin American armed forces, and with
the past and present nature of U.S. policies towards these groups. The
first is narrowly comparative. The second is sharply analytical and
critical, and urges de-emphasis of the support of the military in the
future. [HLAS 23: 2800]

536.
------------. THE UNITED STATES AND THE CHALLENGE TO SECURITY IN LATIN
AMERICA. Columbus, Ohio State University Press, 1966. 98p. $1.50
   Professor Lieuwen sees the challenge exclusively in terms of communist
effectiveness in the area. This single issue is discussed extensively,
but with little more detail than is generally known. [HLAS 29: 6140]

537.
------------. U.S. POLICY IN LATIN AMERICA: A SHORT HISTORY. New York,
Praeger, 1965. 150p. $1.95
   Traces the history of U.S. policy from the Monroe Doctrine to the Good
Neighbor Policy. It also offers a balanced view of present U.S. policy in
Latin America.

538.
Lipset, Seymour M., and Aldo Solari, eds. ELITES IN LATIN AMERICA. New
York, Oxford, University Press, 1967. 531p. $2.95
   A collection of monographs on various elite groups (labor, military,
business, intellectuals, church, etc). Many are papers originally
presented at the June 1965 Montevideo Seminar on Elites and Development in
Latin America.

539.
Liss, Sheldon B. THE CANAL; ASPECTS OF UNITED STATES-PANAMANIAN RELATIONS.
Notre Dame, Ind., University of Notre Dame Press, 1967. 310p. maps.
$2.25
    Studies relations between the U.S. and Panama from 1903 to 1966, center-
ing around the Panama Canal. The author emphasizes the socio-economic
factors which contributed to the turbulent relationship between the two
countries culminating in the 1964 crisis.

540.
---------------. A CENTURY OF DISAGREEMENT: THE CHAMIZAL CONFLICT, 1864-
1964. Washington, University Press 1965. 167p. maps., tables. $4.00
    Documented history of the controversy between Mexico and the U.S. over
the Chamizal tract between Ciudad Juárez and El Paso, with texts of the
relevant treaties, including the settlement of 1963.

541.
List, G. and J. Orrego-Salas, eds. MUSIC IN THE AMERICAS. Bloomington,
Indiana University Press, 1971. 452p. $10.00
    Compiles information on music in the western hemisphere.

542.
Locker, Michael, ed. PATRIA O MUERTE! CUBA: THE ROAD TOWARD A NEW SOCIALISM.
New York, Grossman, 1970. 352p. $3.95
    The editor, and the contributors (William Rose, Peter Rose, Pat Fineran,
Edward Boorstein, and Robin Blackburn) analyze the Cuban Revolution.

543.
Lockwood, Lee. CASTRO'S CUBA, CUBA'S FIDEL: AN AMERICAN JOURNALIST'S
INSIDE LOOK AT TODAY'S CUBA. New York, Random House, 1969. 363p. illus.
$2.95
    Presents an unusual view of Fidel Castro and Cuba based on personal
interviews with the Premier and many members of his government. The text
is accompanied by numerous photographs depicting everyday life. This book
should be of great interest to those studying contemporary Cuba.

544.
López-Lavalle, Maria Esther, comp. BILATERIAL TREATY DEVELOPMENT IN LATIN
AMERICA, 1953-1955. Washington, Pan American Union, Legal Division, Dept.
of International Law, 1956. 158p. (Treaty series, 2; PAU 327-E-5504)
$1.00
    This reference work lists bilateral treaties, conventions, and agree-
ments entered into by the Latin American republics from 1953 through
1955.

545.
López y Fuentes, Gregorio. EL INDIO. Translated by Anita Brenner. New
York, Ungar, 1961. 256p. illus. $1.45
    First published in 1935, this novel epitomizes all that is the essence
of Mexico from pre-Conquest days to the present. Attractive drawings by
Diego Rivera illustrate this prize-winning novel.

546.
-------------------------. EL INDIO. Edited by E. H. Hespelt. New York,
Norton, 1970. 271p. $3.25
    This is an annotated textbook edition of a Mexican classic containing
notes and a vocabulary.

547.
Lummis, Charles Fletcher. LAND OF POCO TIEMPO. Foreword by P. A. Walter.
Albuquerque, University of New Mexico Press, 1952. 236p. $2.25
    This is a facsimile edition of the 1928 classic which deals with
New Mexico's Spanish heritage, the Pueblo Indians, and role of the
Franciscans in the Spanish Southwest. It also includes texts of Spanish
folk songs.

548.
McGann, Thomas F. ARGENTINA: THE DIVIDED LAND. Princeton, N.J., Van
Nostrand, 1966. 127p. $1.45
    A thoughtful and compact study of contemporary Argentina analyzing the
country's national and international situation in light of its geography,
history, and cultural background. A good bibliography is included.

549.
McGavran, Donald, John Huegel, and Jack Taylor. CHURCH GROWTH IN MEXICO.
Grand Rapids, Mich., Eerdmans, 1963. 136p. map, tables. $1.95
    An interpretation of the causes of the expansion of the Protestant
movement in Latin America. Discusses the factors that tend to stimulate
church growth, as well as those that indicate church stagnation.
[Charles Fleener]

550.
Mcgowan, Kenneth, and Joseph A. Hester, Jr. EARLY MAN IN THE NEW WORLD.
Rev. ed., with drawings by Cambell Grant. Garden City, N. Y. Doubleday,
1962. 33p. illus. $1.45
    A popularized discussion of the advent of man to the New World, based
on well-known sources. With limited reservations, this is an informative
introductory volume.

551.
Machado, Manuel A. AN INDUSTRY IN CRISIS: MEXICAN-UNITED STATES COOPERATION
IN THE CONTROL OF FOOT-AND-MOUTH DISEASE. Berkeley, University of California
Press, 1968. 99p. $3.50
    A detailed account of the foot-and-mouth disease (fiebre aftosa) epidemic
introduced into Mexico through Brazilian bulls in 1946, and not totally
eradicated until 1954. Bases on primary sources, this is an important study
of Mexican agriculture and of international agricultural cooperation.

552.
Machado de Assis, Joaquim Maria. DOM CASMURRO. Translated by Helen Caldwell.
Berkeley, University of California Press, 1966. 269p. $1.50
    First published in 1900, Dom Casmurro did not become available in English
until 1953. It is an enchanting, lucid, humorous love story set in 19th
century Rio de Janeiro.

553.
--------------------------------. EPITAPH OF A SMALL WINNER. Translated
from the Portuguese by William L. Grossman. New York, Noonday Press, 1955.
223p. $1.95
    English translation of Memórias póstumas de Brás Cubas (1881), first
published in 1952, in which Machado de Assis initiated his technique of
short chapters and brief sentences of a fanciful and humoristic tone with
emphasis on psychological analysis. It is one of his great novels.

554.
--------------------------------. THE PSYCHIATRIST AND OTHER STORIES.
Translated by William L. Grossman and Helen Caldwell. Berkeley, University
of California Press, 1963. 147p. $1.95
    These 12 selections should serve to explain to the English-reading public
why many critics rate Machado de Assis higher as a short story writer than
as a novelist. The four translations by Grossman are excellent, while the
others are somewhat literal.

555.
McIntyre, A. CARIFTA: A STEP TOWARD A CRIBBEAN ECONOMIC COMMUNITY. New
York, Taplinger, 1971. 88p. $0.60
    Outlines the aims and accomplishments of the Caribbean Free Trade
Association.

556.
McMillion, Ovid M. GEOGRAPHY OF MIDDLE AMERICA; A WORKBOOK. Dubuque, Iowa,
William C. Brown, 1968. 142p. $3.75
    Designed to supplement the standard textbooks in college level courses,
this spiral-bound workbook provides the instructor and student with a
flexible teaching aid. The first 80 pages deal with Latin America in general;
the remaining sections concentrate on Mexico, Central America, and the West
Indies. [Charles Fleener]

557.
------------------. GEOGRAPHY OF SOUTH AMERICA: A WORKBOOK. Dubuque, Iowa,
William C. Brown, 1968. 247p. $4.95
    Designed to supplement the standard textbooks in college courses. The
first 80 pages cover Latin America in general; the rest concentrate on
the North and Central Andean nations, the Southern republics, and end with
Brazil. [Charles Fleener]

558.
McNeely, John H. THE RAILWAYS OF MEXICO: A STUDY IN NATIONALIZATION. El
Paso, Texas Western Press, 1964. 56p. illus., map. $2.00
    A study dealing with the development of the major railroads of Mexico,
placing particular emphasis on the railroad policies of the Mexican government. [Charles Fleener]

559.
McVicker, C. D., and O. N. Soto. TEMAS DE ARCINIEGAS: INVITACIÓN A CON-
VERSAR, LEER Y ESCRIBIR. New York, Harcourt, Brace and World, 1971. 421p.
$3.95
    Essays by Arciniégas are presented here in a book of readings with good
vocabularies.

560.
McWhiney, Grady, and Sue McWhiney, eds. TO MEXICO WITH TAYLOR AND SCOTT,
1845-1847. Waltham, Mass, Blaisdell, 1969. 214p. (Primary sources in
American history) $2.25
    Presents nearly 30 eyewitness accounts by American soldiers of the
Mexican War. These primary sources, in the form of letters, diaries,
reports, and memoirs, describe and analyze the major compaigns and reveal
the actions of the participants in the war.

561.
McWilliams, Carey. BROTHERS UNDER THE SKIN. Rev. ed. Boston, Little,
Brown, 1964. 364p. $1.95

562.
------------------. MEXICANS: A STUDENTS' GUIDE TO LOCALIZED HISTORY.
Edited by C. Lord. New York, Columbia University Teachers College, 1968.
32p. $1.50

563.
Madariaga, Salvador, de. BOLÍVAR. New York, Schocken Books, 1969. 711p.
$4.50
    This is an English translation of the challenging and provocative bio-
graphy of South America's hero of the independence wars, published in 1952.

564.
----------------------. THE RISE OF THE SPANISH-AMERICAN EMPIRE. New York,
Free Press, 1965. 408p. illus. $2.95
    Not too critical of sources, weak in many aspects of institutional life,
and somewhat apologetic about Spain, this book is written from a first-hand
examination of contemporary accounts by one of Spain's most interesting
historians. Madariaga makes many stimulating interpretations and presents
Spain to the outside world during the formation of its vast overseas empire.

565.
Maddison, Angus. ECONOMIC POLICY AND PROGRESS IN DEVELOPING COUNTRIES.
New York, Norton Books, 1970. 313p. $6.50
   Latin America is included in this general analysis on economic policy
in developing countries.

566.
Madsen, William. THE MEXICAN-AMERICANS OF SOUTH TEXAS. New York, Holt,
Rinehart and Winston, 1965. 112p. illus., $1.75
   A careful study of the Mexican-American way of life sponsored by the
Hidalgo Project on Differential Culture Change and Mental Health, which
examines the difficulty Mexican-Americans experience in the process of
Anglicization.

567.
Magoffin, Susan Shelby. DOWN THE SANTA FE TRAIL AND INTO MEXICO:THE DIARY
OF SUSAN SHELBY MAGOFFIN, 1846-1847. Edited by Stella M. Drumm, with a
foreword by Howard A. Lamar. New Haven, Yale University Press, 1962. 294p.
illus., maps. $1.95
   A new edition of the diary of Susan Shelby Magoffin covering her frontier
journey from Independence, Missouri, along the Santa Fe Trail to Chihuahua,
Mexico. Her trip was historically significant because she kept an excellent
record and because she traveled at a crucial time in the trans-Mississippi
West.

568.
Maier, George. THE ECUADORIAN PRESIDENTIAL ELECTION OF JUNE 2, 1968: AN
ANALYSIS. Washington, D.C., Institute for the Comparative Study of
Political Systems, 1969. 90p. tables. $2.50
   Describes the dynamics of Ecuador's political process. Maintains that
personalismo has played a large part in Ecuadorean politics. José María
Velasco Ibarra's election was reflection of the president's personality
rather than his platform.

569.
Maier, Joseph B., and Richard W. Weatherhead, eds. POLITICS OF CHANGE IN
LATIN AMERICA. New York, Praeger, 1964. 268p. $2.25
   A collection of 13 essays by five Latin and eight North Americans re-
flecting good will and the hope that change can come with minimal upset.
Mexico, Brazil, and international relations in general receive somewhat
extended treatment.

570.
Mallin, Jay. FORTRESS CUBA: RUSSIA'S AMERICAN BASE. Chicago, H. Regnery,
1965. 101p. illus. $0.75
   Written by a correspondent who covered Havana for Time magazine from 1952
until 1962, this is a journalistic account of Castro's Cuba.

571.
Mandel, Ernest, ed. FIFTY YEARS OF WORLD REVOLUTION, 1917-1967; AN INTER-
NATIONAL SYMPOSIUM. New York, Merit Publishers, 1968. 366p. $2.45
   A Trotskyite view of communism over the last 50 years. The Latin
American contributors include Luis Vitale (Chile), Nahuel Moreno
(Argentina), and Hugo González Moscoso (Bolivia). The latter is represented
by an essay on "The Cuban Revolution and its lessons." [Charles Fleener]

572.
Mannix, Daniel P., and Malcolm Cowley. BLACK CARGOES: A HISTORY OF THE
ATLANTIC SLAVE TRADE, 1518-1865. New York, Viking Press, 1965. 306p.
illus., map, tables. $1.85
   First published in 1962, this is a description of the Atlantic slave
trade based on contemporary sources. Includes a very good bibliography.

573.
Mansbach, Richard. DOMINICAN CRISIS 1965. New Haven, Conn., Facts on File, 1970. 270p. $1.95
Presents the complete story of the 1965 uprising in the Dominican Republic and of the U.S. and O.A.S. intervention.

574.
Marban, Edilberto. EL MUNDO IBEROAMERICANO: SUS PUEBLOS Y SUS TIERRAS. New York, Regents Pub. Co., 1968. 192p. $2.95
A description of the Spanish-American countries and their cultures. This is a general treatment for use in survey courses and by the general public.

575.
Mármol, José, AMALIA. GRADED SPANISH READER. Edited by J. C. Babcock and M. B. Rodriguez. Boston, Houghton, Mifflin, 1970. 231p. $1.50
The novel Amalia is presented here for use in Spanish courses.

576.
Martí, José. THE AMERICA OF JOSÉ MARTÍ: SELECTED WRITINGS. Translated by Juan De Onís. New York, Funk and Wagnalls, 1968. 335p. $2.50
Cuba's José Martí (1853-1895) was an influential poet of 19th-century Latin America. He was also an essayist, public speaker, and chronicler, who fought for Cuba's liberty and died on the battlefield.

577.
Martínez, Rafael V. MY HOUSE IS YOUR HOUSE. New York, Friendship Press, 1964. 127p. illus. $1.95
This is a popularized study of the background and influence on U.S. culture of the five million North Americans of Hispanic descent.

578.
Mart, John D. THE VENEZUELAN ELECTIONS OF DECEMBER 1, 1963: Part I: AN ANALYSIS. Part II: CANDIDATE BIOGRAPHIES AND PARTY PLATFORMS. Part III: FINAL PROVINCIAL ELECTION RETURNS, BROKEN DOWN BY REGION AND STATE. Washington, D.C., Institute for the Comparative Study of Political Systems, 1964. 46p., 64p., 26p., map, tables. (Election analysis series, 2) $1.00
A through survey of the 1963 election in Venezuela.

579.
Mason, Bruce B., ed. THE POLITICAL-MILITARY DEFENSE OF LATIN AMERICA. Tempe, Arizona State University, 1963. 63p. $1.50
Seven papers presented at a 1962 conference on the title topic are included in this volume. The introduction is by Marvin Alinsky. Russell H. Fitzgibbon, James L. Busey, and Ronald Hilton, among others, have contributed papers to the conference [Charles Fleener]

580.
Mason, John Alden. ANCIENT CIVILIZATIONS OF PERU. Baltimore, Penguin Books, 1957. 330p. plates. $2.25
Written for the layman and full of up-to-date information, this is a well organized and readable book with excellent plates. It is divided into background, history of Peruvian culture, the Inca, arts and crafts, appendix and a bibliography.

581.
Master, Robert V. PERU IN PICTURES. New York, Sterling Pub. Co., 1966. 64p. illus., map. $1.00
Many photographs illustrate the text about the Peruvian land, history, people, government, and business for the layman. [Charles Fleener]

582.
------------------. PUERTO RICO IN PICTURES. Rev. ed. New York, Sterling Pub.
Co., 1967. 67p. $1.00
    An attractive introductory description of Puerto Rico, the land and its
people.

583.
Mathews, Thomas G. LUIS MUÑOZ MARÍN; A CONCISE BIOGRAPHY. New York, Corner-
stone Library, 1967. 61p. illus. $1.00
    This is a clear, concise biography of Puerto Rico's creative ex-governor,
Luis Muñoz Marín, the architect of the island's current prosperity.

584.
Mathiessen, Peter. THE CLOUD FOREST: A CHRONICLE OF THE SOUTH AMERICAN
WILDERNESS. New York, Pyramid Publications, 1966. 288p. illus., maps.
$0.75
    A U.S. naturalist describes his travels through the jungles and mountains
of South America.

585.
Mathis, E. John. ECONOMIC INTEGRATION IN LATIN AMERICA. Austin, University
of Texas Press, 1969. 112p. illus. $3.00
    A brief discussion of economic integration in Latin America in which the
author analyzes the success and propects of regional common markets.

586.
Matthews, Herbert L. FIDEL CASTRO. New York, Clarion Press, 1970. 382p.
$2.95
    This book is the result of long conversations that took place in Havana
in 1967 between New York Times reporter Matthews and Fidel Castro. This
political biography sheds new light on Castro and his government.

587.
------------------, ed. THE UNITED STATES AND LATIN AMERICA. 2d. ed.
Englewood Cliffs, N.J., Prentice-Hall, 1963. 179p. illus., maps, tables.
$1.95
    Contains the text of the final report of the 16th American Assembly, Oct.
15-18, 1959 (Columbia University), and background papers for the meeting,
prepared by Edward W. Barrett and Penn T. Kimball (press and communications);
Reynold E. Carlson (economic relations); Herbert L. Matthews (diplomatic
relations); K. H. Silvert (political change in Latin America); and Frank
Tannenbaum (on understanding Latin America). [HLAS 23: 2759]

588.
May, Herbert K. THE CONTRIBUTORS OF U.S. PRIVATE INVESTMENT TO LATIN AMERICA'S
GROWTH. New York, Council for Latin America, 1970. 100p. tables. $1.50
    The author outlines the contributions by the U.S. private sector to the
economies of various Latin American countries.

589.
Mayers, Marvin Keene, ed. THE LANGUAGES OF GUATEMALA. New York, Humanities
Press, 1966. 318p. $13.75
    This collection of studies deals with indigenous languages of Guatemala.

590.
Mecham, J. Lloyd. CHURCH AND STATE IN LATIN AMERICA: A HISTORY OF POLITICO-
ECCLESIASTICAL RELATIONS. Rev. ed. Chapel Hill, University of North
Carolina Press, 1966. 465p. $3.45
    First published in 1934, this is a revised edition of the best survey of
church-state relations in the national period of Latin American history. The
emphasis in this scholarly and readable book is on the political significance
of church-state relations.

591.
Mende, Tibor. THE INTER-AMERICAN BANK; A FORERUNNER AMONG FINANCIAL
INSTITUTIONS. Washington, Inter-American Development Bank, 1965.
Free to libraries
    This is a popular account of the Bank's activities, aims and organiza-
tional structure.

592.
Merk, Frederick. MANIFEST DESTINY AND MISSION IN AMERICAN HISTORY: A RE-
INTERPRETATION. New York, Random House, 1963. 265p. $1.95
    The author analyzes Mexican and Caribbean examples of "manifest destiny"
and presents an appraisal of varying North American opinions regarding U.S.
expansionism in the 19th century.

593.
Mesa-Lago, Carmelo. AVAILABILITY AND RELIABILITY OF STATISTICS IN SOCIALIST
CUBA. Pittsburgh, University of Pittsburgh, Center for Latin American Studies,
1969. 29p. (Latin American studies occasional papers, 1) $1.00
    Professor Mesa-Lago briefly studies statistical sources available for
Castro's Cuba for the last decade.

594.
Métraux, Alfred. HISTORY OF THE INCAS. Translated by George Ordish. New
York, Schocken Books, 1970. 221p. illus. $2.45
    A comprehensive survey of the Incas from the cultures of the Mochica and
Chimu through the empire and Spanish rule to the 20th century. The original
French edition is entitled Les Incas (1961).

595.
MEXICO " 68: THE STUDENTS SPEAK. New York, U.S. Committee for Justice to
Latin American Political Prisoners, 1969. 32p. illus. $1.00
    Supports the June-October 1968 student strike in Mexico City and condemns
what they call the Mexican governments's "repression." Timothy Harding
presents an introduction and the strike committee of the Faculty of the
University of New Mexico provides a position paper on "The Mexican Student
Movement: Its Meaning and Perspectives." [Charles Fleener]

596.
Mezerik, Avrahm. G. CUBA AND THE UNITED STATES. New York, International
Review Service, 1960. 110p. maps. $5.00
    A chronological survey of U.S.-Cuban relations.

597.
------------------. CUBA, U.S., AND U.S.S.R. RELATIONS. New York, International Review Service, 1969. 92p. maps. $5.00
    Chronological review of U.S. diplomacy towards Cuba and the U.S.S.R.
since the Cuban Revolution.

598.
Midwest Council of the Association for Latin American Studies. THE COMMUNITY
IN REVOLUTIONARY LATIN AMERICA. Lawrence, University of Kansas, Center
for Latin American Studies, 1963. 36p. $2.00
    Includes three papers presented at the 1963 meeting of the Council at
Western Michigan State University: "The Latin American Community in Revolution and Development," by Richard N. Adams; "Land and Politics in Rural
Guatemala: a Study of a Highland Agricultural Community," by Oscar Horst
and Roland H. Ebel; and "Problems and Prospects for Community Development
in Northeast Brazil, "by Belden Paulson.

599.
------------. CURRENT DEVELOPMENTS IN BRAZIL. East Lansing, Michigan
State University, Latin American Studies Center, 1967. 65p. $2.00
    Five papers on Brazil encompassing broad topics from "Reflection on the
Brazilian Northeast" to Ambassador Vasco Leitão de Cunha's explanation
of "Brazilian Policies Today." All were delivered originally at the
Council's 1966.

meeting in East Lansing, Michigan.

600.
Milla, José. CUADROS GUATEMALTECOS. Edited by G. J. Edberg. New York,
Macmillan, 1965. 115p. $1.95

601.
Miller, Theodore R. GRAPHIC HISTORY OF THE AMERICAS. New York, J. Wiley,
1969. 72p. maps, tables. illus. $3.95
    While the U.S. is the principal subject of this volume, 16 large maps
of the Western Hemisphere depict the flow of history from Cape Horn to Baffin
Bay. This is a convenient, graphic source for students of the Americas.
[Charles Fleener]

602.
Millon, Robert P. ZAPATA: THE IDEOLOGY OF A PEASANT REVOLUTIONARY. New
York, International Publishers, 1969. 159p. $2.25
    Emiliano Zapata and land reform symbolized the essence of the Mexican
Revolution of 1910. Although agrarian reform was their main objective, the
zapatistas also had a program of social and political reforms. The author
presents a rather superficial study of the zapatista movement against the
background of political ideologies.

603.
Milne, Jean. FIESTA TIME IN LATIN AMERICA. Los Angeles, Ritchie Press,
1968. 236p. illus. $2.95
    "Fiestas (Spanish America), festas (Brazil), or fêtes (Haiti) are given
for just about every reason that one might think of .." and they can be
divided into three groups: religious, civil, and tribal. This book
describes a great number of celebrations in a general way. A useful appendix
outlines the fiestas by countries.

604.
Mistral, Gabriela [pseud.] SELECTED POEMS OF GABRIELA MISTRAL, Translated
by Langston Hughes. Bloomington, Indiana University Press, 1966. 119p.
$1.75
    This translation is the product of one poet's liking for another. The
simplicity of Hughes' own style is a perfect medium to allow Gabriela
Mistral's own to come through with a minimum of distortion. The work is
prefaced by an introduction by Hughes and the citation by the Nobel Prize
Committee. Mistral was awarded the Nobel Prize for Literature in 1945.

605.
-------------------------- SELECTED POEMS OF GABRIELA MISTRAL. Translated
and edited by Doris Dana. Introd. by Francisco Aguilera. Woodcuts by
Antonio Frasconi. Baltimore, Johns Hopkins University Press, 1971. 235p.
illus. $2.95
    Bilingual edition of the most representative poems by the Chilean Nobel
Prize winner. The Library of Congress has simultaneously issued a record-
ing by Gabriela Mistral reading her poetry. It may be obtained from the
Music Division, Library of Congress, Washington, D.C. 20540 $4.95 post-paid.

606.
Moerner, Magnus, ed. THE EXPULSION OF THE JESUITS FROM LATIN AMERICA.
New York, Knopf, 1965. 220p. $2.50
    A collection of 18 essays on the expulsion of the Jesuits from Spanish
(1767) and Portuguese (1759) America. The editor's introduction and bibliographical notes are excellent.

607.
----------------. RACE MIXTURE IN THE HISTORY OF LATIN AMERICA. Boston,
Little, Brown, 1967. 178p. $3.25
    One of the foremost scholars on race relations analyzes the race mixture
in Latin America from a historical perspective.

608.

Montejo, Esteban. AUTOBIOGRAPHY OF A RUNAWAY SLAVE. Edited by Miguel Barnet; translated by Jocasta Innes. New York, World Pub. Co., 1969. 223p. $2.25

Translation of Biografía de un cimarrón (1966), it deals with the personal impressions of a perceptive man who observed the impact of the abolition of slavery in Cuba, his thoughts on the independence movement (1895-98), its various leaders, and their efforts to form a government after 1901. Includes his views on 20th century Cuba and insightful remarks on the Cuban Revolution of 1959. Montejo lived to be over 100 years old, and the translation compassionately portrays his humanity and political commitments. For graduate students as well as undergraduates a valuable document for understanding the perspectives of the lower class swept up in major events. [Vincent C. Peloso]

609.

Moreno, Francisco José, and Barbara Mitrani, eds. CONFLICT AND VIOLENCE IN LATIN AMERICAN POLITICS: A BOOK OF READINGS. New York, Crowell, 1971. 275p. $2.95

Includes essays and short studies on violence's role in the political processes of various Latin American countries.

610.

Morison, Samuel Eliot. CHRISTOPHER COLUMBUS: MARINER. New York, New American Library, 1956. 160p. $0.60

This is a condensation and rewriting of the well-known biography Admiral of the Ocean Sea (1942). The book was written after the author, for many years a yachtsman, had made four voyages in which he went over much of the route of Columbus in a sailing vessel and as far as possible at the same time of the year.

611.

Morley, Sylvanus Griswold. THE ANCIENT MAYA. Edited by George W. Brainerd. 3d ed. rev. Stanford, Calif., Stanford University Press, 1969. 507p. illus., maps, tables. $3.85

This is a classic work on the Mayas for the non-specialists. The author presents the magnificent world of the Mayas, and includes material on the wall paintings of Bonampak and the Palenque tomb. The text is enhanced with beautiful illustrations.

612.

Morrison, Roy F. TRAILERING IN MEXICO. Rev. ed. Berverly Hills, Calif., Trail-R Club of America, 1968, 184p. illus. $3.50

A guide to visiting Mexico by trailer which contains detailed information on camp sites and travel tips.

613.

Morse, Jim, comp. FOLK SONGS OF THE CARIBBEAN. New York, Bantam Books, 1960. 208p. $0.50

Includes love songs, work songs, game songs, ballads, and calypsos from the Caribbean islands. Guitar chords, words, and melodies for each song facilitate the use of this work.

614.

Morse, Richard M., ed. THE BANDEIRANTES: THE HISTORICAL ROLE OF THE BRAZILIAN PATHFINDERS. New York, Knopf, 1965. 224p. $2.50

A useful compilation of documents and essays on the bandeirantes and on the Brazilian frontier expansion, preceded by a fine essay on the phenomenon.

615.

Nach, James. GUATEMALA IN PICTURES. New York, Sterling Pub. Co., 1966. 64p. illus., maps. $1.00

One of an excellent series of popular introductory texts to different countries. The author presents the land, history, government, people, and economy of Guatemala in convenient and handsomely illustrated booklet.

616.
Naipaul, Vidiadhar Surojprasad, **and others**. ISLAND VOICES: STORIES FROM THE
WEST INDIES. Edited with an introd. By Andrew Salkey. New York, Liveright,
1970. 256p. $2.45
    This collection of recent short stories from Caribbean authors includes
such authors as Samuel Selvon and John Hearns.

617.
Nance, A. D. A STUDY OF MEXICO AND CENTRAL AMERICA. Menlo Park, Calif.,
Pacific Coast Publications, 1970. 250p. illus. $1.85
    A general description of Mexico and Central America.

618.
Nance, J. PRE-SPANISH TRADE IN THE BAY ISLANDS. Birmingham, Ala., Southern
University Press, 1969. 281p. illus. $1.00
    Studies trading patterns in the Bay Islands based on evidence which
survived conquest and colonization.

619.
Nash, Manning. MACHINE AGE MAYA: THE INDUSTRIALIZATION OF A GUATEMALA
COMMUNITY. Chicago, University of Chicago Press, 1967. 155p. maps, tables.
$1.95
    Describes an Indian mountain community which has successfully adapted
to the establishment of Central America's largest textile mill in its midst.
The author combines a descriptive analysis with problem-oriented research
in this scholarly and well-organized study. [Charles Fleener]

620.
--------------. PRIMITIVE AND PEASANT ECONOMIC SYSTEMS. San Francisco,
Chandler Pub. Co., 1970. 166p. $2.50
    Studies primitive and peasant economic systems and their adaptation into
industrialized society.

621.
Neale-Silva, Eduardo. HORIZONTE HUMANO: VIDA DE JOSÉ EUSTASIO RIVERA.
Madison, University of Wisconsin Press, 1960. 506p. illus. $2.25
    A biography of the Colombian poet and novelist, exhaustively documented
and brilliantly executed by a professor who specialized in studying the man,
the work and the period. It would be difficult to find a Spanish-American
writer who has been favored with a biography comparable to this in scope and
quality.

622.
Nearing, Scott, **and** Joseph Freeman. DOLLAR DIPLOMACY: A STUDY IN AMERICAN
IMPERIALISM. New York, Monthly Review, 1969. 353p. maps. $3.95
    Written more than 45 years ago, the authors coined the phrase that has
been used subsequently to describe the first decades of U.S. expansion.
They analyze cases in which the U.S. economic and diplomatic interest have
intervened in certain countries such as Panama, Mexico, Haiti, the Dominican
Republic, Nicaragua, and Cuba. [Charles Fleener]

623.
Needler, Martin Cyril. ANATOMY OF A COUP D'ETAT: ECUADOR 1963. Washington,
Institute for the Comparative Study of Political Systems, 1964. 54p. $2.50
    With firsthand knowledge of many personalitits, the author has written
an accurate analysis of the 1963 coup in Ecuador which deposed Carlos Julio
Arosemena as President.
624.
------------------------. LATIN AMERICAN POLITICS IN PERSPECTIVE. 2d. ed.
Princeton, N.J., Van Nostrand, 1970. 200p. $2.40
    A good general study by an experienced Latin Americanist, describing
Latin American politics. It includes a good bibliography.

625.

———————————————. POLITICAL DEVELOPMENT IN LATIN AMERICA: INSTABILITY, VIOLENCE, AND EVOLUTIONARY CHANGE. New York, Random House, 1968. 210p. $3.25

An analysis of political development, institutions, and processes in contemporary Latin America. It covers in sequence the problem of stability and instability, violence, and the strategies by which change is consciously sought.

626.

Nehemkis, Peter. LATIN AMERICA: MYTH AND REALITY. Rev. ed. New York, New American Library, 1966. 286p. $1.25

In a general treatment, written for the lay reader, the author points out the fascinating diversity of Latin America and attempts to unmask the mythology that blocks understanding of Latin Americans by North Americans.

627.

Neruda, Pablo. THE HEIGHTS OF MACCHU PICCHU. Translated by Nathaniel Tarn. New York, Noonday Press, 1969. 75p. $1.95

An excellent translation of one of Neruda's longer poems presented here in a bilingual edition. It is a song to indigenous Hispanic-America.

628.

———————————. PABLO NERUDA: A NEW DECADE, POEMS 1958-1960. Translated by Ben Belitt and Alistair Reid. New York, Grove Press, 1971. 274p. $2.95

Professor Belitt states that this edition was culled from six volumes of poetry, and that the selections recall "the true measure of Neruda's long traffic with the democracy of letter."

629.

———————————., and César Vallejo. SELECTED POEMS. Edited by R. Bly. Boston, Beaxon, 1971. 198p. $2.25

Contains a selection of poems by two leading Latin American poets.

630.

———————————. SELECTED POEMS OF PABLO NERUDA. Edited by Ben Belitt. Introd. by Luis Monguió. New York, Grove Press, 1963. 319p. $2.95

These translations of Ben Belitt and the excellent study by Luis Monguió constitute much more than just an introduction of Pablo Neruda to the North American public. For the student of Hispanic poetry, however, they prove how difficult it is to translate Neruda. The selection is very representative.

631.

———————————. TWENTY LOVE POEMS AND A SONG OF DESPAIR. New York, Grossman Publications, 1971. 250p. $1.50

First published in 1924 as Veinte poemas de amor y una canción desesperada, this is a collection of lyric poems by the most important Latin American poet alive today.

632.

———————————. WE ARE MANY. Translated by Alistair Reid. Illustrated by Hans Ehrmann. New York, Grossman, Publications, 1967. 32p. 2 plates, illus. $2.50

633.

Nettl, Bruno. FOLK AND TRADITIONAL MUSIC OF THE WESTERN CONTINENTS. Englewood Cliffs, N.J., Prentice-Hall, 1965. 213p. illus. $2.95

The first two chapters introduce the subject. Three others deal with the traditional music of the American Indians, the music of the Afro-Latins in the New World, and Western and Western-descended folk music in the Americas. This comprehensive work includes a good bibliography. [Charles Fleener]

634.
Newcomb, William. THE INDIANS OF TEXAS: FROM PREHISTORIC TO MODERN TIMES.
Austin, University of Texas Press, 1961. 404 p. illus. $2.95
   Traces the many tribes who have lived in what today is Texas from the
pre-Columbian period to the present.

635.
Nicholls, William H., and Ruy Miller Paiva. NINETY-NINE FAZENDAS: THE
STRUCTURE OF BRAZILIAN AGRICULTURE, 1963. Nashville, Vanderbilt University
Press, 1966-69. 5 v. maps. tables. $3.50, $5.50, $6.50, $7.50, $9.00
respectively.
   The authors study the causes of low productivity in Brazilian agricul-
ture. This is a massive and important project which surveys individual
regions of Brazil.

636.
Nicholson, Irene. A GUIDE TO MEXICAN POETRY: ANCIENT AND MODERN. New
York, International Publications Service, 1968. 96 p. illus. $2.00
   A guide to Mexican poetry which starts with pre-Columbian works and
brings it up to the present.

637.
Nicholson, Norman L. CANADA IN THE AMERICAN COMMUNITY. Princeton, N. J.,
1963. 128 p. maps $1.75
   Canada is part of the Commonwealth by tradition, yet is American by location and sentiment. This book explores to what extent Canada forms part
of Western Hemisphere economic, social, and cultural life.

638.
Niemeier, Jean Gilbreath. THE PANAMA STORY. Portland, Ore., Metropolitan
Press,1968. 303 p. illus. $2.95
   A simplified historical study of the republic of Panama intended for the
generalist.

639.
Niggli, Josephina. MEXICAN VILLAGE. Chapel Hill, University of North
Carolina Press, 1970. 491 p. illus. $2.95
   The author artfully depicts life in Hidalgo, Nuevo León.

640.
--------. UN PUEBLO MEXICANO: SELECTIONS FROM MEXICAN VILLAGE. Translated and edited by Justina Ruiz de Conde. Designs by Marion Fitz-Simons.
New York, Norton, 1969. 267 p. $3.75
   The stories center in the village of Hidalgo, one of the five towns in
the Sabinas Valley in northern Mexico and the same characters appear and
reappear until the life of the village is an authentic folk life. Christian and pagan elements mix to form a unique cultural picture.

641.
Nisbet, Charles T. LATIN AMERICA: PROBLEMS IN ECONOMIC DEVELOPMENT. New
York, Free Press, 1969. 357 p. $4.95
   Presents a systematic outline of Latin American economic development
within the socio-cultural context of the hemisphere.

642.
Noel, Bernard. MEXICAN ART, I: FROM THE BEGINNING TO THE OLMECS. New
York, Tudor Pub. Co., 1969. 64 p. illus. (Petite encyclopédie de l'art,
88) $1.25
   A brief eight-page text introduces the 24 photographs of pre-classic,
Pacific coast, and Olmec art objects. [Charles Fleener]

643.
--------. MEXICAN ART, II: TEOTIHUACAN TAJIN, MONTE ALBAN. New York,
Tudor Pub. Co., 1968. 64 p. illus. (Petite encyclopédie de l'art, 89)
$1.25
   A brief survey of these cultures precedes the 25 photographic illustra-
tions of examples of their sculptured and architectural art.

644.
--------. MEXICAN ART, III; MAYA. New York, Tudor Pub. Co., 1968. 64 p.
illus. (Petite encyclopédie de l'art, 90). $1.25
   Attrative black and white photographs illustrate the architectural,
ceramic, and stone work triumphs of the most brilliant of the pre-Columbian
civilizations. The author provides a brief introduction. [Charles Fleener]

645.
--------. MEXICAN ART, IV; TOLTECS, AZTECS. New York, Tudor Pub. Co.,
1968. 64 p. illus. (Petite encyclopédie de l'art, 91). $1.25
   Following a nine-page introduction, this small but handsome book presents nine examples of Toltec art, six representations of Mixtec-Puebla
achivement, and nine photographs of Aztec works of art. [Charles Fleener]

646.
North, Lisa. CIVIL-MILITARY RELATIONS IN ARGENTINA, CHILE, AND PERU.
Berkeley, University of California, Institute of International Relations,
1966. 86 p. tables $1.75
   Analyzes civilian political communities through an examination of the
patterns of military organizations in Peru, Chile, and Argentina. The
latter two are often compared and contrasted. Peru is treated separately.
The appendixes list the military revolts in each nation chronologically
from 1900 through 1963. [Charles Fleener]

647.
Nowell, Charles E. THE GREAT DISCOVERIES AND THE FIRST COLONIAL EMPIRES.
Ithaca, N. Y., Cornell University Press, 1954. 150 p. maps $1.75
   Describes the historical and cultural background of the first colonial
empires. This is a good summary of the age of discovery. Includes a
good bibliography.

648.
Nun, José. LATIN AMERICA: THE HEGEMONIC CRISIS AND THE MILITARY COUP.
Berkeley, Institute of International studies, University of California,
1969. 73 p. $1.50
   Analyzes the frequent military coups in Latin America in connection
with the rapid changes experienced by the middle sectors. Argentina,
Uruguay, Chile, Brazil, and Mexico receive special attention [Charles
Fleener]

649.
Nye, Joseph A., Jr. CENTRAL AMERICAN REGIONAL INTEGRATION. New York,
Carnegie Endowment, Distributed by Taplinger Pub. Co., 1967. 66 p.
tables, map $0.60
   Surveys the accomplishments of Central America's economic integration.
Trade has quadrupled during the first five years of the Common Market's
existence. The author warns the reader that "a political upheaval in one
member country could swamp the fragile bark."

650.
Nystrom, J. Warren, and Nathan A. Haverstock. THE ALLIANCE FOR PROGRESS:
KEY TO LATIN AMERICA'S DEVELOPMENT. Princeton, N. J., Van Nostrand, 1966.
126 p. maps. $1.45
   This is a perceptive and somewhat optimistic analysis of the Alliance
for Progress.

651.
Oakes, Maud. TWO CROSSES TO TODOS SANTOS: SURVIVALS OF MAYAN RELIGIOUS
RITUALS. Princeton, N. J., Princeton University Press, 1969. 274 p.
illus., map, tables. $2.95
   First published in 1951, this is a scholarly study of the religious
customs of the Mayas in the Cuchumantes mountains. The author has uncov-
ered much data on the Mayan culture of Guatemala and presents it in an
interesting and artful style that holds the reader's attention. [Charles
Fleener]

652.
Ordish, George. MAN CROPS, AND PESTS IN CENTRAL AMERICA. New York, Pergamon Press, 1966. 119 p. illus. plates. $2.95
The general problems of losses of agricultural produce owing to the attack of pests, are the main concern of this book. It will prove extremely interesting and informative to economists and sociologists.

653.
Organization of American States. Dept. of International Law. APPLICATIONS OF THE INTER-AMERICAN TREATY OF RECIPROCAL ASSISTANCE. Washington, Pan American Union, 1957. 247 p. map. $1.75
Surveys the Inter-American system of peace and security and its operation within the international diplomatic structure. It also includes examples of the application of the treaty of reciprocal assistance from 1948 through 1956.

654.
Ortega, P. R. CHRISTMAS IN OLD SANTA FE. Santa Fe., N. M., Ancient City Book Shop, 1971. 250 p. illus. $2.50
Compiles and describes various Christmas celebrations in Santa Fe.

655.
Ortiz, E. COMPLETE BOOK OF MEXICAN COOKING. New York, Bantam, 1969. 161 p. illus. $0.95
Compiles recipes and instructions for the preparation of well-known Mexican main courses and desserts.

656.
Ortiz, Fernando. CUBAN COUNTERPOINT: TOBACCO AND SUGAR. New York, Random House, 1970. 352 p. $1.95
The author maintains that Cuba's two main crops, tobacco and sugar have shaped Cuban society and together have formed the backbone of Cuban economy. This important study was first published in 1940 under the title Contrapunteo cubano del tabaco y del azúcar.

657.
Ovchynnk, Michael. FRESHWATER FISHES OF ECUADOR AND PERSPECTIVE FOR DEVELOPMENT OF FISH CULTIVATION. East Lansing, Latin American Studies Center, Michigan State University, 1967. 44 p. illus., map. $1.00
The first part of this study is devoted to the task of describing Ecuadorean fish. The final section studies the lack of protein in the diet of most Ecuadoreans and suggests how this might be improved through the introduction of modern techniques of fish cultivation. [Charles Fleener]

658.
Pachter, Henry Maximilian. COLLISION COURSE; THE CUBAN MISSILE CRISIS AND CO-EXISTENCE. New York, Praeger, 1963. 261 p. $2.25
A detailed account of the Cuban missile crisis of October, 1962. Contains a thoughtful analysis of implications of U.S.-Soviet co-existence. The last part of the book contains a concise chronology of the crisis and a useful collection of documents, as well as bibliographies.[HLAS 27:3429]

659.
Padgett, Leon Vincent. THE MEXICAN POLITICAL SYSTEM. Boston, Houghton, Mifflin, 1966. 244 p. maps. $3.25
This is a concise and thorough study of the Mexican system of government. Thanks to its stable political system for the last four decades Mexico has seen great economic and social progress. Includes bibliographies.

660.
Painter, Murill Thayer. EASTER AT PASCUA VILLAGE. Tucson, University of Arizona Press, 1960. 35 p. illus. $1.00
Describes traditional easter celebrations in an Arizona village.

661.
--------. FAITH, FLOWERS, AND FIESTAS. Tucson, University of Arizona Press, 1970. 250 p. illus. $1.00
   Includes a description of traditional Arizona festivals and folk art.

662.
Pan American Union. COPYRIGHT PROTECTION IN THE AMERICAS: UNDER NATIONAL LEGISLATION AND INTER-AMERICAN TREATIES. 3d ed. rev. and enl. Washington, Pan American Union, 1968. 301 p. $2.45
   Outlines copyright legislation in the Latin American republics and contains the text of relevant inter-American treaties.

663.
Pan American Union. Division of Law and Treaties. BILATERAL TREATY DEVELOPMENTS IN LATIN AMERICA, 1942-1952. Washington, 1953. 243 p. (Law and treaty series, 38; PAU 327-E-5071) $1.50
   Includes bilateral treaties, conventions, and agreements entered into by the Latin American republics during 1942-1952.

664.
--------. BILATERAL TREATY DEVELOPMENTS IN LATIN AMERICA, 1938-1948. Washington, 1950. 154 p. (Law and treaty series, 32; PAU 341-E-4483) $1.50
   Includes bilateral treaties, agreements, and conventions for the period of 1938-1948 entered into by the Latin American republics.

665.
--------. BILATERAL TREATY DEVELOPMENTS IN LATIN AMERICA, 1953-1955. Washington, 1956. 158 p. (Law and treaty series, 2) $1.00
   Includes bilateral treaties, agreements, and conventions for the period of 1953-1955 entered into by the Latin American republics.

666.
Papadake, S. OSCAR NIEMEYER. New York, Braziller, 1970. 149 p. illus. $2.95
   Studies the famed Brazilian architect, the most influential trend setter of contemporary Latin America.

667.
Pariseau, Earl J., ed. CUBAN ACQUISITIONS AND BIBLIOGRAPHY; PROCEEDINGS AND WORKING PAPERS OF AN INTERNATIONAL CONFERENCE HELD AT THE LIBRARY OF CONGRESS, April 13-15, 1970. Washington, Library of Congress, Hispanic Foundation, 1971. 195 p. Free upon request.
   Surveys Cuban holdings of the Library of Congress, including newspapers, periodicals, and manuscripts. It also contains articles on Cuban sources available in England, Spain, Germany and other foreign depositories.

668.
Parkes, Henry Bamford. HISTORY OF MEXICO. Rev. ed. (Boston, Houghton, Mifflin, 1969. 460 p. illus. $2.85
   Since 1938 Parkes' History of Mexico has been the standard one-volume survey in English. This revised edition in paperback will be very useful for students of Mexico. It covers the history of Mexico from earliest times to the presidency of Díaz Ordaz. [Charles Fleener]

669.
Parra, Nicanor. POEMS AND ANTIPOEMS. Edited by Miller Williams. Translated by Fernando Alegría and others. New York, New Directions, 1967. 149 p. $1.95
   Bilingual edition of poems taken from Poemas y antipoemas (1938-1953); Versos de salón (1953-1962); and Canciones rusas (1963-1964). Parra is a poet and professor of theoretical physics who has shaken the rigid structure of poetic theory with his antipoems. He is one of the most original and audacious contemporary poets and is widely read in the U. S. and in Europe. One of the most outstanding poems included is "Soliloquy of the Individual" in which the poet concludes that "life has no meaning."

670.
Parra, Teresa de la. MAMA BLANCA'S SOUVENIRS. Translated by Harriet
de Onís. Washington, Pan American Union, 1959. 129 p. $1.50
   The Venezuelan novelist Teresa de la Parra (1891-1936) describes beautifully rural life in an old society. Las memorias de Mamá Blanca (1929) are
memories of life on a sugarcane plantation near Caracas. It is a tender
and vivid novel.

671.
Parry, John Horace and P. M. Sherlock. A SHORT HISTORY OF THE WEST INDIES.
2d ed. New York, St. Martin's Press, 1968. 316p. illus., maps. $2.50
   An excellent account of the history of the islands in the Caribbean sea
from 1492 to 1962. While treating the story of these islands as a connected
whole, it is addressed to readers in the British Caribbean [Charles Fleener]

672.
Parson, Francis. EARLY 17th CENTURY SPANISH MISSIONS OF THE SOUTHWEST.
Tucson, Ariz., Dale Stuart King, 1968. 120p. illus. $2.45
   Description of the early missions of west Texas, New Mexico, and
northern Arizona with attractive drawings and photos.

673
Pasadena, Calif., Art Museum. SANTOS. NEW MEXICAN FOLK ART. Introd. by
L. P. Frank. Foreword by T. W. Leavitt. La Jolla, Calif., McGilvery, 1970.
192p. illus. $1.50
   An illustrated guide to New Mexican folk art which can be found at the
Pasadena Art Museum.

674.
Pauline, Lawrence J. LATIN AMERICA: HISTORY, CULTURE, PEOPLE. Bronxville,
N.Y., Cambridge Book Co., 1969. 250p. illus. maps, tables. $0.85
   This extensive general survey of Latin America is designed for high
school use. The author aims to "provide background for the understanding
of important concepts concerning Latin America." Questions and activities
are suggested at the end of each chapter. [Charles Fleener]

675.
Payne, Arnold. THE PERUVIAN COUP D' ETAT OF 1962: THE OVERTHROW OF MANUEL
PRADO. Washington, Institute for the Comparative Study of Political Systems,
1968. 85p. tables. $2.00
   Places the 1962 coup de' état into perspective as it describes other
coups which may be considered turning points in Peruvian history. It then
analyzes the coup of July 8, 1962 and suggests the significance of this
event.
676.
Paz, Octavio. ¿ÁGUILA O SOL? EAGLE OR SUN? Translated by Eliot Weinberger.
New York, October House, 1970. 125p. $2.95
   A bilingual edition of essays by one of Mexico's outstanding poets. It
includes Trabajos del poeta (1949), Arenas movedizas (1949); and ¿Águila o
sol? (1950). The essays explore Mexico, the relations between language
and poetry, and the poet and history.

677.
-----------. THE LABYRINTH OF SOLITUDE; LIFE AND THOUTHT IN MEXICO. Translated by Lysander Kemp. New York, Grove Press, 1963. 212p. $1.95
   In this penetrating examination of the nature of Mexico and Mexicans, by
a distinguished Mexican poet and intellectual, the basic theme is the
universal alienation of all mankind. The author studies the Mexican manifestations of this universal ill in a series of nine essays.

678.
Pearcy, George Etzel. THE WEST INDIAN SCENE. Princeton, N.J., Van Nostrand,
1968. 136p. maps. $1.45
   The author presents brief, timely sketches of each political entity in
the West Indies. The emphasis is on the political, economic, and social
aspects as well as on the islands' relations with the United States.

679.
Peavy, Charles D. CHARLES A. SIRINGO; A TEX'S PICARO. Austin, Texas,
Stack-Vaughn 1967. 41p. $1.00

680.
Pendle, George. A HISTORY OF LATIN AMERICA. Baltimore, Penguin Books,
1963. 249p. maps. $1.25
General treatment of Latin America, useful for review purposes. Includes
a bibliography.

681.
Perkins, Dexter. HISTORY OF THE MONROE DOCTRINE. Rev. ed. Boston, Little,
Brown, 1968. 462p. $2.95
First published in 1941 as Hands off: a history of the Monroe Doctrine,
this is a historical analysis of the famous doctrine.

682.
Pesman, Michiel Walter. MEET FLORA MEXICANA: AN EASY WAY TO RECOGNIZE
SOME OF THE MORE FREQUENTLY MET PLANTS OF MEXICO AS SEEN FROM THE MAIN
HIGHWAYS. Globe, Ariz., D.S. King, 1962. illus., map. $5.00
The author describes and catalogs the numerous plants and flowers that
one is apt to see in Mexico. This is a helpful guide, complete with good
illustrations.

683.
Peterson, Frederick. ANCIENT MEXICO; AN INTRODUCTION TO THE PRE-HISPANIC
CULTURES. New York, Putnam, 1962. 313p. illus., maps. $2.45
This is a popularized general account of pre-Hispanic Mesoamerican
culture, with special emphasis on Mexico during the last few centuries
before the conquest.

684.
Petras, James. CHILEAN CHRISTIAN DEMOCRAEY: POLITICS AND SOCIAL FORCES.
Berkeley, Institute of International Studies, University of California,
1967. 61p. $1.50
Deals with Christian Democracy as a contemporary political movement in
Latin America. The author analyzes Frei's government with its heterogenous
backing and examines the behavioral characteristics of the party and its
role in government.

685.
----------, and Maurice Zeitlin eds. LATIN AMERICA: REFORM OR
REVOLUTION? A READER. New York, Fawcett Publications, 1968. 511p. $1.95
Includes a introduction by the editors and 23 papers of varying views,
premises, and quality. The authors include both Latin Americans and North
Americans. An important book for college courses on contemporary Latin
American problems.

686.
Phillips, Ruby Hart. CUBA: ISLAND OF PARADOX. New York, Astor-Honor, 1970.
129p. $2.45

687.
Picón-Salas, Mariano. A CULTURAL HISTORY OF SPANISH AMERICA: FROM CONQUEST
TO INDEPENDENCE. Translated by Irving A. Leonard. Berkeley, University of
California Press, 1962. 192p. $1.95
This is a well-known work on Spanish colonial culture, skillfully
translated by Irving A. Leonard.

688.
Pike, Fredrick B., ed. CONFLICT BETWEEN CHURCH AND STATE IN LATIN AMERICA.
New York, Knopf, 1964. 239p. $2.50
A short compilation of 20 previously published papers on the topic in
question, divided chronologically, dealing with the colonial, 19th century,
and modern periods. Includes a bibliography.

689.
----------. ed. FREEDOM AND REFORM IN LATIN AMERICA. Notre Dame, Ind.,
University of Notre Dame Press, 1967. 308p. $3.25
   The 11 papers included in this work deal with both freedom and reform
in Latin America as a whole and in relation to specific nations. Professor
Pike provides a new introduction to this book which was first published in
1959.

690.
----------. ed. LATIN AMERICAN HISTORY: SELECT PROBLEMS, IDENTITY, INTE-
GRATION, AND NATIONHOOD. New York, Harcourt, Brace and World, 1969. 482p.
illus., maps. $5.95
   Contains readings on the discovery of the New World; the problem of con-
flicting Spanish imperial ideologies; the impact of Iberic culture on the
indigenous populations; the roots of revolution; slavery; questions of
national identity; current social problems, etc. The selection of materials,
some from primary sources, is excellent.

691.
Pitt, Leonard. THE DECLINE OF THE CALIFORNIOS: A SOCIAL HISTORY OF THE
SPANISH-SPEAKING CALIFORNIANS, 1846-1890. Berkeley, University of
California Press, 1966. 324p. illus. $2.65
   A thoughtful, exhaustively documented social history of Spanish-Americans
in California from 1846 through 1890.

693.
Pohl, Irmgard, and Joseph Zepp. LATIN AMERICA; A GEOGRAPHICAL COMMENTARY.
Edited by Kempton Webb. New York, Dutton, 1967. 315p. maps, plates,
tables. $2.35
   The present edition has been adapted from the German work Amerika (1955)
for English-speaking readers. The book provides a geographical and
sociological analysis of all the countries of Latin America.

694.
Pomeroy, William J. ed. GUERRILLA WARFARE AND MARXISM. Introd. by William
J. Pomeroy. New York, International Pub. Co., 1969. 336p. $2.50
   Several authors discuss current controversies over the strategy and
tactics of guerrila warfare. Also published in hard cover.

695.
Poppino, Rollie E. BRAZIL: THE LAND AND THE PEOPLE. Illus. by Caribe and
Poty. New York, Oxford University Press, 1968. 370p. illus., maps, tables.
$2.50
   A concise study of Brazil from the Portuguese conquest to modern times.
Social and economic history receive special emphasis, a fact which makes
this book more valuable than the standard accounts of successions of
political events. Includes a good general bibliography.

696.
Pozas Arciniégas, Ricardo. JUAN THE CHAMULA; AN ETHNOLOGICAL RECREATION
OF THE LIFE OF A MEXICAN INDIAN. Translated by Lysander Kemp. Berkeley,
University of California Press, 1962. 115p. illus. $1.50
   Translation of Juan Pérez Jolote; biografía de un tzotzil (1952), by a
prominent Mexican anthropologist. It is a thorough biographic study of a
Tzotzil Indian in the 20th century.

697.
Prado, Caio, Jr. THE COLONIAL BACKGROUND OF MODERN BRAZIL. Translated
by Suzette Macedo. Berkeley, University of California Press, 1969. 439p.
$3.45
   This is an important book about colonial Brazil which will be very useful in college level courses. The translation is excellent.

698.
Pratt, Julius W. EXPANSIONISTS OF 1898; THE ACQUISITION OF HAWAII AND THE
SPANISH ISLANDS. Chicago, Quadrangle Books, 1964. 393p. $2.95
   A study of United States expansion in the Pacific and Caribbean areas

emphasizing the influence of business interests on diplomacy. It is based
on primary sources, and it contains a useful bibliography.

699.
Prescott, William Hickling. THE CONQUEST OF MEXICO; THE CONQUEST OF PERU,
AND OTHER SELECTIONS. Edited and abridged, and with an introd. by Roger
Howell. New York, Washington Square Press, 1966. 406p. map. $1.45
   Selections from Prescott's four histories.

700.
----------. THE CONQUEST OF PERU. Abridged and edited by Victor W. Von
Hagen. New York, New American Library, 1961. 416p. $0.75
   Abridged version of the well written and well researched account of the
conquest of Peru by the famous 19th century historian.

701.
----------. HISTORY OF THE CONQUEST OF MEXICO. Introd. by C. Harvey
Gardiner. Chicago, University of Chicago Press, 1966. 413p. illus.
$3.45
   The classic 19th century account of the conquest of Mexico. It is ex-
tremely well written. Includes a bibliography.

702.
----------. PORTABLE PRESCOTT. THE RISE AND DECLINE OF THE SPANISH EMPIRE.
Edited by Irwin R. Blacker. New York, Viking Press, 1966. 568p. maps.
$1.85
   This volume offers selections from Prescott's four histories, The
conquest of Mexico; Ferdinand and Isabella; The conquest of Peru; and
Philip II.

703.
Prince-Williams, D. R., ed. CROSS-CULTURAL STUDIES. Baltimore, Penguin
Books, 1970. 254p. $2.75
   Explores research into psychological variables as they appear in Latin
American, African, and other non-Western cultures.

704.
Quirk, Robert E. AN AFFAIR OF HONOR; WOODROW WILSON AND THE OCCUPATION OF
VERACRUZ. New York, Norton, 1967. 184p. $2.25
   First published in 1962, this is a well-documented account of the American
occupation of Veracruz in 1914, which received deserved recognition from the
Mississippi Valley Historical Association. Mexicans may object to the title
but will have no quarrel with the author's conclusion that the Wilson policy,
however admirable in theory, was impossible in practice. Includes bibliographies. [HLAS 26:655]

705.
----------. THE MEXICAN REVOLUTION, 1914-1915. New York, Norton, 1969.
325p. $1.95
   Significant, well-written volume describing the origin, development,
program, and collapse (owing to dissension and defeat) of the Revolutionary
Convention of Aguascalientes. The work is based on primary sources, including the private papers of Convention leader Roque González Garza. It
was first published in 1960.

706.
Rabinovitz, Francine F., Felicity M. Trueblood, and Charles J. Savio.
LATIN AMERICAN POLITICAL SYSTEMS IN AN URBAN SETTING; A PRELIMINARY BIB-
LIOGRAPHY. Gainesville, University of Florida Press, 1967. 42p. Free of
charge.
   A bibliography to aid scholars interested in the study of the political
systems of Latin America and students of the field of comparative urban
development. 434 items are listed. [Charles Fleener]

707.
Ramos, Samuel. PROFILE OF MAN AND CULTURE IN MEXICO. Translated by Peter
G. Earle. Introd. by Thomas B. Irving. Austin, University of Texas Press,

1970. 198p. $1.95
First published in 1934, this evaluation of Mexican character by a
philosopher has both literary merit and penetration, and is required
reading for understanding modern Mexico.

708.
Rappaport, Armin, ed. THE MONROE DOCTRINE. New York, Holt, Rinehart and
Winston, 1964. 122p. $2.25
A variety of divergent opinions on this subject makes the editor's task
easier. Raúl Díaz de Medina and Luis Quintanilla present Latin American
evaluations.

709.
----------. ed. THE WAR WITH MEXICO; WHY DID IT HAPPEN? Chicago, Rand
McNally, 1964. 60p. $1.00
A selection of contemporary documents presenting the advocates of
manifest destiny, the slave interest, and President Polk as chief culprits.
Includes a bibliography.

710.
Ray, Philip A. SOUTH WIND RED: OUR HEMISPHERE CRISIS. Chicago, H. Regnery,
1962. 242p. $2.00
The author argues for a foreign economic policy toward Latin America
based upon "enlightened private entrepreneurship" in place of massive
government-to-government aid. The latter policy is said to place the U.S.
in alignment with the left in most parts of Latin America. [HLAS 25:5348]

711.
Read, William R. NEW PATTERNS OF CHURCH GROWTH IN BRAZIL. Grand Rapids,
Mich., Eerdmans Pub. Co., 1965. 240p. tables. $2.45
A statistical and descriptive work which provides a comparative analysis
of the rapid growth of several Protestant denominations in Brazil.

712.
Redfield, Robert. CHAN KOM: A MAYA VILLAGE. Abridged ed. Chicago,
University of Chicago Press, 1962. 236p. $1.95
Originally published in 1934, this is the abridged version of a scholarly
anthropological study of a Maya village in Yucatán.

713.
----------. THE LITTLE COMMUNITY AND PEASANT SOCIETY AND CULTURE. Chicago,
University of Chicago Press, 1962. 177, 88p. $2.45
This is a reissue of two studies: The little community: viewpoints for the
study of a human whole (1955), and Peasant society and culture; an anthropological approach to civilization (1956), which study the culture and
ethnology of Yucatán.

714.
----------. THE PRIMITIVE WORLD AND ITS TRANSFORMATION. Ithaca, N.Y.,
Cornell University Press, 1957. 198p. $1.95
First published in 1953, this book is a general study of the people who
existed before the rise of the first cities, the ones the author refers to
as "precivilized" or "folk societies" and their transformation.

715.
----------. THE VILLAGE THAT CHOSE PROGRESS: CHAN KOM REVISTED. Chicago,
University of Chicago Press, 1962. 187p. illus., maps. $1.50
First published in 1950, this is a description of socio-economic
development of a Yucatán village from 1930 through 1948, by a well-known
anthropologist.

716.
Reed, John. INSURGENT MEXICO. New York, International Publishers, 1969.
235p. $2.65
John Reed was sent to cover the Mexican Revolution for the New York
World. He joined the Revolution and fought with the guerrillas, earned
the confidence and trust of many of the participants and wrote this moving

account about the Revolution in 1914. He later became internationally
famous for his book about the Soviet Revolution, <u>Ten days that shook the
world.</u>

717.
Reed, Nelson. THE CASTE WAR OF YUCATÁN. Stanford Calif., Stanford
University Press, 1967. 308p. illus., maps. $2.95
    The author describes in detail the Caste War which lasted from 1847 to
1855. He also analyzes the social and economic systems of Yucatán in the
19th and 20th centuries. The work is based on solid documentary evidence
and it includes a good bibliography. First published in 1964.

718.
Reedy, Daniel R. THE POETIC ART OF JUAN DEL VALLE CAVIEDES. Chapel Hill,
University of North Carolina Press, 1964. 152p. (Romance languages and
literature series, 46) $5.00
    This is a study of the life and times of the satirical poet of colonial
Peru (1652?-1697?), together with a discussion of critical commentaries on
his work since 1791, and an analysis of his collected writings. Includes
a bibliography.

719.
Reeve, Frank Driver. NEW MEXICO; A SHORT HISTORY. Denver, A. Swallow,
1966. 112p. illus. $2.00
    This is an illustrated history of New Mexico and its Hispanic heritage.

720.
Reina, Rubén E. THE LAW OF THE SAINTS; A POKOMAN PUEBLO AND ITS COMMUNITY
CULTURE. Indianapolis, Bobbs-Merrill, 1966. 338p. illus., tables, maps.
$3.25
    This book represents a prolonged study of the descendants of a group of
Maya Indians called Pokoman. The author concentrates on the pueblo of
Chinautla, 16 miles north of Guatemala City, and stresses the economic
activities and <u>cofradía</u> customs of the Chinautlans. [Charles Fleener]

721.
Remmling, Günter W. SOUTH AMERICAN SOCIOLOGISTS; A DIRECTORY. Austin,
University of Texas Press, 1970. 59p. $1.00
    This reference book will be welcomed and treasured by Sociologists and
librarians alike.

722.
Research Institute for the Study of Man, <u>New York, N.Y.</u> PAPERS OF THE
CONFERENCE ON RESEARCH AND RESOURCES OF HAITI. New York, 1969. 624p.
tables. $3.00
    Papers presented at the Conference on Research and Resources of Haiti,
November 1-4, 1967, New York. The topics covered include demography and
human resources; language and literacy; physical and mental health; and
Haitian institutions. Many of the participants were Haitian. A very
valuable contribution to the study of Haiti.

723.
Revueltas, José, FROM A MEXICAN PRISON: THE YOUTH MOVEMENT AND THE
ALIENATION OF SOCIETY. New York, Merit Publishers, 1969. 34p. $0.35
    In 1968 Revueltas was accused of being the intellectual leader of the
student revolts that broke out in Mexico. He was arrested and subsequently
wrote this essay which represents his interpretation of the student
rebellion and its implications from a Marxist point of view. [Charles
Fleener]

724.
Ring, Henry. HOW CUBA UPROOTED RACE DISCRIMINATION. New York, Merit
Publishers, 1961. 15p. $0.25
    A report on Cuba's attempt to abolish racial discrimination.

725.
Rivera, Julius. LATIN AMERICA; A SOCIOCULTURAL INTERPRETATION. New York,
Appleton-Century-Crofts, 1971. 204 p. illus. $2.95
    An objective and imaginative analysis of a complex continent. The empha-
sis is on society and norms governing social relationships, as well as on
the multiple cultures of Latin America.

726.
Robb, John Donald. HISPANIC FOLK SONGS OF NEW MEXICO; WITH SELECTED SONGS
COLLECTED, TRANSCRIBED, AND ARRANGED FOR VOICE AND PIANO. Albuquerque, University of New Mexico Press, 1954. 83 p. $2.00
    Includes folk songs with corresponding English translations. It also
contains a general discussion of Hispanic folk songs and a detailed examination of a few specific tunes.

727.
Roberts, Edwin A., Jr. LATIN AMERICA. Brunswick, N. J., Dow Jones, National Observer, 1964. 202 p. illus. $2.00
    Sixteen Latin American nations and certain common topics are surveyed in
this general journalistic treatment of the hemisphere.

728.
Robertson, Donald. PRE-COLUMBIAN ARCHITECTURE. New York, Braziller, 1963.
128 p. illus., maps. $2.95
    This is a short, well-written discussion of characteristics and differ-
ences of architecture in Middle America and the Andean region.

729.
Robertson, William Spence. THE RISE OF THE SPANISH-AMERICAN REPUBLICS AS
TOLD IN THE LIVES OF THEIR LIBERATORS. New York, Free Press, 1965. 348 p.
maps. $2.95
    Paperback edition of a book first published in 1918. It has been super-
seded in some details by recent scholarship, but it still is the best short
survey of its subject in English.

730.
Robinson, Harvey. LATIN AMERICA: A GEOGRAPHICAL SURVEY. New York, Praeger,
1967. 499 p. illus., tables, maps. $4.95
    A contemporary survey describing both the geographical unity and diver-
sity of Latin America. The introductory section deals with the physical
and cultural background of the hemisphere. In the second, larger section,
each nation is described in terms of its physical, human, and economic
geography. [Charles Fleener]

731.
Robock, Stefan Hyman. BRAZIL'S DEVELOPING NORTHEAST; A STUDY OF REGIONAL
PLANNING AND FOREIGN AID. Washington, Brookings Institution, 1963. 213 p.
maps. $2.00
    This is an important study of the economic problems of Brazil's North-
east. Robock's work had great impact on the Development Bank of the Northeast and later upon the Superintêndencia do Desenvolvimento de Nordeste
(SUDENE).

732.
Rockefeller, Nelson Aldrich. THE ROCKEFELLER REPORT ON THE AMERICAS.
Introd. by Tad Szulc. Chicago, Quadrangle Books, 1969. 144 p. tables,
maps. $1.25
    New York State's Governor Rockefeller warns President Nixon in this re-
port that the hemisphere is again in the throes of violent political, economic, and social upheaval. He emphasizes the importance of Latin America
to the U.S.

733.
Rodman, Selden. MEXICAN JOURNAL; THE CONQUERORS CONQUERED. Carbondale,
Southern Illinois University Press, 1965. 298 p. $2.45
    First published in 1958, this account of a trip to Mexico (1956-57) de-
scribes ancient ruins and records talks with José Vasconcelos, Diego Rivera,
Clemente Orozco, Carlos Fuentes and David Siqueiros.

734.
Rodriguez, Mario. CENTRAL AMERICA. Englewood Cliffs, N.J., Prentice-Hall, 1965. 178p. maps. $1.95
This excellent survey of Central American history in the 19th and 20th centuries provides a background for an understanding of the present. A very useful contribution and careful synthesis of a complex area. Includes a bibliography.

735.
----------, and Vincent C. Peloso, eds. A GUIDE FOR THE STUDY OF CULTURE IN CENTRAL AMERICA; HUMANITIES AND SOCIAL SCIENCES. Washington, Pan America Union, 1968. 88p. (Basic bibliographies, 5) $2.00
This bibliography is a thorough compilation of works on Central America. The 934 entries have been selected carefully; outstanding works have been evaluated with brief annotations. This is an especially useful reference aid for scholars, researchers, and librarians. Highly recommended.

736.
Rodriguez-Alcalá, Hujo, and Sally Rodriguez Alcalá, eds. CUENTOS NUEVOS DEL SUR: ARGENTINA, CHILE, URUGUAY, PARAGUAY. Englewood Cliffs, N.J., Prentice-Hall, 1967. 234p. $3.95
Contains a selection of outstanding short stories from South America.

737.
Rogers, Francis M., and David T. Haberly. BRAZIL, PORTUGAL, AND OTHER PORTUGUESE-SPEAKING LANDS; A LIST OF BOOKS PRIMARILY IN ENGLISH. Cambridge, Mass., Harvard University Press, 1968. 73p. $1.00
Contains over 800 entries of books in English published since World War II. No books in Portuguese are included, but a few of the most important works in Catalan, Dutch, French, German, Italian, Latin, Russian, and Spanish are present. This is a very useful guide.

738.
Rojas, Arnold R. THE LAST OF THE VAQUEROS. Sausalito, Calif., Academy Guild Press, 1960. 165p. illus. $1.95

739.
Rojo, Ricardo. CHE GUEVARA: VIE ET MORT D'UN AMI. Port Washington, N.Y., Paris Publications, 1969. 209p. illus. $1.20
French translation of Mi amigo el Che by an Argentine fellow-revolutionary of Guevara. It includes much information on the history of the Cuban Revolution.

740.
----------. MY FRIEND CHE. Translated from the Spanish by Julian Casart. New York, Grove Press, 1970. 220p. illus. $1.25
A fellow political activist from Argentina discusses his friend Che Guevara with whom he was closely associated through the 1950's and especially through the Cuban Revolution. It is an important study.

741.
Romanell, Patrick. THE MAKING OF THE MEXICAN MIND. Notre Dame, Ind., University of Notre Dame Press, 1967. 213p. $2.45
This is a reprint of a work which was published in 1952. It traces rapidly the development of Mexican philosophy from colonial times to the present, concentrating on the works of Caso and Vasconcelos, and the new trends such as perspectivism and existentialism. It includes a lengthy bibliography.

742.
Romero, José Luis. A HISTORY OF ARGENTINE POLITICAL THOUGHT. Translated by Thomas McGann. Stanford, Calif., Stanford University Press, 1968. 274p. maps. $2.95
A study of Argentine political thought from colonial times to 1955, in which the author synthesizes social and economic perceptions into political trends. Professor McGann's introduction stresses the comparisons that may be made with the U.S. A translation of Las ideas políticas en Argentina

(1963), it includes a good bibliography.

743.
Romney, Kimball, and Romaine Romney. THE MIXTECANS OF JUXTLAHUACA, MEXICO.
New York, J. Wiley, 1966. 150p. illus., maps. (Six cultures, 4) $2.95
Explores patterns of child-rearing and subsequent effects on the
personality in a small barrio of Oaxaca. The author studies the ethnographic
background of the people as well as their customs.

744.
Ronning, C. Neale, ed. INTERVENTION IN LATIN AMERICA. New York, Knopf,
1970. 220p. $2.75
The editor has selected 23 essays which trace various aspects of U.S.
intervention in Latin America. The book has been divided into two parts:
"Intervention; Motives, Methods, and Consequences;" and "Non-intervention:
the Evolution of a Doctrine." The editor has written an excellent introduction and prepared a chronology of U.S. armed intervention in Latin
America from 1798 to 1945.

745.
Roosevelt, Theodore. THE ROUGH RIDERS. New York, New American Library,
1961. 215p. illus. $0.75
This is Theodore Roosevelt's own account of the Rough Riders' partici-
pation in the Spanish-American War.

746.
Ross, Stanley R., ed. IS THE MEXICAN REVOLUTION DEAD? New York, Knopf,
1966. 255p. $2.50
Without settling the title's issue, the editor's introduction is a
thoughtful analysis, providing a general framework for 22 selections,
emphasizing various aspects of the Revolution. A good selective bibliography
enhances this teaching aid [Howard F. Cline]

747.
Ruiz, Ramón Eduardo. CUBA: THE MAKING OF A REVOLUTION. New York, Norton,
1970. 190p. $1.65
Professor Ruiz contends that the Cuban Revolution does not represent a
sharp break with the island 's past, but grew out of events and circumstances
that had been developing for well over half a century. This is an excellent
and well-documented analysis of the background of Castro's Revolution.
[Charles Fleener]

748.
-----------, ed. INTERPRETING LATIN AMERICAN HISTORY; FROM INDEPENDENCE TO
TODAY. New York, Holt, Rinehart and Winston 1970. 453p. $2.95
Section one of this book of readings covers the histories of Argentina,
Brazil, Mexico, and Cuba. The second section includes readings on Chile,
Peru, Bolivia, and Venezuela. Section three contains topical issues that
cut across national boundaries. The readings were written by prominent
historians, economists, and thinkers.

749.
-----------. ed. THE MEXICAN WAR: WAS IT MANIFEST DESTINY? New York, Holt,
Rinehart, and Winston, 1963. 118p. $2.25
Hubert Bancroft and Justo Sierra present Mexican view points but they are
outnumbered by U.S. historians discussing national problems. The editor ably
directs the questions.

750.
Rulfo, Juan. EL LLANO EN LLAMAS. 8th ed. Austin, University of Texas Press,
1969. 192p. $1.50
Rulfo is one of Mexico's most gifted writers. He works on rural themes and
and the rugged life of Mexican peasants. This is a very attractive edition.

751.
-----------. PEDRO PÁRAMO. Edited by Luis Leal. New York, Appleton-Century-

Crofts, 1970. 178p. $2.95

Pedro Páramo was first published in 1955 by the Mexican novelist Juan Rulfo. It depicts the life of a Mexican peasant from infancy to death. It is a violent, b tal, vengeful, and sensual life, dignified by his love for Susana. Brutal is an annotated textbook edition which includes a vocabulary.

752.
----------. PEDRO PÁRAMO. Translated by Lysander Kemp. New York, Grove Press, 1959. 123p. $1.25

This is a very good English translation of the above.

753.
Sábato, Ernesto. EL TÚNEL. Edited by Louis C. Perez. New York, Macmillan, 1965. 124p. $2.25

This is a textbook edition of this contemporary Argentine novel about alienation.

754.
Sable, Martin H. COMMUNISM IN LATIN AMERICA; AN INTERNATIONAL BIBLIOGRAPHY: 1900-1945, 1960-1967. Los Angeles, University of California Press, 1968. 220p. $2.00

Designed to supplement and update Ludwig Lauerhass' Communism in Latin America; a bibliography, the post-war years (1945-1960), this select bibliography includes more than 2,000 items in 22 languages, most of which are avialable in major university libraries. The entries have been arranged chronologically and by countries.

755.
----------. A GUIDE TO LATIN AMERICAN STUDIES. Los Angeles, University of California Press, 1967. 783p. tables. $25.00

This oversize reference work is an annotated bibliography that covers the humanities, as well as the social, natural, and applied sciences. It contains 51,024 entries of English, Spanish, and Portuguese sources. The introduction is in English and Spanish. [Charles Fleener]

756.
Samora, Julian, ed. LA RAZA: FORGOTTEN AMERICANS. Notre Dame, Ind., University of Notre Dame Press, 1969. 218p. tables. $2.50

In the U.S. Southwest there are more than four million Spanish-speaking citizens. The seven authors of the essays in this volume deal with religion, political activity, civil rights, and the emerging middle class. The editor summarizes the current status of the Chicanos and suggest paths for future development.

757.
Sánchez, Florencio. REPRESENTATIVE PLAYS OF FLORENCIO SÁNCHEZ. Translated by Willis Knapp Jones. Washington, Pan American Union, 1961. 326p. $2.50

Considered one of Spanish America's greatest playwrights, Sánchez produced the 11 plays included here between 1903 and 1909. Included are the classics My son the lawyer (M'hijo el dotor); The immigrant girl (La gringa); Down the gully (Barranca abajo); and Our children (Nuestros hijos).

758.
Sánchez, George Isadore. MEXICO. Boston, Ginn, 1966. 112p. illus. maps. $1.60

A general and concise text about Mexico intended for young readers, or for survey courses. Contains a brief bibliography

759.
Sánchez, José. ACADEMIAS Y SOCIEDADES LITERARIAS DE MEXICO. Chapel Hill, University of North Carolina Press, 1951. 277p. $6.50

Contains a historical listing of Mexican literary societies. Of great interest for the specialist.

760.
Sanders, William T., and Barbara J. Price. MESOAMERICA: THE EVOLUTION OF A
CIVILIZATION. New York, Random House, 1969. 265p. illus., maps. $4.50
    The authors analyze the factors and processes of growth that shaped
culture history in Mexico and Guatemala long before the advent of the white
man. It is a valuable book on the theory of civilization, and it points
out that nowhere is the societal structure of several layers of ancient
civilizations as well documented as in Mesoamerica and in Peru.

761.
Sanderson, Ivan Terence. CARIBBEAN TREASURE. New York, Pyramid Publications,
1963. 292p. illus. $0.75
    Describes the fascinating world of the Caribbean jungle animals. It was
first published in 1939.

762.
Sarfatti, Magali. SPANISH BUREAUCRATIC-PATRIMONIALISM IN AMERICA. Berkeley,
University of California, Institute of International Studies, 1966. 129p.
tables. $1.75
    Describes the main characteristics of the Spanish bureaucratic-patrimonial
system during the colonial period. Using a generalized Weberian model of
patrimonial authority, the author has examined the interrelationships
between normative and structural, theoretical and empirical aspects of the
Spanish traditional system.

763.
Sarmiento, Domingo Faustino. LIFE IN THE ARGENTINE REPUBLIC IN THE DAYS OF
THE TYRANTS; OR CIVILIZATION AND BARBARISM. Translated by Mrs. Horace Mann.
New York, Hafner, 1960. 400p. $2.45
    Mrs. Mann's English translation of Civilización i barbarie; vida de Juan
Facundo Quiroga (1845) was first published in 1868. Sarmiento's book provides
an interesting insight into the first decades of Argentina as an independent
nation. It also occupies an important place in Spanish-American literature.

764.
----------. LIFE IN THE ARGENTINE REPUBLIC IN THE DAYS OF THE TYRANTS; OR
CIVILIZATION AND BARBARISM. With a biographical sketch of the author by
Mrs. Horace Mann. New York, Macmillan, 1961. 288p. $1.50
    See above.

765.
----------. TRAVELS; A SELECTION. Translated by Inés Muñoz. Washington,
Pan American Union, 1963. 297p. $1.50.
    Contains a selection of travel accounts by Sarmiento. He undertook the
trips from 1845 to 1848 as a representative of the Chilean government. The
selection is taken from the 3 volume work dealing with the U.S., which he
regarded as a model for Argentina.

766.
Sasser, Elizabeth Skidmore. ARCHITECTURE OF ANCIENT PERU. Illus. by Nolan
E. Barrick. Lubbock, Texas Technological College, International Center for
Arid and Semi-Arid Land Studies, 1969. 79p. illus. $2.95
    The scope of this survey extends from the Chavín Cult around 900 B.C.
to the Imperialist Period of the Inca until the arrival of the Spaniards
in the 16th century. An important and useful contribution.

766A.
Sawyer, A. R. TIAHUANACO TEXTILE DESIGN. New York, Museum of Primitive
Art, 1970. Distributed by the New York Graphic Arts Society. 195p. illus.
$1.50
    The text explains the many attractive textile designs from Tiahuanaco
which are reproduced here.

767.
Scobie, James R. ARGENTINA; A CITY AND A NATION. New York, Oxford University Press, 1964. 294p. maps. $2.50
An excellent general survey of Argentine history which emphasizes the economic, cultural, and social factors involved in the rivalry between Buenos Aires and the provinces. The author interprets Argentina's long struggle for unity. Includes a very good 26-page select bibliography.

768.
Semmel, Bernard. DEMOCRACY VERSUS EMPIRE: THE JAMAICA RIOTS OF 1865 AND THE GOVERNOR EYRE CONTROVERSY. New York, Doubleday, 1969. 200p. $1.45
A thorough study of the 1865 Jamaica riots and its political implications which will be welcome by students of Caribbean history.

769.
Senior, Clarence. THE PUERTO RICANS: STRANGERS, THEN NEIGHBORS. Chicago, Quadrangle Books, 1965. 128p. tables. $1.95
The present study analyzes the problems of education, job discrimination, and social acceptance which confronts the Puerto Ricans in the U.S. mainland, and points out what progress has been made. Includes an introduction by Hubert Humphrey and an endorsement by the B'nai B'rith.

770.
Sexton, Patricia Cayo. SPANISH HARLEM: ANATOMY OF POVERTY. New York, Harper & Row, 1966. 208p. map. $1.60
The author probes into the many problems of the Puerto Rican slum-dwellers in New York City.

771.
Schell, Rolfo F. DE SOTO DIDN'T LAND AT TAMPA. Rev. ed. Fort Myers Beach, Fla., Island Press, 1966. 96p. $1.00

772.
Schmitt, Karl M., and David Burks, EVOLUTION OR CHAOS: DYNAMICS OF LATIN AMERICAN GOVERNMENT AND POLITICS. Introd. by Ronald M. Schneider. New York, Praeger, 1963. 320p. $2.95
This is a useful overview of Latin American politics up to 1963.

773.
Scholes, Walter V. MEXICAN POLITICS DURING THE JUÁREZ REGIME; 1855-1872. Columbia, Mo., University of Missouri Press, 1969. 190p. illus. $2.50
This is a scholarly interpretation of the Mexican political scene from 1855 through 1872, especially as it was influenced by the Reform Program. He concludes that the economic and political power of the Church was circumscribed and republican institutions such as free speech and free press were attained. [Charles Fleener]

774.
Schulz, Herbert Clarence et al. TEN CENTURIES OF MANUSCRIPTS IN THE HUNTINGTON LIBRARY. San Marino, Calif., Huntington Library, 1962. 87p. illus., maps. $1.50

775.
Schurz, William Lytle. THE CIVILIZATION OF LATIN AMERICA. New York, Dutton, 1964. 429p. maps. $1.95
The author presents a popularized general study of Latin American cultural backgrounds. It was first published in 1954.

776.
-----------. LATIN AMERICA: A DESCRIPTIVE SURVEY. Rev. ed. New York, Dutton, 1964. 373p. maps. $1.95
This is a revised edition of a 1941 work with good personal insights into the history, land, and society of Latin America. It is a readable introductory text.

777.
----------. THE MANILA GALLEON. New ed. New York, Dutton, 1959. 453p.
$2.45
    First published in 1939, this is an account of the Acapulco-Manila galleon
trade from 1565 to 1815. Contains interesting descriptions of the navigation
of the Pacific and the Spanish empire in the Orient.

778.
Scott, Robert E. MEXICAN GOVERNMENT IN TRANSITION. Rev. ed. Urbana, University of Illinois Press, 1964. 345p. $2.25
    A good analysis of the changing pattern of government in Mexico over the
past half century. Useful for courses on Mexico. Includes a bibliography.

779.
Shafer, Robert Jones. MEXICO: MUTUAL ADJUSTMENT PLANNING. Syracuse, N.Y.,
Syracuse University Press, 1966. 214p. $4.25
    This excellent large-scale examination of Mexican economic development
planning emphasizes its sectional and regional nature.

780.
Shapiro, N., and E.S. Simha eds. NEGRITUDE: BLACK POETRY FROM AFRICA AND THE
CARIBBEAN. Introd. by W. Cartey. New York, October House, 1970. 240p.
$2.95
    Includes a well-chosen selection of contemporary Black poetry from the
Caribbean.

781.
Shapiro, Samuel, ed. CULTURAL FACTORS IN INTER-AMERICAN RELATIONS. Notre
Dame, Ind., University of Notre Dame Press, 1968. 368p. $3.45
    These papers delivered at the 5th annual meeting of the Catholic Inter-
American Cooperation Program in St. Louis, in 1968, addressed themselves to
the problems facing Latin America and to the general question of inter-American
cultural relations. The contributors include Ricardo Arías Calderón, Lyle N.
McAlister, Eugene J. McCarthy, John Plank, and others.

782.
----------, ed. INTEGRATION OF MAN AND SOCIETY IN LATIN AMERICA. Notre Dame,
Ind., Notre Dame University Press, 1968. 356p. $3.35
    Includes papers presented at the 4th annual meeting of the Catholic Inter-
American Cooperation Program. The authors include J. Mayone Stycos (on
population problems); Arturo Bonilla (on trade unions); Henry Landsberger
(labor problems); and others. Includes bibliographical notes.

783.
Sherlock, Philip M. WEST INDIES. New York, Walker, 1966. 215p. illus.,
maps. $3.50
    This interpretative history and anlysis hails from Trinidad. The author
analyzes the ten islands' achievements as a whole in light of the special
economic and political di ficulties which face these societies. [Charles
Fleener]

784.
Sherwood, Frank P. INSTITUTIONALIZING THE GRASS ROOTS IN BRAZIL. San
Francisco, Chandler Pub. Co., 1967. 173p. illus. $3.75
    Surveys Brazilian popular politics.

785.
Sierra, Justo. POLITICAL EVOLUTION OF THE MEXICAN PEOPLE. Introd. by Edmundo
O'Gorman. Prologue by Alfonso Reyes. Austin, University of Texas Press,
1970. 406p. $2.95
    This classical synthesis written on the eve of the Mexican Revolution
influenced greatly the leaders of the Revolution. Sierra was the first
historian to show sympathy for the plight of the masses.

786.
Sigmund, Paul E., Jr., ed. THE IDEOLOGIES OF THE DEVELOPING NATIONS.
New York, Praeger, 1963. 326p. $3.95

One fourth of this work is devoted to Latin America. It is valuable because it makes available English translations of writings and speeches by leading figures of the region such as Haya de la Torre, Betancourt, Frei, Latendorf, Kubitschek, and Castro, expressing their political theories.

787.
----------., ed. MODELS OF POLITICAL CHANGE IN LATIN AMERICA. New York Praeger, 1970. 338p. $3.95
Mexico, Bolivia, and Cuba were chosen by the author as models of regimes that derived their political character from revolution. Argentine, Brazil, and Peru are examples for military regimes, while Colombia, Venezuela, and Chile are presented as the leading constitutional democracies. It should be kept in mind that Mexico is now a democracy and that Bolivia is currently under military rule.

788.
Silverberg, Robert. LOST CITIES AND VANISHED CIVILIZATIONS. New York, Batam Books, 1964. 177p. $0.60
This work was first published in 1962 in hard cover; Chichén Itzá is one of the lost cities studied.

789.
Silvert, Kalman H. CHILE, YESTERDAY AND TODAY. New York, Holt, Rinehart and Winston, 1965. 218p. illus., maps. $2.00
A popular, intelligent account a country not adequately studies in recent years. The author intends to introduce the reader to Chile's past and present.

790.
----------. THE CONFLICT SOCIETY: REACTION AND REVOLUTION IN LATIN AMERICA. Rev. ed. New York, American Universities Field Staff, 1966. 289p. $2.25
First published in 1961, this revised edition contains several new essays entitled " National Political Change in Latin America," "The Costs of Antinationalism," "Argentina," "The University Students," and "Peace, Freedom, and Stability in the Western Hemisphere." A valuable source of information on contemporary Latin America.

791.
Simpson, Lesley Bird. MANY MEXICOS. 3d ed. rev. and enl. Berkeley, University of California Press, 1959. 349p. $1.95
Prof. Simpson, long a student of Mexico and a thorough scholar and observer of Mexican life, has turned out one of the truly good books about Mexico. This revised edition was first published in 1952.

792.
Sinclair, Andrew. CHE GUEVARA. Edited by Frank Kermods. New York, Viking Press, 1970. 128p. $1.95
The author has prepared a study of Guevara's ideas and influence on Latin American politics.

793.
Singletary, Otis A. THE MEXICAN WAR. Chicago, University of Chicago Press, 1960. 181p. $1.95
This is a brief, readable account of the Mexican War. No new ground is broken, and the author plunges directly into the events of 1845 with only a scant six pages devoted to the historical background [HLAS 25:3324]

794.
Skidmore, Thomas. POLITICS IN BRAZIL, 1930-1964; AN EXPERIMENT IN DEMOCRACY. New York, Oxford University Press, 1968. 446p. maps. $2.50
A thorough review of Brazilian politics and government during a crucial period of Brazilian history. It is based on extensive scholarly research, and it is a major contribution to the field of Brazilian studies. Includes bibliographical footnotes.

795.
Slater, Jerome. A REEVALUATION OF COLLECTIVE SECURITY: THE OAS IN ACTION.

Columbus, Ohio State University Press, 1965. 56p. $1.50
  Contends that collective security is workable under certain circumstances
and that some appropriate revisions of the theory of collective security will
be necessary.

796.
Smiley, Terah Leroy, and others. FOUNDATION FOR THE DATING OF SOME LATE
ARCHAEOLOGICAL SITES IN THE RIO GRANDE AREA; NEW MEXICO. Tucson, University
of Arizona Press, 1953. 66p. illus. maps. $1.00
  Studies archaeological dating in the Rio Grande area of New Mexico. A
very interesting monograph.

797.
Smith, Buckingham, trans. NARRATIVES OF THE CAREER OF HERNANDO DE SOTO, by
a Gentleman of Elvas. Introd. by A. Lythe. Gainesville, Fla., Kallman Pub.
Co., 1969. 243p. illus. $2.25
  Examines the career of Hernando de Soto one of the early explorers of
Florida.

798.
Smith, Robert Freeman, ed. BACKGROUND TO REVOLUTION: THE DEVELOPMENT OF
MODERN CUBA. New York, Knopf, 1965. 224p. $2.50
  A selection of essays concerning Cuban history of the past three centuries
showing that from the beginning of European contact the island has captured
the interest of foreign powers that believed Cuba was vital to their interest.
It provides historical perspective to counteract simplistic views of Cuba's
political history.

799.
----------. UNITED STATES AND CUBA: BUSINESS AND DIPLOMACY, 1917-1961. New
Haven, Conn., College and University Press, 1962. 256p. $2.25
  Published in 1961, this is a review of U.S.-Cuban relations since 1898.
Special attention is given to the important problems raised by the interplay
of private business and governmental agencies in the formulation of foreign
policy. The author has made extensive use of official documents and archival
sources. [HLAS 24:3551]

800.
Stycos, J. Mayone, and Jorge Arias, eds. POPULATION DILEMMA IN AMERICA.
New York, Columbia Books, 1966. 249p. maps. $2.45
  Contains 11 papers on population problems in Latin America presented as
background reading at the 1965 Pan American Assembly on Population in Cali,
Colombia, sponsored by the Pan American Assembly of Columbia University,
New York.

801.
Suárez, Andrés. CUBA: CASTROISM AND COMMUNISM, 1959-1966. Cambridge,
Massachusetts Institute of Technology Press, 1969. 266p. $2.45
  This highly praised work surveys the course of political events in Cuba
from early revolutionary days to the mid-1960's. It is a comprehensive,
objective, and scholarly book on Fidel Castro's Cuba.

802.
Suassuna, Ariano. THE ROGUES' TRIAL; THE CRIMES OF JOHN CRICKET AND OTHER
ROGUES; THEIR TRIAL AND THE INTERCESSION OF MARY, OUR LADY OF MERCY. A
SATIRE ON HUMAN FRAILTIES IN THE FORM OF A MIRACLE PLAY BASED ON BALLADS AND
FOLK TALES OF NORTHEASTERN BRAZIL. Translated by Dillwyn F. Ratcliff.
Berkeley, University of California Press, 1963. 107p. $1.50
  English translation of the prize-winning play Auto da Compadecida (1957)
in which the playwright combines the technique of a puppet shoe, the miracle
play, and the commedia dell' arte with Brazilian folklore. Although based
on the 15th century auto of Gil Vicente, this work is thoroughly Brazilian
in feeling and social satire.

803.
Summer, William Graham. THE CONQUEST OF THE UNITED STATES BY SPAIN, AND

OTHER ESSAYS. Chicago, H. Regnery, 1965. 250p. $1.45
    One of the essays in this work describes Spain's colonization of North
America.

804.
Sundel, Alfred. CHRISTOPHER COLUMBUS; A CONCISE BIOGRAPHY. New York, American
R.D.M. Corp., 1968. 67p. illus., maps. $1.00
    This is a popularized account of efforts by Columbus to gain support in his
enterprise, and of his four voyages to the New World.

805.
-----------. HISTORY OF THE AZTECS AND THE MAYAS AND THEIR CONQUEST. New York,
American R. D. M. Corp., 1967. illus., maps. $1.00
    Describes the two great nations of Middle America and their conquest.
Intended for the generalist.

806.
Swan, B. F. EARLY PRINTING IN THE CARIBBEAN. Edited by C. Clair. New York,
A. Schram, 1971. 420p. illus., $8.25
    Surveys early printing in the Caribbean area.

807.
Szulc, Tad. LATIN AMERICA. New York, Atheneum, 1966. 185p. map. $1.65
    A New York Times correpondent introduces the reader to the changing Latin
American scene. It is a popularized essay divided into background, the present
and the future, and Latin America and the world.

808.
Tambs, Lewis A., and others, ed. LATIN AMERICAN GOVERNMENT LEADERS. Tempe,
Arizona State University Center, 1970. 65p. $2.00
    The editors have assembled 350 biographies of political and governmental
leaders in 12 Latin American countries. A much needed and useful reference
work.

809.
Tannenbaum, Frank. PEACE BY REVOLUTION; MEXICO AFTER 1910. Drawings by
Miguel Covarrubias. New York, Columbia University Press, 1966. 316p. illus.,
maps. $2.45
    Tannenbum's excellent appraisal of the Mexican Revolution was first pub-
lished in 1933. He emphasizes the two decades following 1910.

810.
-----------. SLAVE AND CITIZEN; THE NEGRO IN THE AMERICAS. New York, Random
House, 1963. 128p. $1.45
    First published in 1946, it rests on the thesis that when the moral equality
of the Negro was accepted by the governing society slavery was abolished peace-
fully, but when that egalitarianism was lacking, social change and abolition
were produced by force, war, or revolution.

811.
-----------. TEN KEYS TO LATIN AMERICA. New York, Random House, 1966. 237p.
$1.95
    The key subjects in this collection of essays are "race" and "religion."
Emphasis is placed on current problems and their historical roots by a
sympathetic critic who has spent a lifetime studying such matters.

812.
Tarn, Nathaniel, ed. CON CUBA: AN ANTHOLOGY OF CUBAN POETRY. New York,
Grossman, 1969. 144p. $2.95
    Cuba according to the editor is a land "where poets are as abundant as
trees and books as leaves." This collection presents 30 Cuban poets, more
than half of them born after 1935. They range from Felix Pita (b. 1909) to
Lina de Feria and Eduardo Lolo (b. 1945). The poems appear in the original
Spanish with English translations.

813.
Tate, Bill. MOUNTAIN CHANTS: THE SECRET OF THE PENITENTES. Truchas, N.M.,
Tate Gallery Publications, 1970. 59p. illus. $3.00
    In this brief study the author describes several rites of the Penitentes,
a sacred Spanish-American brotherhood.

814.
----------. THE PENITENTES OF THE SANGRE DE CRISTOS: AN AMERICAN TRAGEDY.
2d. ed. Truchas, N.M., Tate Gallery Publications, 1968. 56p. illus., maps.
$3.00
    The Penitentes are members of a secret and ancient Spanish-American
brotherhood who live in the mountains of northern New Mexico and Southern
Colorado. The author, who lives among the Penitentes in the village of
Truchas attempts to portray and to clarify the Penitentes' way of life.
The illustrations by the author are very good. [Charles Fleener]

815.
----------. TRUCHAS: VILLAGE WITH A VIEW, LIFE IN A SPANISH VILLAGE. Truchas,
N.M., Tate Gallery Publication, 1969. 49p. illus. $2.50
    The author, who is an artist, moved to Truchas in 1963. This personal
essay about his experiences contains prose, poetry, recipes, and drawings.

816.
Taylor, Barbara Howland. MEXICO: HER DAILY AND FESTIVE BREADS. Edited by
Ruth S. Lamb. Claremont, Calif., Creative Press, 1969. 98p. illus. $1.50
    In words and pictures the author describes the varieties of breads of
Mexico and interprets what they tell about the country and the people. Many
attractive illustrations enhance the text.

817.
Taylor, Philip B. Jr. THE VENEZUELAN GOLPE DE ESTADO OF 1958: THE FALL OF
MARCOS PÉREZ JIMÉNEZ. Washington, Institute for the Comparative Study of
Political Systems, 1968. 98p. tables. $2.00
    Analyzes the barracks revolt which brought down the dictatorship of Pérez
Jiménez. Venezuelan society and politics, as well as the nature of the
dictorship are studies. Professor Taylor concludes that "Venezuela has burst
from its shell of past authoritarianism with enormous energy."

818.
Tebbel, John William, and Ramón Eduardo Ruiz. SOUTH BY SOUTHWEST; THE MEXICAN-
AMERICAN AND HIS HERITAGE. New York, Doubleday, 1969. 122p. illus. maps.
$1.45
    A thoughtful study of Mexican-Americans and their cultural heritage.

819.
Terry, Robert H. ed. SELECTED READINGS ON LATIN AMERICA. Berkeley, Calif.,
McCutchan Pub. Co., 1969. 188p. maps. $3.95
    This volume contains essays by Frank Tannenbaum, Hubert Herring, Victor
L. Urquidi, and others. The readings deal with social, economic, and
diplomatic topics.

820.
Thiesenhusen, William C. CHILE'S EXPERIMENTS IN AGRARIAN REFORM. Madison,
University of Wisconsin Press, 1966. 230p. maps, tables. $3.00
    Analyzes several land reform experiments in Chile where the traditional
latifundia-minifundia agrarian structure still predominates. It is predicated
on the idea that when a more inclusive agricultural restructuralization comes,
technicians will benefit from having studied how reform works on a small
scale.

821.
Thomas, Aaron Joshua. DOMINICAN REPUBLIC CRISIS, 1965. Edited by John Carey.
New York, Oceana Pub. Co., 1967. 164p. $2.45
    Analyzes the Dominican crisis of 1965 and the intervention of the Inter-
American Peace Force.

822.
Thompson, Edward Herbert, and J. R. Murie. HIGH PRIEST'S GRAVE: CHICHÉN
ITZÁ YUCATÁN, MEXICO. New York, Kraus Reprints, 1970. 320p. illus. $5.00
   An archaeological study of a Maya grave with attractive illustrations.

823.
Thompson, Edward Herbert. PEOPLE OF THE SERPENT; LIFE AND ADVENTURE AMONG
THE MAYAS. New York, Putnam, 1965. 301p. (Capricorn, 123) $1.65
   This is a book of personal memoirs, essentially a volume on archaeology,
written by one of the most famous explorers of Yucatán, the archaeologist who
established the ritual significance of the Sacred Cenote of Chichén Itzá.

824.
Tinkle, Lon. THE ALAMO; THIRTEEN DAYS TO GLORY. New York, New American
Library, 1958. 176p. illus. $0.50
   This is a factual yet considerably dramatized day-by-day account of the
1836 battle for the Alamo.

825.
Tolstoy, Paul. SURFACE SURVEY OF THE NORTHERN VALLEY OF MEXICO; THE CLASSIC
AND POST-CLASSIC PERIODS. Philadelphia, American Philosophical Society,
1958. 108p. illus. map. $2.00
   This is a thorough study of classic and post-classic art in northern
Mexico.

826.
Tomasek, Robert Dennis, ed. LATIN AMERICAN POLITICS; STUDIES OF THE CON-
TEMPORARY SCENE. 2d. ed. rev. and updated. Garden City, N.Y., Doubleday,
1970. 584p. $2.45
   First published in 1966, this is a new edition of a selection of essays
which present a many-sided view of the power groups, the political process,
and the violent nature of Latin American politics. Chosen from the writings
of well-known authorities, they provide a good background from the understanding of Latin American politics.

827.
Tornöe, J. K. COLUMBUS IN THE ARCTIC? AND THE VINELAND LITERATURE. New York,
Humanities Press, 1965. 92p. maps. $5.00
   The author assumes that the sagas of the Norse discovery can be interpreted
as factual reports of historical events. He further states that first-hand
knowledge of North America persisted in Europe for many centuries. Thus he
theorizes that Columbus actually knew about North America before "accidentally"
discovering the Western Hemisphere. [Charles Fleener]

828.
Torres Ríoseco, Arturo, ed. ANTOLOGÍA DE LA LITERATURA HISPANO-AMERICANA;
SELECCIÓN, COMENTARIOS, NOTAS Y GLOSARIO. 2d. ed. New York, Appleton-
Century Crofts, 1961. 311p. $3.25
   This is a very useful and representative anthology of Spanish-American
literature. It includes samples from novels, short stories, essays, and
poetry by great literary figures.

829.
----------. THE EPIC OF LATIN AMERICAN LITERATURE. Berleley, University of
California Press, 1959. 277p. $1.50
   Originally published in 1942, this is an excellent survey of the history
of Latin American literature from the colonial period to the mid-20th century.
It includes a chapter on Brazilian literature.

830.
Trend, John Brande. BOLIVAR AND THE INDEPENDENCE OF SPANISH AMERICA. New
York, Harper and Row, 1970. 289p. $1.45
   A fresh view of Simon Bolívar and the independence of South America is
presented here. It will be very useful for studying the independence period.

831.
Turner, Frederick C. THE DYNAMIC OF MEXICAN NATIONALISM. Chapel Hill,
University of North Carolina Press, 1968. 350p. $2.95
   This is an important study of the nature and some of the functions of
nationalism in Mexican society by a political scientist. He analyzes the
extent to which nationalism has been relevant in Mexican national life,
particularly since the Revolution of 1910.

832.
Turner, M.C. LA EMPRESA DEL LIBRO EN AMERICA LATINA. New York, Bowker, 1970.
451p. $7.00
   Surveys Latin American publishing. This will be a useful work for persons
engaged in acquisitions.

833.
Ulloa, Jorge Juan and Antonio de Ulloa. A VOYAGE TO SOUTH AMERICA. The
John Adams translation abridged. Introd. by Irving A. Leonard. New York,
Knopf, 1964. 245p. $2.50
   Translation of a controversial 18th century report emphasizing defects
in the Spanish empire in its waning days. Two young Spanish officers describe
vividly their visit to the important Spanish cities and settlements of South
America.

834.
United Nations. Economic Commission for Latin America. ECONOMIC BULLETIN FOR
LATIN AMERICA. Washington, $2.50
   This is a biennial publication, containing a wealth of statistical data.

835.
U.S. Agency for International Development. Office of Technical Cooperation
and Research. A STUDY OF PRESENT AND NEEDED BOOK ACTIVITIES IN NATIONAL
DEVELOPMENT: CHILE. Pittsburgh, University of Pittsburgh, School of Education,
1967. 141p. $1.00
   This report is the result of a survey of "book development" in Chile. A
team of four researchers investigated the needs for, and potentials of textbooks in the Chilean educational system.

836.
----------. A STUDY OF PRESENT AND NEEDED BOOK ACTIVITIES IN NATIONAL
DEVELOPMENT: PERU. Pittsburgh, University of Pittsburgh School of Education,
1967. 141p. $1.00
   Surveys who is publishing, distributing, and utilizing books in the various
educational and development programs in Peru. Recommendations are also made
for future projects to encourage Peruvian publishing.

837.
Urquidi, Víctor . FREE TRADE AND ECONOMIC INTEGRATION IN LATIN AMERICA: THE
EVOLUTION OF A COMMON MARKET POLICY. Translated by Marjory M. Urquidi.
Berkeley, University of California Press, 1962. 190p. $3.75
   A Mexican economist traces the steps leading to the Central American
integration treaties and the organization of LAFTA. This is an English
translation of Trayectoria del mercado común latino-americano (1960),
complete with a bibliography, appendixes, a chronology, and the text of the
Treaty of Montevideo.

838.
Usigli, Rodolfo. CORONA DE LUZ. Edited by Rex Edward Ballinger. New York,
Appleton-Century-Crofts, 1967. 217p. illus. $2.95
   This is the Mexican playwright's latest work published in 1965. The present
edition includes a vocabulary and notes.

839.
----------. CORONA DE SOMBRA; PIEZA ANTIHISTÓRICA EN TRES ACTOS. Edited by
Rex Edward Ballinger. New York, Applet n-Century-Crofts, 1961. 206p. illus.
$2.65
   Usigli is probably the most professional Mexican playwright. He calls
Crona de sombra (1943) an anti-historical work with a historical theme; the

tragic fate of Maximilian and Carlota. This is a textbook edition of the play.

840.
----------. EL GESTICULADOR. Edited by Rex Edward Ballinger. New York, Appleton-Century-Crosts, 1963. 178p. illus. $2.65
According to the preface "this textbook edition of El Gesticulador (1937) is designed to furnish English speaking students of Hispanic literature with an interesting play by the most distinguished playwright of Mexico.

841.
Uslar Pietri, Arturo. CATORCE CUENTOS VENEZOLANOS. Philadelphia Center for Curriculum Development, 1969. 320p. $2.40

842.
----------. LAS LANZAS COLORADAS. Edited by Donald Devernish Walsh. New York, Norton, 1964. 219p. $2.75
This is a historical novel by the Venezuelan writer who was born in 1905. It was first published in 1931. In this novel Uslar Pietri's rich prose describes barbarism and chaos with the figure of Bolívar vaguely outlined.

843.
Vaillant, George Clapp. AZTECS OF MEXICO: ORIGIN, RISE, AND FALL OF THE AZTEC NATION. Rev. by Suzannah B. Vaillant. Baltimore, Penguin, 1962. 333p. $2.95
New edition of the book, first published in 1941, that has come closest to becoming the standard account of Central Mexican archaeology and the culture of the native peoples of the area at Contact. The archaeological portion has been considerably revised to bring the account up-to-date.

844.
Valdés, Nelson, and Edwin Lieuwen, comps. THE CUBAN REVOLUTION; A RESEARCH-STUDY GUIDE, 1959-1969. Albuquerque, University of New Mexico Press, 1971. 230p. $3.95
Contains 3,839 items essential for scholars working in the humanities and social sciences. It is the first systematic and comprehensive guide which includes all relevant sources, both primary and secondary, for the study of revolutionary Cuba. Included are official documents, eyewitness reports, dissertations, books, periodicals, and newspapers.

845.
Vallejo, César. POEMAS HUMANOS. HUMAN POEMS. Translated by Clayton Eshleman. New York, Grove Press, 1969. 326p. $2.95
Poemas humanos was first published posthumously in Paris in 1939. The poems were inspired by the Spanish Civil War. The poet expressed through his verses the great pity he felt for the oppressed and turned his hopes toward redemption through Marxism. In this edition Spanish and English texts face each other.

846.
Vallier, Ivan. CATHOLICISM, SOCIAL CONTROL, AND MODERNIZATION IN LATIN AMERICA. Santa Cruz, University of California, 1970. 171p. tables. $2.95
Analyzes how Catholicism is affecting the processes of change in Latin America. A number of individuals and groups have become symbols for the "new Church" such as Dom Helder Cámara, the bishop of Recife, the priest-turned guerrillero Camilo Torres, Ivan Illich of the Center for Intercultural Formation in Cuernavaca, Mexico, and others.

847.
Van Deusen, Glyndon G. THE LIFE OF HENRY CLAY. Boston, Little, Brown, 1937. 448. $2.45
Latin America remains on the periphery in this classic biography of one of her earliest advocates in the U.S. Some interesting background information on U.S. attitudes towards Latin America for the 1800-1850 period. [Charles Fleener]

848.
Van Loon, Hendrick Willem. FIGHTERS FOR FREEDOM: JEFFERSON AND BOLIVAR.
New York, Apollo Editions, 1962. 243p. illus. $1.95
    Originally published in 1948 as two works under the titles: Thomas
Jefferson, and The life and times of Simón Bolívar, respectively, this edition
combines the two towering figures. It is a popular treatment for the lay
reader.

849.
Vargas Valdés, José Joaquín. ARTÍCULOS Y ENSAYOS. Edited by Aníbal Vargas
Barón. Eugene, University of Oregon Press, 1963. 197p. $3.50
    Includes essays and articles by a Colombian journalist, politician, and
philosopher.

850.
Veliz, Claudio, ed. OBSTACLES TO CHANGE IN LATIN AMERICA. New York, Oxford
University Press, 1969. 263p. $1.95
    Contains papers presented at the Conference on Obstacles to Change in
Latin America, London, 1965. The papers were written by leading authorities
on Latin America and are provocative and interesting. The contributors
include Torcuato Di Tella, Celso Furtado, Orlando Fals Borda, Victor Urquidi,
and Felipe Herrera.

851.
----------, ed. THE POLITICS OF CONFORMITY IN LATIN AMERICA. New York,
Oxford University Press, 1970. 304p. $2.25
    The eight essays and excellent introduction comprising this volume
examine the principal political problems of development in Latin America. The
topics include the military, peasant, and rural migrants in politics, the
church and social change, European immigrants, university students, etc.

852.
Veríssimo, Érico. GATO PRETO EM CAMPO DE NEVE. Edited by L. Kasten and C.
E. Leroy. New York, Harcourt, Brace and World, 1969. 296p. $2.95
    A novel by the well-known contemporary Brazilian author.

853.
Violette, Paul E. SHELLING IN THE SEA OF CORTEZ. Tucson, Ariz., D.S. King,
1964. 95p. illus. $1.95
    This is a handsomely illustrated guide to shellfish in the Gulf of
California.

854.
Vogan, Grace Dawson. MERRY-GO-ROUND OF GAMES IN SPANISH. Skokie, Ill,,
National Textbook Corp., 1962. 30p. illus. $1.00

855.
Vogt, Evon Zartman. THE ZINACANTECOS OF MEXICO; A MODERN MAYA WAY OF LIFE.
New York, Holt, Rinehart and Winston, 1970. 113p. illus. maps. $3.95
    Zinacantan is one of 21 Tzotzil-speaking towns in Chiapas, Mexico, in the
highlands near the Guatemalan border. The Zinacantecos are modern Mayas who
have been converted to Catholicism. Their life is highly ceremonialized and
the Spanish Catholic observances and rites have synthesized smoothly with
Mayan usages. The result is a unique, elaborate, and highly integrated
cultural system. This study is an important contribution to the field of
cultural anthropology.

856.
Von Hagen, Victor W. THE AZTEC: MAN AND TRIBE. New York, New American
Library, 1958. 222p. illus. $0.75
    Popularized account of late pre-Hispanic central Mexican native culture
with a brief archeological background. It is an error-studded and superficial
work, valuable only for its fine line drawings by Alberto Beltrán, which
capture the spirit of Aztec pictorial style. [HLAS 22:612]

857.
----------. DESERT KINGDOMS OF PERU. New York, New American Library, 1969.
218p. illus. $1.50
Describes the kingdoms of ancient Peru in a popular style.

858.
----------. THE REALM OF THE INCAS. New York, New American Library, 1957.
231p. illus. $0.75
Deals with the ancient cultures of Peru culminating with the Incas. A
brief discussion of the geographical and historical background of per-Incaic
cultures is followed by the Incas and their achievements. Unfortunately, it
often overstretches the data and contains some inaccuracies. This volume
should be used with caution. [HLAS 21:340]

859.
----------. THE WORLD OF THE MAYA. New York, New American Library, 1960.
270p. illus. $0.50
Popular and superficial account of pre-Hispanic Maya civilization, based
in part on the documentary sources. Contains numerous errors of fact and
interpretations. [HLAS 24:1161]

860.
Wagley, Charles. AMAZON TOWN; A STUDY OF MAN IN THE TROPICS. New York,
Knopf, 1964. 338p. illus. $2.95
First published in 1953, this is a fully rounded description of a small
community on the lower Amazon river system, based on intermittent visits
between 1942 and 1948. It is of great value in understanding the relationship of humans and their institutions to the tropical habitat. A new
epilogue by the author brings the book up-to-date.

861.
----------. AN INTRODUCTION TO BRAZIL. New York, Columbia University Press,
1965. 322p. $2.50
An excellent work by a well-known social anthropologist with extensive
background on Brazil, which provides a basic understanding of that country.
Includes a good bibliography.

862.
----------, and Marvin Harris. MINORITIES IN THE NEW WORLD; SIX CASE STUDIES.
New York, Columbia University Press, 1964. 320p. $2.45
The authors wrote an incisive book on Indians, Negroes, Jews, and other
minority groups in the Americas. The book was written in 1956 and first
published in 1958, thus the chapter on blacks in the United States is somewhat outdated.

863.
Wagner, C. Peter. LATIN AMERICAN THEOLOGY; RADICAL OR EVANGELICAL? THE
STRUGGLE FOR THE FAITH IN A YOUNG CHURCH. Grand Rapids, Mich., Eerdmans,
1970. 118p. $2.45
The Associate Director of the Andes Evangelical Mission describes the
current crisis in theological circles in the Latin American Protestant
churches. The author analyzes the "radical left" and concludes that the
theology of its exponents has become secularized.

864.
Wakefield, Dan. ISLAND IN THE CITY; PUERTO RICANS IN NEW YORK. New York,
Corinth Books, 1960. 149p. $1.95
Presents a disturbing but excellent journalistic account of Spanish Harlem
and other Puerto Rican ghettos. It was first published in 1957.

865.
Walsh, Donald D., and Lawrence B. Kiddle, eds. CUENTOS AMERICANOS CON ALGUNOS
POEMAS. 3d. ed. New York, Norton, 1970. 267p. $2.30
This reader first appeared in 1942 under the title Cuentos y versos
americanos. The material included is intended for first year students of
Spanish. It contains excerpts from Gregorio López y Fuentes, Alberto Guillén,

Alfonsina Storni, Horacio Quiroga, Arturo Uslar Pietri, and others. Included
are exercises and an extensive vocabulary.

866.
Walters, Elsa H., and E. B. Castle. PRINCIPLES OF EDUCATION WITH SPECIAL
REFERENCE TO TEACHING IN THE CARIBBEAN. New York, Humanities Press, 1967.
211p. $3.00
    This introduction to the theory and practice of education is intended for
students in teachers' colleges of the British West Indies. Examples and
illustrations have been taken from Dr. Walter's decade of first-hand experience
in West Indian schools.

867.
Wauchope, Robert, ed. THE INDIAN BACKGROUND OF LATIN AMERICAN HISTORY; THE
MAYA, AZTEC, INCA, AND THEIR PREDECESSORS. New York, Knopf, 1970. 211p.
map. $2.95
    This excellent selection of readings treats a wide range of ancient
cultures. The editor has concentrated on the native civilizations that most
concern Latin American historians. The introduction summarizes the earlier
cultures that preceded those described in the readings.

868.
Weaver, Jerry L., ed. LATIN AMERICAN DEVELOPMENT: A SELECTED BIBLIOGRAPHY,
1950-1967. Santa Barbara, Calif., American Bibliographical Center, Clio
Press, 1969. 87p. $7.25
    Lists articles and books dealing with the political, economic, and social
development of Latin America. It contains a total of 1,853 entries, classified
by region or country with lists arranged alphabetically by author.
[Charles Fleener]

869.
----------., ed. THE POLITICAL DIMENSIONS OF RURAL DEVELOPMENT IN LATIN
AMERICA: A SELECTED BIBLIOGRAPHY, 1950-1967. Long Beach, California State
College, 1968. 92p. $5.00
    This bibliography of studies dealing with the various facets of rural
development in Latin America, contains books, monographs, articles, dissertations, and bibliographies. Lists 1,506 entries. [Charles Fleener]

870.
Webb, Kempton E. BRAZIL. Boston, Ginn, 1970. 122p. illus., maps. $1.60
    This is a general discussion of Brazil's history, geography, economy,
and culture. It is a useful introduction to the country for survey courses
or for a high school audience.

871.
Weinberg, Albert K. MANIFEST DESTINY: A STUDY OF NATIONALIST EXPANSIONISM
IN AMERICAN HISTORY. Chicago, Quadrangle Books, 1963. 559p. $2.95
    An excellent study based on public records, newspapers, and diplomatic
correspondence. It contains data on U.S.-Mexican relations, the Spanish-
American War, the Panama Canal, and "Dollar Diplomacy." Includes bib-
liographical notes.

872.
Werstein, Irving. 1898: THE SPANISH-AMERICAN WAR AND THE PHILIPPINE
INSURRECTION TOLD WITH PICTURES. New York, Cooper Square Publishers, 1966.
191p. illus. maps. $2.50
    This is an illustrated and popularized study of the Spanish-American
War and the Philippine insurrection.

873.
Whitaker, Arthur P. ARGENTINA. Englewood Cliffs, N.J., Prentice-Hall, 1964.
184p. $1.95
    Two chapters on the 19th century serve as an introduction to this political
survey of Argentina since 1880. Contains a helpful bibliography.

874.
----------., ed. LATIN AMERICA AND THE ENLIGHTENMENT. 2d. ed. Ithaca,
N.Y., Cornell University Press, 1965. 156p. $1.75
    Originally published in 1942, this standard volume contains a collection of
essays by prominent Latin Americanists such as John Tate Lanning, Harry
Bernstein, Roland D. Hussey, etc. A new essay by Charles Griffin and an
updated bibliography have been added to the present edition.

875.
----------. THE SPANISH-AMERICAN FRONTIER; 1783-1795: THE WESTWARD MOVEMENT
AND THE SPANISH RETREAT IN THE MISSISSIPPI VALLEY. Introd. by Samuel E.
Morison. Lincoln, University of Nebraska Press, 1969. 255p. $1.95
    First published in 1927 this is a thorough analysis of Spain in North
America towards the end of the 18th century and the gradual displacement of
Spanish power by the Westward Movement.

876.
----------. THE U.S. AND THE INDEPENDENCE OF LATIN AMERICA, 1800-1830.
New York, Norton, 1964. 630p. $3.25
    Based on official records, document collections, and contemporary sources,
this work focuses on the diplomatic role of the U.S. in encouraging independence movements in Latin America. It was first published in 1941.

877.
----------. THE WESTERN HEMISPHERE IDEA: ITS RISE AND DECLINE. Ithaca, N.Y.,
Cornell University Press, 1965. 208p. $1.95
    This work contains eight essays which analyze the cultural and intellectual
implications of the "Western Hemisphere Idea" from the 18th century to the
present.

878.
Whitten, Norman E., and John F. Szwed. AFRO-AMERICAN ANTHROPOLOGY: CON-
TEMPORARY PERSPECTIVES. Foreword by Sidney Mintz. New York, Free Press,
1970. 468p. illus. $5.95
    Contains articles by prominent anthropologists dealing with Africans in
the Americas. The topics covered include ethnohistory and self-image,
cultural and linguistic ambiguities, patterns of performance, and others.
This is a very important contribution, with a good bibliography.

879.
Wiarda, Howard J. DICTATORSHIP AND DEVELOPMENT; THE METHODS OF CONTROL IN
TRUJILLO'S DOMINICAN REPUBLIC. Gainesville, University of Florida Press,
1968. 224p. maps. $3.75
    This analysis focuses on the methods and nature of Rafael Trujillo's
dictatorial control of the Dominican Republic, 1930-61. Professor Wiarda
seeks to offer some conclusions concerning the legacy bequeathed to the
island republic by the despot's rule.

880.
Wilbur, W. Allan, and Van R. Halsey, eds. THE MONROE DOCTRINE. Boston,
Heath, 1965. 180p. $1.80
    The editors have assembled 65 selections from documents and secondary
sources tracing the history of the Monroe Doctrine. Includes a helpful
chronology of the evolution of this doctrine. A teacher's edition is also
available from the publisher.

881.
Wilder, Thornton Niven. THE BRIDGE OF SAN LUIS REY. New York, Washington
Square Press, 1960. 117p. illus. $0.60
    First published in 1927, this novel was inspired by a short play by
Prosper Merimée, Le carrosse du Saint Sacrement. The novel is set in
colonial Lima of the 18th century, and it centers around a group of people
precipitated into a gulf when a bridge breaks.

882.
Wilgus, Alva Curtis, and Raul d'Eça. LATIN AMERICAN HISTORY: A SUMMARY OF

POLITICAL, ECONOMIC, SOCIAL, AND CULTURAL EVENTS FROM 1492 TO THE PRESENT.
5th ed. New York, Barnes & Noble, 1963. 466p. $2.75
   This is the fifth edition, completely revised, of an outline which first
appeared in 1939.

883.
Wilkerson, Loree A. R. FIDEL CASTRO'S POLITICAL PROGRAMS FROM REFORMISM TO
MARXISM-LENINISM. Gainesville, University of Florida Press, 1965. 100p.
$2.00
   This is a serious study of the evolution of Castro's program from the tenets
of Orthodoxia to Communism.

884.
Williams, Eric Eustace. CAPITALISM AND SLAVERY. New York, Putnman, 1966.
285p. $1.85
   First published in 1944, this is an economic history of slavery with a
Marxist orientation. It also covers abolition in the West Indies. The author
is now Prime Minister of Trinidad and Tobago.

885.
----------. EDUCATION IN THE BRITISH WEST INDIES. Pref. by John Dewey.
New York, University Place Book Shop, 1969. 259p. $3.75
   Outlines education and possibilities of improving the school systems in the
West Indies.

886.
----------. HISTORY OF THE PEOPLE OF TRINIDAD AND TOBAGO. New York, Trans-
atlantic Arts, 1965. 292p. maps. $2.95
   First published in 1962, this is a concise history based on primary sources.
It is the most complete and scholarly contribution in this field.

887.
Williams, Miller, ed. CHILE: AN ANTHOLOGY OF NEW WRITINGS. Kent, Ohio, Kent
State University Press, 1968. 210p. $1.95
   An anthology of poetry, one play, and two short stories giving an excellent
insight into contemporary Chilean literature. The following writers have
been included: Miguel Arteche, Efraín Barquero, Enrique Lihn, Pablo Neruda,
Nicanor Parra, and others. The editor's translations are very good and he
has included reproductions of the author's signatures.

888.
Winsberg, Morton D. COLONIA BARON HIRSCH: A JEWISH AGRICULTURAL COLONY IN
ARGENTINA. Gainesville, University of Florida Press, 1963. 71p. maps, tables.
$2.00
   This is a study of a colony of Northern European Jews in Argentina from 1905
to 1962. The emphasis is on the sociological aspects of the community.

889.
----------. MODERN CATTLE BREEDS IN ARGENTINA; ORIGINS, DIFFUSION, AND CHANGE.
Lawrence, University of Kansas Press, 1968. 59p. maps. $2.00
   The aim of this monograph is to explain the diffusion of modern breeds of
cattle throughout Argentina, the high concentrations of distinct breeds within
physical regions, and why the popularity of various breeds has fluctuated.

890.
Wolf, Eric Robert. SONS OF THE SHAKING EARTH. Chicago, University of Chicago
Press, 1959. 302p. $1.95
   An exciting and authoritative account of the peoples and cultures of Middle
America from the earliest times to the present. The presentation of the
archaeological evidence, particularly in the valley of Mexico, is first-rate.
The author's ideas on the importance of irrigation in Mexican prehistory are
of great significance. [HLAS 23:159]

891.
Wolf, Bertram David. THE FABULOUS LIFE OF DIEGO RIVERA. New York, Stein and
Day, 1969. 457p. illus. $3.95

Diego Rivera (1886-1957) is considered Mexico's most important contemporary artist. This is an excellent account of the artistic and personal life of this important figure. It has 164 black and white illustrations of persons and paintings.

892.
Womack, John, Jr. ZAPATA AND THE MEXICAN REVOLUTION. New York, Random House, 1970. 480p. illus. $2.95
This highly readable, scholarly book won the 1970 Bolton Prize of the Conference of Latin American History. It presents the revolution in Morelos as an exciting story of simple people caught up in a great moment of history. Zapata emerges as the cunning campesino and charismatic leader who guides his people through a successful revolution.

893.
Wood, Bryce. THE MAKING OF THE GOOD NEIGHBOR POLICY. New York, Norton, 1967. 438p. $2.95
Traces the origin of the Good Neighbor Policy to the U.S. intervention in Nicaragua in 1926-1927. The book has been documented with case studies and previously unpublished material from the archives of the State Department and the Franklin D. Roosevelt Library at Hyde Park, N.Y., and probably will remain the standard reference work on the period.

894.
Wood, Robert, Brother. MISSIONARY CRISIS AND CHALLENGE IN LATIN AMERICA. New York, Herder and Herder, 1964. 92p. $1.25
This is thoughtful study about the shortage of priests in Latin America and an analysis of the many challenges which the contemporary church faces.

895.
Woods, Eugene. HOW TO RETIRE IN MEXICO. San Diego, R. R. Knapp, 1967. 126p. illus., maps. $1.95
This book outlines the advantages of retiring in Mexico. It contains useful information on food, lodging, places to see, and customs of the country.

896.
Woodward, Ralph Lee., Jr. CLASS PRIVILEGE AND ECONOMIC DEVELOPMENT. THE CONSULADO DE COMERCIO OF GUATEMALA, 1793-1871. Chapel Hill, University of North Carolina Press, 1966. 155p. $2.50
This carefully researched monograph describes the functions and operations of the Consulado of Guatemala and attempts to indicate the extent and significance of its role in the economic and political history of Central America.

897.
Worcester, Donald E., and Wendell G. Schaeffer. THE GROWTH AND CULTURE OF LATIN AMERICA. 2d ed. New York, Oxford University Press, 1970. 2 v. $4.50 each
The first edition published in 1956 has been updated here. This textbook sythesizes a great body of recent monographic material and reflects modern trends of historiography. It is especially useful for coverage of 17th century developments.

898.
----------. SEA POWER AND CHILEAN INDEPENCENCE. Gainesville, University of Florida Press, 1962. 87p. $2.00
Based on published sources, this is an interesting, well-balanced treatment of a topic whose significance extends beyond the independence of Chile alone.

899.
Yañez, Agustín. AL FILO DEL AGUA. Austin, University of Texas Press, 1970. 209p. illus. $2.25
This is the great contemporary Mexican novelist's best known book. It was first published in 1947. The book depicts the atmosphere in a small Mexican village on the eve of the Mexican Revolution. In masterful strokes Yañez has etched the deep religiosity and the collective lethargy of the people.

900.
Yates, Donald A., _and_ J. Dalbor, _eds_. IMAGINACIÓN Y FANTASÍA; CUENTOS DE
LAS AMÉRICAS. Rev. ed. New York, Harcourt, Brace, and World, 1970. 378p.
$2.95
   Includes a representative selection of Latin American short stories.

901.
----------. Joseph Sommers, _and_ Julian Palley, _comps_. TRES CUENTISTAS
HISPANOAMERICANOS: HORACIO QUIROGA, FRANCISCO ROJAS GONZÁLEZ, MANUEL ROJAS.
New York, Macmillan, 1969. 211p. $3.25
   Includes several short stories by a Uruguayan, a Mexican, and a Chilean,
this providing a good cross-section in idioms and social customs. Each of
these writers depicted the country-side and the psychology of the people
with accuracy. Intended as a reader for intermediate Spanish classes.

902.
Zárate, Agustín de. THE DISCOVERY AND CONQUEST OF PERU. Translated by John
Michael Cohen. Baltimore, Penguin Books, 1968. 279p. maps. $1.45
   This is a translation of the first four books of Historia del descubrimiento
y conquista del Perú (1955). The translator has interpolated much first-hand
material by six people who took part in the conquest as well as material by
Cieza de León, Garcilaso de la Vega, and José de Acosta.

903.
Zeitlin, Maurice, _and_ Robert Scheer. CUBA: TRAGEDY IN OUR HEMIPSHERE. New
York, Grove Press, 1963. 316p. $0.95
   This is an account of the Cuban Revolution by two authors who have traveled
in Cuba since Castro came to power. It is based on documents and news
sources.

904.
----------. REVOLUTIONARY POLITICS AND THE CUBAN WORKING CLASS. New York,
Harper and Row, 1970. 306p. $1.95
   First published in 1967, this book is based on data drawn from interviews
with industrial workers in revolutionary Cuba in 1962.

905.
Zelayeta, Elena Emilia. ELENA'S FIESTA RECIPES. Rev. ed. Foreword by Helen
E. Brown. Los Angeles, W. Ritchie Press, 1968. 126p. $1.95
   The author has assembled a wonderful variety of recipes for Mexican
dishes and some Central American favorites.

906.
----------. ELENA'S SECRETS OF MEXICAN COOKING. New York, Doubleday, 1970.
204p. illus. $1.95
   Includes a good assortment of recipes and hints on how to master Mexican
cooking.

907.
Zorrilla de San Martín, Juan. TABARÉ AN INDIAN LEGENT OF URUGUAY. Translated by Walter Woen. Washington, Pan American Union, 1956. 366p. $2.75
   This is an English translation of Tabaré by the Uruguayan poet and e
essayist Zorrilla de San Martín (1885-1931). Tabaré, a _mestizo_ born of a
Charrúa chief and a captive Spanish woman, is the tragic protagonist of
this epic poem about the Spanish spiritual conquest of the Indians.

908.
Abbruzzese, M. GOYA. New York, Grosset & Dunlap, 1970. 100p. $1.50
   Contains an overview of the Spanish painter's work and an introduction
to his life and times.

909.
Abreu-Gómez, Ermico, and J. S. Flores. HISTORIAS DE DON QUIJOTE. New York,
Van Nostrand, 1970. 261p. $2.25
   This is a textbook edition of stories from Don Quijote to be used in
Spanish language instruction.

910.
Adams, Nicholson Barney, and John E. Keller. HISTORY OF SPANISH LITERATURE:
A BRIEF SURVEY. Paterson, N.J., Littlefield, Adams, 1962. 206p. map.
$1.95
   This is a succinct overview of Spanish literature from the early Middle
Ages to the present. A useful book for survey courses.

911.
Agoncillo, Teodoro A. A SHORT HISTORY OF THE PHILIPPINES. New York, New
American Library, 1969. 319p. $1.50
   This short history of the Philippines includes detailed information about
the period when the Philippines were part of the Spanish colonial empire
(from the time of contact to 1899).

912.
Ainaud de Lasarte, Juan. ROMANESQUE CATALAN ART. PANEL PAINTING. New
York, Tudor Pub. Co., 1965. 95p. illus. $1.50
   A brief introduction prefaces the 15 small but excellent reproductions
of superb examples of romanesque panel paintings that still survive in
Catalonia.

913.
Alarcón, Pedro Antonio de. EL SOMBRERO DE TRES PICOS. Edited by Edmund V.
de Chasca. 2d ed. Boston, Ginn-Blaisdell, 1969. 322p. illus. $3.50
   Alarcón's most successful novel was based on a popular ballad, El moli-
nero de Arcos. It deals with the tale of the corregidor's love for the
miller's wife, set in the early 19th century. The descriptions of a small
town and its people are humorous.

914.
----------. EL SOMBRERO DE TRES PICOS. Edited by E.P. Crawford. New York,
Macmillan, 1962. 200p. $1.95
   This edition of the Three-cornered hat is intended for classroom use.

915.
----------. THE THREE CORNERED HAT. Translated by Harriet de Onis.
Woodbury, N. Y., Barron's, 1964. 198p. $1.25
   Mrs. de Onis has given us an excellent translation of this witty Spanish
classic. It is intended for classroom use.

916.
Alarcón, Pedro Antonio de. THE THREE CORNERED HAT. A modern translation, with notes, edited by Glenn Wilbern. New York, American RDM, 1966. 250p. $1.25
   This is an English-language textbook edition of Alarcón's classic work.

917.
Alas, Leopoldo. LA REGENTA, by Clarín [pseud.] Philadelphia, Center for Curriculum Development, 1969. 240p. $2.40
   This is a textbook edition of one of the most important novels written in Spain in the 19th century. It was first published in 1885, and it depicts life in Oviedo (Vetusta in the book), swirling around a love story in which "La Regenta," a married woman, is the coveted prize. The picture that emerges is a minutely detailed canvas reminding one of Zola and Flaubert.

918.
_____. SU UNICO HIJO, by Clarín [pseud.] Philadelphia, Center for Curriculum Development, 1970. 131p. $1.20
   This is Clarín's second full-length novel published in 1890, presented here in abridged form. In it one can find naturalistic influences as well as the idealistic tendency which began to affirm itself in the author's work towards the end of the century.

920.
Alberti, Rafael. SELECTED POEMS. Translated by Ben Belitt. Introduction by Luis Monguió. Berkeley, University of California Press, 1966. 219p. illus. $1.75
   Alberti was born near Cádiz, Spain, in 1902, and has been living in Buenos Aires since the Spanish Civil War. This volume contains a bilingual edition of some 50 poems which originally appeared between 1929 and 1954. The poet's own drawings serve as illustrations. Monguió's introduction captures the poet's work and his personality.

921.
Aldecoa, Ignacio. SANTA OLAJA DE ACERO Y OTRAS HISTORIAS. New York, Philadelphia, Chilton Book Co., 1968. 167p. $0.90
   Aldecoa is one of the most influential novelists of present-day Spain. He returns to a traditional posture in the novel.

922.
Allen, John Jay. DON QUIXOTE: HERO OR FOOL? A STUDY IN NARRATIVE TECHNIQUE. Gainesville, University of Florida Press, 1969. 90p. $2.00
   The author analyzes widely divergent critical opinions toward Don Quixote throughout the history of literature. Don Quixote has been studied by many outstanding literary critics of the last two centuries.

923.
Allen, J. H. OLD PORTUGUESE VERSIONS OF THE LIFE OF SAINT ALEXIS; CODICES ALCOBACENCES Nos. 36 and 266. Urbana, University of Illinois Press, 1970. 200p. illus. $3.00

924.
Alpern, Hymen, ed. THREE CLASSIC SPANISH PLAYS: SHEEP WELL, by Lope de Vega; LIFE IS A DREAM, by Calderón de la Barca; NONE BENEATH THE KING, by Rojas Zorrilla. New York, Washington Square Press, 1963. 229p. $0.60
   Includes English translations of three well-known and important plays of the Spanish Golden Age: Fuente Ovejuna by Lope de Vega; La vida es sueño by Calderón de la Barca; and Del rey abajo ninguno by Rojas Zorrilla.

925.
Alpert, Michael, ed. TWO SPANISH PICARESQUE NOVELS. Edited and translated by Michael Alpert. Baltimore, Penguin Books, 1969. 213p. $1.45
 The editor presents new translations of El Lazarillo de Tormes (1554) and Francisco de Quevedo's Vida del buscón (1626). Both classics depict social conditions in 16th and 17th century Spain and each has rascally heroes living by their wits.

926.
Anderson, G., and others, eds. PROSAS Y POESIA DE ESPAÑA E HISPANOAMERICA; LECTURAS INTERMEDIAS. New York, Harper and Row, 1970. 304p. $3.95
 An anthology of prose and poetry selections from Spain and Spanish America.

927.
Anderson-Imbert, Enrique, eds. VEINTE CUENTOS ESPAÑOLES DEL SIGLO VEINTE. New York, Appleton-Century-Croft, 1970. 250p. $3.50
 The editor has assembled a very good, brief anthology of Spanish short stories of the 20th century.

928.
Andrian, Gustave W., ed. MODERN SPANISH PROSE AND POETRY. 2d ed. New York, Macmillan, 1969. 233p. $3.25
 Includes a representative sample of contemporary Spanish prose and poetry.

929.
Apollonio, Umbro. PICASSO. Translated from the Italian by Cesare Foligno. New York, Crown Publishers, 1965. 26p. illus. (10 mounted col.) $1.45
 This is a handsome brief book reproducing representative works by the great Spanish master of the 20th century.

930.
Arjona, Doris King, and Edith F. Helman, eds. CUENTOS CONTEMPORANEOS. New York, Norton, 1958. 182p. $2.30
 The editors have assembled Spanish short stories of the 19th and 20th centuries, intended for students in their second year of Spanish. The authors include Armando Palacio Valdés, Ramón del Valle Inclán, Azorín, Emilia Pardo Bazán, Ramón Gómez de la Serna, Ramón Pérez de Ayala, and others.

931.
Arnett, Willard Eugene. GEORGE SANTAYANA. New York, Washington Square Press, 1968. 184p. $0.75
 This is a lucid and succinct study of the life and works of the Spanish-born philosopher.

932.
Arrabal, Fernando. THE ARCHITECT AND THE EMPEROR OF ASSYRIA, Translated from the French by Everart d'Harnoncourt and Adele Shank. New York, Grove Press, 1970. 93p. $1.95
 Includes two English translations of two plays by the most controversial Spanish playwright of the last decade.

933.
_____. GUERNICA AND OTHER PLAYS. Translated by Barbara Wright. New York, Grove Press, 1969. 126p. $1.95
 Includes English translations of Labyrinth; Picnic on the battlefield; and Tricycle, in addition to Guernica, by Spain's young and internationally acclaimed avant garde playwright.

934.
Atkinson, William C. HISTORY OF SPAIN AND PORTUGAL. Baltimore, Penguin Books, 1969. 382p. $1.45
 This is a useful survey of the history of the Iberian Peninsula to 1956.

935.
Auclair, Marcelle. TERESA OF AVILA. Translated by Kathleen Pond, New York,
Doubleday, 1959. 480p. (Imagebooks, D79) $1.45
   First published in 1953, this is a thorough study of the great mystic of
the Spanish counter-reformation. In her works Saint Teresa opened up new
vistas of mystical experience.

936.
Augier, D., and M. Tuñon De Lara. SPAIN. Translated by N. C. Klegg, New
York, Viking Press, 1970. 159p. illus. $1.65
   This is a succinct description of Spain.

937.
Ayala, Francisco. LA CABEZA DEL CORDERO. Edited by Keith Ellis. Englewood Cliffs, N. J., Prentice-Hall, 1968. 196p. port. $3.50
   This is a textbook edition of four short stories by one of the outstanding writers of Spanish fiction. The Spanish Civil War is at the center of
these stories. Ayala examines the tragic effects of civil conflicts on
society, and the resulting deterioration of human relationships. Includes
an extensive vocabulary.

938.
_____. MUERTES DE PERRO. Philadelphia, Center for Curriculum
Development, 1969. 150p. $1.20

939.
Baker, J. F., and I. Almeida Ariza, eds. ESPAÑA A LA VISTA. New York,
Pergamon Press, 1970. 200p. illus. $2.50

940.
Barnes, Richard G., ed. THREE SPANISH SACRAMENTAL PLAYS. Translated and
with an introduction by Richard G. Barnes. San Francisco, Chandler Pub.
Co., 1969. 103p. $2.25
   Includes For our sake by Lope de Vega; King Belshazzar's feast by
Calderón de la Barca; and The Bandit Queen by Maestro Josef de Valdivielso.
Barnes' introduction describes briefly the auto sacramental and synthe-
sizes the careers of the three playwrights.

941.
Baroja y Nessi, Pió. EL ARBOL DE LA CIENCIA. Edited by Gerard G. Flynn.
New York, Appleton-Century-Crofts, 1970. 250p. $2.75
   Pío Baroja, after Benito Pérez Galdós, the leading novelist of modern
Spanish literature. First published in 1911, this novel deals with the
incongruities of the modern world and its growing technology.

942.
_____. EL ARBOL DE LA CIENCIA. Philadelphia, Center for Cur-
riculum Development, 1968. 200p. $1.20
   See above.

943.
_____. THE RESTLESSNESS OF SHANTI ANDIA, AND SELECTED STORIES.
Translated by Anthony and Elaine Kerrigan. New York, New American Library,
1962. 330p. (Signet, CT-149) $0.75
   This is an English translation of the fast-moving novel about the wanderings of a Basque sailor. Also included are six short stories and an extensive introduction to the world of Pío Baroja by Anthony Kerrigan.

944.
Barrett, Linton Lomas. BARRON'S SIMPLIFIED APPROACH TO CERVANTES' DON
QUIXOTE. Woodbury, New York, Barron's Educational Series, 1968. 124p. $0.95
   This is an annotated and greatly simplified edition of the Spanish classic.

945.
Barrett, Linton Lomas, ed. FIVE CENTURIES OF SPANISH LITERATURE: FROM THE
CID THROUGH THE GOLDEN AGE. New York, Dodd, Mead, 1968. 352p. $5.95
Includes representaive selections of Spanish prose and poetry from the
Middle Ages through the 17th century.

946.
Barrios, Miguel de. LA POESIA RELIGIOSA DE MIGUEL DE BARRIOS. Columbus,
Ohio State University Press, 1962. 357p. $5.00
Miguel de Barrios was the pseudonym of Daniel Levi de Barrios (1625?-
1701), born in Montilla, Spain. He lived in Amsterdam for most of his life.
In his writings this convert to Catholicism from Judaism returns to a primi-
tive mysticism.

947.
Basdekis, Demetrios. MIGUEL DE UNAMUNO. New York, Columbia University
Press, 1970. 48p. $1.00
Provides a critical study of the writings of the great Spanish novelist
and philosopher.

947A.
Beene, Gerrie and Lourdes Miranda King. DINING IN SPAIN. Rutland, Vt.,
C. E. Tuttle, 1969. 197p. $2.50
The recipes in this book are authentic and more than half of them are
for specialties served in Madrid's most distinctive restaurants. It in-
cludes a guide to and a description of the wines of Spain.

948.
Bell, Aubrey F. G. BALTASAR GRACIAN. New York, Hispanic Society of America, 1968. 100p. $2.00
This is a study of Baltasar Gracián y Morales, Spanish moral philosopher
and stylist of the 17th century, and his concern for ethical principles
and rules of conduct for leaders.

949.
_____. BENITO ARIAS MONTANO. New York, Hispanic Society of
America, 1969. 120p. $2.00
This is a very good study of Arias Montano, theologian, writer, philosopher, and naturalist of 16th century Spain. He knew several Oriental languages and was one of the most erudite men of his century. He was professor of Oriental languages at the Escorial monastery, and the author of many
learned treatises.

950.
_____. CERVANTES. New York, Macmillan, 1961. 247p. $0.95
The author bases his biography largely on the works of Cervantes, search-
ing the author's words for a revelation of the poet and the philosopher.

951.
_____. FERNAN LOPEZ. New York, Hispanic Society of America,
1969. 90p. $2.00
Fernán López was a Portuguese chronicler of the 15th century, whose work
about the reigns of Pedro I, Fernando I, and Juan I is outstanding.

952.
_____. GIL VICENTE. New York, Hispanic Society of America,
1967. 140p.
Gil Vicente (1470?-1536?), a renaissance dramatist and lyric poet, born
in Portugal, wrote his most important works in Spanish. He wrote more than
40 plays, only seven were in Portuguese.

953.
_____. JUAN GINES DE SEPULVEDA. New York, Hispanic Society of
America, 1969. 106p. $2.00
Sepúlveda was a philosopher and outstanding classicist of the 16th cent-
ury. Erasmus considered him the most erudite man of his time. His work on
philosophy and theology were controversial and created heated polemics.

954.
Bell, Aubrey F. G. LUIS DE CAMOES. New York, Hispanic Society of America, 1969. 152p. illus. $2.00
Camões (1524-1580) is considered Portugal's greatest poet. Some critics consider that Camões reached his height as a lyric poet. Undoubtedly, his best known work remains Os Lusíadas, an epic poem of the Portuguese empire.

955.
Belso, Ramiro. LIVING SPAIN. A GUIDE TO THE SPANISH PEOPLE. Translated by Harold Null, New York, Crown Publications, 1968. 173p. illus., tables. $2.95
A guide to Spain and the cultural characteristics of its people.

956.
Bemis, Samuel Flagg. PINCKNEY'S TREATY. AMERICA'S ADVANTAGE FROM EUROPE'S DISTRESS, 1783-1800. Rev. ed. New Haven, Conn., Yale University Press, 1960. 372p. $1.75
The diplomatic winning of the American west is explained in terms of Great Britain and Spain's need for American neutrality during the wars of the French Revolution.

957.
Benavente, Jacinto. BONDS OF INTEREST. Introd. by Hymen Alpern; translated by J. G. Underhill. New York, Ungar, 1967. 160p. $1.75
This is a bilingual edition of Los intereses creados (1907) by the Nobel Prize-winning Spanish playwright Jacinto Benavente (1886-1954). In addition to having written over 150 plays, he also found time to write literary and political essays. Los intereses creados is a charming allegorical and morality plan, generally considered Benavente's masterpiece.

958.
_____. LOS MALHECHORES DEL BIEN. Edited by Irving A. Leonard and Robert K. Spaulding. New York, Macmillan, 1963. 126p. $1.95
This is a textbook edition, with notes and vocabulary, of a play written in 1905 in which Benavente shows depth and intensity.

959.
_____. LA MALQUERIDA. Edited by Paul T. Manchester, New York, Appleton-Century-Crofts, 1959. 143p. $2.25
This is a rustic tragedy, simple yet masterly in its dramatic construction. It was published in 1913.

960.
Benedikt, Michael, and George E. Wellworth, eds. MODERN SPANISH THEATRE. AN ANTHOLOGY OF PLAYS. New York, Dutton, 1969. 416p. $2.95
Includes eight Spanish plays of the 20th century which, according to one critic, combine the theater of magic and the theatre of anguish. Valle-Inclán, García Lorca, Casona, and Arrabal are represented among these dramas that span the period 1913-1963.

961.
Bentley, E. ed. SIX SPANISH PLAYS: THE CELESTINA, by Fernando de Rojas; THE SIEGE OF NUMANTIA, by Miguel de Cervantes Saavedra; FUENTEOVEJUNA, by Félix Lope de Vega; THE TRICKSTER OF SEVILLE, by Tirso de Molina; LOVE AFTER DEATH; [and] LIFE IS A DREAM, by Pedro Calderón de la Barca. New York, Doubleday, 1969. 380p. $1.95
This edition contains the six greatest Spanish plays of the Golden Age.

962.
Berger, John. THE SUCCESS AND FAILURE OF PICASSO. Baltimore, Penguin Books, 1965. 210p. illus. $2.25
Picasso's life and work, from his "Blue Period" through Cubism and the compositions that culminated in "Guernica" up to the present day, are presented in this serious study of the man and the artist. The 120 illustrations add depth to both the biographical and critical aspects of the work.

963.
Birmingham, David. THE PORTUGUESE CONQUEST OF ANGOLA. New York, Oxford
University Press, 1965. 51p. bibl., maps $1.00
A brief survey of the establishment of Portuguese hegemony in Angola
from 1483 to the late 18th century.

964.
Blanco Aguinaga, Carlos, ed. LISTA DE LOS PAPELES DE EMILIO PRADOS EN LA
BIBLIOTECA DEL CONGRESO DE LOS ESTADOS UNIDOS DE AMERICA. Con pref. de
Howard F. Cline. Baltimore, Johns Hopkins Press, 1967. 46p. port. $3.50
After the death of the Spanish poet Emilio Prados in 1962 his papers were
deposited in the Library of Congress where they were cataloged and micro-
filmed. Professor Blanco arranged the papers and prepared the present listing. The papers include drafts of poems and autobiographical papers from
1925 to 1962. An appendix lists Prados' published works.

965.
Blasco Ibañez, Vicente. LA BARRACA. Edited by P. T. Manchester. New York,
Macmillan, 1965. 229p. $1.75
This is an essentially descriptive and historic novel which established
Blasco Ibañez' reputation as the Spanish Zola.

966.
_____. BLOOD AND SAND. Translated by Frances Partridge.
Introd. by Isaac Goldberg. New York, Ungar, 1964. 240p. $1.45
Sangre y arena, of which this book is a translation, was published in
1908. It is a picturesque and romantic novel.

967.
Bohl de Faber, Cecilia. LA GAVIOTA, by Fernán Caballero, [pseud.] Edited
by G. W. Umprey and F. Sánchez y Escribano. Boston, Heath, 1970. 321p.
$3.50
Fernán Caballero (1796-1877) was born in Switzerland and died in Seville;
the daughter of a Spanish mother and German father, she had lived in Andalusia from the age of 17. She wrote her first novel, La Gaviota, in 1849
in French and then translated it into Spanish.

968.
_____. LA GAVIOTA. THE SEA GULL, by Fernán Caballero,
[pseud.] Translated by J. MacLean, Woodbury, N. Y., Barron's Educational
Series, 1966. 246p. $1.75
This is a textbook edition of La gaviota (1849), a romantic story of a
peasant girl who marries a German surgeon, becomes an opera singer, falls in
love with a bullfighter and, after the death of both husband and lover,
marries a village barber.

969.
Bonet, Juan. TAMBIEN EN PALMA CRECEN LOS NIÑOS. Edited by Vera F. Beck-
Aguilar and Harry Kurz. New York, Scribner, 1967. 211p. illus. $2.95
This textbook edition contains notes and vocabulary. The readings were
taken from the author's Historia para unas manos (1962).

970.
Booton, Harold W. ARCHITECTURE OF SPAIN. Chester Springs, Pa., Dufour,
1970. 130p. illus. $1.95
This is an attractive book about Spanish architecture with handsome
illustrations.

971.
Borkenau, Franz. SPANISH COCKPIT: AN EYE-WITNESS ACCOUNT OF THE POLITICAL
AND SOCIAL CONFLICT OF THE SPANISH CIVIL WAR. Ann Arbor, University of
Michigan Press, 1963. 303p. $2.25
Originally published in 1937, this book was written by a political ana-
lyst. It describes accurately the specific characteristics of the Spanish
conflict and forms a gripping picture of those critical times.

972.
Bosquet, Alain. CONVERSATIONS WITH DALI. Translated by Joachim Neugroschel.
New York, Dutton, 1969. 123p. $1.45
    Ten conversations with the modern Spanish painter Salvador Dalí. Typi-
cally mercurial and quotable Daliisms abound, as well as shrewd and knowing
observations on the history and craft of painting. An added attraction is
a new translation of Dalí's essay "The Conquest of the irrational" in which
he comments on the place of surrealism in 20th century culture.

973.
Boxer, Charles R. FOUR CENTURIES OF PORTUGUESE EXPANSION: A SUCCINCT SUR-
VEY. Berkeley, University of California Press, 1961. 102p. illus. map,
port. $1.65
    The text of four lectures given by the author in South Africa in 1960.
Some documentation has been added in the present edition.

974.
_____. FRANCISCO VIEIRA DE FIGUEIREDO: A PORTUGUESE MERCHANT-
ADVENTURER IN SOUTH EAST ASIA, 1624-1667. The Hague, Martinus Nijhoff,
1967. 118p. illus. $2.35
    Studies Francisco Vieira de Figueiredo and the role of the Portuguese in
Macassar and Timor during the 1640-1668 period. More than half of this vol-
ume is devoted to the 19 Portuguese and Dutch documents which illustrate
Professor Boxer's account. [Charles Fleener]

975.
Bradford, Saxtone E. SPAIN IN THE WORLD. Princeton, N. J., Van Nostrand,
1962. 121p. maps. (Searchlight, 3) $1.45
    Analyzes Spain as a cultural and political entity in the modern world.

976.
Braider, Donald. PRIVATE LIFE OF EL GRECO. New York, Dell, 1969. 461p.
$1.25
    Studies the tormented life of a great artist whose life seemed cursed
with misfortune. He witnessed the depletion of his family fortunes, the
mental collapse of María, his young bride, and the public condemnation of
the woman he loved. Although born in Greece, he has become identified with
Spain. His paintings represent masterfully the counter-reformation period
of Spain.

977.
Brault, Gerard J., ed. CELESTINE: A CRITICAL EDITION OF THE FIRST FRENCH
TRANSLATION OF THE SPANISH CLASSIC LA CELESTINA. Detroit, Wayne State Uni-
versity Press, 1963. 264p. $8.00
    The full title of this work in its earlier editions was Tragicomedia de
Calisto y Melibea, published in Burgos in 1499.

978.
Braymer, Nan, and Lillian Lowenfels, eds. MODERN POETRY FROM SPAIN AND
LATIN AMERICA. New York, Corinth Books, 1964. 63p. $1.45
    Contains Spanish and Spanish American poems.

979.
Brenan, Gerald. THE LITERATURE OF THE SPANISH PEOPLE: FROM ROMAN TIMES TO
THE PRESENT DAY. New York, Meridian Books, 1957. 494p. $3.65
    This is a succinct history of Spanish literature from its origins to the
present.

980.
_____. THE SPANISH LABYRINTH, AN ACCOUNT OF THE SOCIAL AND POLITIC-
AL BACKGROUND OF THE CIVIL WAR. 2d ed. Cambridge, England, University
Press, 1960. 384p. maps $1.95
    First published in 1943, this history of Spain covers the 1874-1936
period. It focuses on the four decades preceding the Spanish Civil War.

115

981.
Buchanan, Milton A., ed. SPANISH POETRY OF THE GOLDEN AGE. 2d ed. rev.
Toronto, University of Toronto Press, 1966. 149p. $4.00
113 poems are included ranging in chronological order from the Marques
de Santillana (1398-1458) to Sor Juana Inés de la Cruz (1651-1695). The
poems appear in the original Spanish, but are exhaustively annotated in
English.

982.
Buero Vallejo, Antonio. EL CONCIERTO DE SAN OVIDIO. Edited by P. N. Trakas.
New York, Scribner, 1965. 215p. $2.95
This is an annotated Spanish edition of this contemporary Spanish play.

983.
_____. EN LA ARDIENTE OSCURIDAD. Edited by S. A. Wofsy.
Introd. by Juan Rodriguez Castellano. New York, Scribner, 1954. 196p.
illus. $2.95
This is an annotated textbook edition of Spain's well-known contemporary
playwright's popular play depicting life of the lower classes of Madrid.

984.
_____. DOS DRAMAS DE BUERO VALLEJO. Edited by Isabel
Magaña Schewill. New York, Appleton-Century-Crofts, 1967. 259p. port.
$3.65
Includes Aventura en los gris and Las palabras en la arena, as well as
notes and a vocabulary.

985.
_____. HISTORIA DE UNA ESCALERA. Edited by J. Sánchez.
New York, Scribner, 1955. 179p. illus. $2.95
This is a play depicting the life and customs of people in the vicinity
of Madrid.

986.
_____. MADRUGADA. Edited by Donald Bleznick and Martha T.
Halsey. Boston, Ginn-Blaisdell, 1969. 111p. port. $2.25
Contains an annotated textbook edition of Buero Vallejo's play.

987.
_____. LAS MENINAS. Edited by J. Rodriguez Castellano.
New York, Scribner, 1963. 237p. $2.95
This is an attractive edition of the Spanish dramatist's play which was
a stunning success in Spain and Spanish-America.

988.
Buñuel, Luis. BUNUEL: THREE SCREENPLAYS. New York, Grossman, 1970. 121p.
illus. $3.50
Includes the screenplays of Viridiana, The exterminating angel, and Simon
of the desert.

989.
Burnshaw, Stanley, ed. THE POEM ITSELF. Edited, and with an introd. by
Stanley Burnshaw, associate eds. Dudley Fitts, et al. New York, Schocken
Books, 1967. 337p. $2.45
First published in 1960, this is a presentation of major French, Spanish,
Portuguese, German, and Italian poets. It includes ten important poets from
Spain and Portugal: Rosalía Castro, Miguel de Unamuno, Antonio Machado, Juan
Ramón Jiménez, León Felipe, Fernando Pessoa, Pedro Salinas, Jorge Guillén,
Federico García Lorca, and Rafael Alberti. This work is highly recommended
for serious students of modern comparative literature. The selection of
poets from the Iberian peninsula is representative; in fact, the editors present a major poetic figure of the 19th century with Rosalía Castro. She is
not widely known outside her homeland because she wrote mostly in Gallegan
(the dialect of her native Galicia) rather than in Castilian Spanish.

990.
Bush, M. L. RENAISSANCE, REFORMATION, AND THE OUTER WORLD. New York,
Harper & Row, 1969. 387p. illus., maps, ports. $2.95

991.
Butler, Richard. THE LIFE AND WORLD OF GEORGE SANTAYANA. Chicago, H.
Regnery, 1960. 205p. $1.45
    Studies the life and work of George Santayana, the Spanish philosopher
who spent most of his life in the United States.

992.
Byne, Arthur and M. Stapley. DECORATED WOODEN CEILINGS IN SPAIN. New York,
Hispanic Society of America, 1960. 90p. illus. $2.00
    This is an attractive description of decorated wooden ceilings in Spain.

993.
_____. SPANISH INTERIORS AND FURNITURE. BRIEF TEXT
BY MILDRED STAPLEY. New York, Dover, 1969. 300p., plates. $5.00
    Spanish interior decorative schemes and furniture are presented here with
taste and an excellent sense of history.

994.
Calderón de la Barca, Pedro. EL ALCALDE DE ZALAMEA. Edited by P. N. Dunn.
New York, Pergamon Press, 1969. 380p. $2.95
    This is a textbook edition of Calderón's most famous tragedy dealing with
honor. Contains notes and vocabulary.
995.
_____. FOUR PLAYS: SECRET VENGEANCE FOR SECRET INSULT:
THE PHANTOM LADY; THE MAYOR OF ZALAMEA; THE DEVOTION TO THE CROSS. Translated by Edwin Honig. New York, Hill and Wang. 1969. 302p. $1.95
    Professor Honig has prepared excellent English translations of these
plays. A secreto agravio secreta venganza (1635) is a tragedy dealing with
the defense of honor; La dama duende (1629) is an amusing comedy revolving
around love, intrigue, and honor; El alcalde de Zalamea (1642) is also a
tragedy about defending honor; and La devoción a la cruz (1633) is a theological play.
996.
_____. LIFE IS A DREAM. Translated by William E. Col-
ford. Woodbury, N. Y., Barron's Educational Series, 1960. 101p. $1.25
    This is a textbook edition of Calderón's beautiful allegorical drama,
whose central character is Segismundo. Through him the playwright explores
the mysteries of human destiny, the illusory nature of everyday existence,
and the conflict between predestination and free will.

997.
_____. THE MAYOR OF ZALAMEA. Translated by William E.
Colford. Woodbury, N. Y., Barron's Educational Series, 1961. 131p. $1.25
    This is a textbook edition, intended for classroom use.

998.
_____. TRAGEDIAS ONE: LA VIDA ES SUEÑO; LA HIJA DEL
AIRE; EL MAYOR MONSTRUO DEL MUNDO. Philadelphia, Chilton, 1969. $1.80
    A textbook edition of the well-known masterpiece La vida es sueño; as well
as the historical comedy about Semiramis, queen of Ninive: La Hija del aire
(1653); and the religious play El mayor monstruo del mundo (1637).

999.
_____. TRAGEDIAS 3: LOS CABELLOS DE ABSALON; LA DEVOCION
DE LA CRUZ; EL MAGICO PRODIGIOSO; LAS CISMAS DE INGLATERRA. Introd. by
Francisco Ruiz Ramón. Philadelphia, Center for Curriculum Development, 1970.
539p. $2.40
    Presents four religious tragedies of the Spanish Golden Age.

1000.

_____. LA VIDA ES SUEÑO; EL ALCALDE DE ZALAMEA.
Edited by Sturgis E. Leavitt. New York, Dell, 1962. 239p. $0.50
    This is a textbook edition with notes and vocabulary, of Calderón's
two masterpieces.

1001.
Calvo Sotelo, Joaquín. LA MURALLA. Edited by Robina E. Henry and Enrique
Ruiz-Fornells. New York, Appleton-Century-Crofts, 1962. 112p. $1.95
    This is a textbook edition of this contemporary Spanish play.

1002.
Camõens, Luís Vaz de. THE LUSIADS. Translated by William C. Atkinson,
Middlesex, England, Penguin, 1952. 249p. $1.95
    This is a very good English translation of the famous Portuguese epic.

1003.
Cano, José Luis. ed. TEMA DE ESPAÑA EN LA POESIA ESPAÑOLA CONTEMPORANEA.
Philadelphia, Center for Curriculum Development, 1964. 300p. $3.94
    The editor has prepared a representative anthology of contemporary Span-
ish poetry.

1004.
Cannon, W. C. ed. MODERN SPANISH POEMS. New York, Macmillan, 1969. 289p.
$2.25
    An anthology of modern Spanish poems which includes the most outstanding
modern poets starting with the late 19th century.

1005.
Carbonell, Reyes. EL HOMBRE SOBRE EL ARMARIO Y OTROS CUENTOS. Prólogo
de Antonio de Zunzunegui. Edited by Leonard C. de Morelos and Adela Lafora.
New York, Harper & Ros, 1967. 230p. $3.25
    Contains the title story, as well as El reloj, Ay! literatura, and El
loro by a Valencian short story writer.

1006.
Casa, Frank Paul. EN BUSCA DE ESPAÑA. New York, Harcourt, Brace & World,
1968. 237p. illus. $3.95

1007.
Casona, Alejandro. EL CABALLERO DE LAS ESPUELAS DE ORO. Edited by José A.
Balseiro and Eliana Suárez Rivero. New York, Oxford University Press,
1968. 176p. $1.95
    The most famous era of Spanish culture, the Golden Age, comes to life
in this play by Casona based on the life of Francisco Quevedo. The editors' preface and introduction provide a rich background for students of
Spanish literature.

1008.

_____. CORONA DE AMOR Y MUERTE. Edited by José A. Balseiro and
J. R. Owre. New York, Oxford University Press, 1969. 269p. $2.75

1009.

_____. NUESTRA NATACHA. Edited by W. H. Shoemaker. New York,
Appleton-Century-Crofts, 1968. 200p. $1.95
    This is a textbook edition of a gay contemporary Spanish play.

1010.
Cela, Camilo José. LA COLMENA. The complete novel edited with notes and
vocabulary by José Ortega. New York, Las Americas Pub. Co., 1966. 311p.
$4.00
    A textbook edition of Cela's most ambitious novel. The editor has added
a vocabulary in the form of footnotes and an appendix of all the madrileñ-
ismos and other idiomatic expressions. Recommended for advanced Spanish
courses.

118

1011.

_____. LA FAMILIA DE PASCUAL DUARTE. Edited by Harold L.
Bodreau and John W. Kronik, New York, Appleton-Century-Crofts, 1967. 175p.
illus. $2.45
    This is a Spanish edition of Cela's masterful book which had a powerful
impact on the Spanish novel of the post-Civil War period. Includes a vocabulary, and is eminently suited for classroom use.

1012.

_____. THE FAMILY OF PASCUAL DUARTE. Translated by Anthony
Kerrigan. 13th rev. ed. New York, Avon Books, 1964. 144p. $0.60
    English translation of Cela's first book, La familia de Pascual Duarte
(1942), a terse and probing account of the harsh life of a poor Spanish
family. It is presented as the autobiography of a murderer about to be
executed. There is a great deal of existential despair in Pascual who
killed the things he loved and hated. The novel has authenticity and humor, and the sometimes brutal popular language makes Pascual very contemporary. Pascual is an anti-hero trying to escape his spiritual crisis. This
novel introduced a literary movement known as tremendismo reflecting the
anguish of everyday life. It also marked the revival of the picaresque
novel, breaking with the innocuous artistry of the decade preceding the
1940's. This work is probably Cela's most popular one and it has been
translated into many foreign languages.

1013.

_____. THE HIVE. Translated by J. M. Cohen, in consultation
with Arturo Barrea. Introd. by Arturo Barrea. New York, Noonday Press,
1965. 247p. (Noonday, 276) $1.95
    English translation of La colmena (1951) which critics consider Cela's
best book. He presents Madrid in the 1940's, in the wake of a devastating
civil war, where hunger is a reality. The characters' tormented existence
presents a penetrating examination of Spanish civilization, and the Hispanic values of virility, personal dignity, honor and a keen sense of life
and death. Cela analyzes the horror of hunger and abjection -- yet his
people are not dehumanized and we get an essentially sympathetic feeling
towards Madrid and Spain.

1014.

_____. MRS. CALDWELL SPEAKS TO HER SON. by J. S. Bernstein,
with the cooperation of the author. Ithaca, N. Y., Cornell University
Press, 1968. 224p. $2.45
    Cela wrote Mrs. Caldwell habla con su hijo in 1953. He used the tech-
nique of letters written by Mrs. Caldwell to her dead son. The brief
topical chapters on an incestuous mother-son relationship are subtle and
poetic.

1015.
Cervantes Saavedra, Miguel de. DECEITFUL MARRIAGE AND OTHER EXEMPLARY
NOVELS. Translated by Walter Starkie. New York, New American Library,
1970. 320p. $0.75
    This is a new translation of El casamiento engañoso with a foreword by
Walter Starkie. Spain's greatest novelist wrote this work in a realistic
style.

1016.

_____. DON QUIJOTE DE LA MANCHA. New York, Mac-
millan, 1960. 410p. $2.25
    Cervantes' masterpiece was published in 1605 under the title El ingenioso
hidalgo don Quijote de la Mancha, the story of a naive country gentleman who
decides to become a knight errant. The book is a satire of the romances of
chivalry.

1017.

_____. DON QUIXOTE DE LA MANCHA. Translated by
John Michael Cohen. Baltimore, Penguin Books, 1960. 390p. $1.95

1018.

_____. DON QUIXOTE DE LA MANCHA. Translated by Charles Jarvis. Abridged and edited with an introd. by Lester G. Crocker. New York, Washington Square Press, 1957. 446p. $0.95

A handsome abridged edition of El ingenioso hidalgo don Quijote de la Mancha (1605).

1019.

_____. DON QUIJOTE DE LA MANCHA. Edited by W. Tardy. Skokie, Ill., National Textbook Corp., 1969. 301p. $1.00 5 or more $0.85 each.

This is a textbook edition of the Spanish classic.

1020.

_____. DON QUIXOTE. Translated by Peter Motteux. New York, Airmont, 1968. 799p. $1.25

Raymond R. Canon provides a brief biographical sketch of the author. The publisher eliptically reveals that this version is "Ozell's revision of the translation of Peter Motteux." [Charles Fleener]

1021.

_____. DON QUIXOTE DE LA MANCHA. Translated by Pierre A. Motteux. Introd. by Henry Grattan Doyle. New York, Modern Library, 1950. 836p. $1.45

The perceptive introduction and a concise biographical note on Cervantes with a select reading list enhance this excellent edition.

1022.

_____. DON QUIXOTE OF LA MANCHA. Translated and edited by Walter Starkie. New York, New American Library, 1968. 324p. $0.95

An abridged edition of Don Quixote, in which the translator provides an excellent introduction to the life and times of Miguel de Cervantes, author of the greatest Spanish classic.

1023.

_____. EXEMPLARY NOVELS OF CERVANTES. Cranbury, N. J., A. S. Barnes, 1960. 143p. illus. $1.25

First published in 1952, this selection includes The generous lover, The little gypsy, and The jealous Estremaduran, from Cervantes' immortal work Novelas ejemplares (1613), a collection of twelve short stories in the style of the Italian novella, but with an ethical purpose.

1024.

_____. INTERLUDES. New translation with foreword by Edwin Honig. New York, New American Library, 1969. 220p. $0.75

This is an outstanding English translation of Entremeses (1615).

1025.

_____. THE PORTABLE CERVANTES. Translated and edited by Samuel Putnam. New York, Viking Press, 1968. 420p. $2.25

First issued in 1949, this well-known translation includes both parts of Don Quijote, complete, with all omitted passages covered by editorial summaries. Also included are two of the exemplary novels and Foot in the Stirrup, as well as an excellent introduction by Samuel Putnam.

1026.

_____. SELECTIONS FROM DON QUIJOTE. Edited by J. D. Ford. Boston, Heath, 1970. 390p. $2.75

This is a useful textbook edition of selections from the Spanish masterpiece.

1027.

_____. SIX EXEMPLARY NOVELS. Translated and edited by Harriet de Onís. Woodbury, N. Y., Barron, 1967. 297p. illus. $1.50

Includes Dialogue of the dogs (Coloquio de los perros); Master Glass (El Licenciado Vidriera); Gypsy maid (La gitanilla); Rinconete y Cortadillo;

Jealous hidalgo (El celoso extremeño); and The illustrious kitchen maid (La ilustre fregona); which are six of a collection of twelve short stories which Cervantes published in 1613 under the title of Novelas ejemplares.

1028.
_____. TALES FROM DON QUIXOTE. New York, Pyramid Books, 1970. 280p. $0.35

1029.
_____. THREE EXEMPLARY NOVELS. Edited by Avellarce. New York, Dell,1968. 295p. $0.50
Includes El Licenciado Vidriera; El Casamiento engañoso, and Coloquio de los perros.

1030.
Chapman, Charles E. A HISTORY OF SPAIN. New York, Free Press, 1965. 559p. $2.95
This excellent history of Spain from its beginnings to 1917, emphasizing Spain in America, 1492-1808, is based on Historia de España y de la civilización española of Rafael Altamira y Crevea. Includes a bibliography.

1031.
Chase, Gilbert. THE MUSIC OF SPAIN. 2d. ed. New York, Dover, 1959. 383p. illus. $2.50
This is an historical study of Spanish music from the Middle Ages to the present.

1032.
Chilcote, Ronald H. ed. EMERGING NATIONALISM IN PORTUGUESE AFRICA: A BIBLIOGRAPHY. Stanford, Calif., Hoover Institute for War and Peace, 1969. 114p. $4.00
This is a useful and important bibliography on nationalism in the Portuguese territories of Africa.

1033.
_____. PORTUGUESE AFRICA. Englewood Cliffs, N. J., Prentice-Hall, 1968. 149p. maps. $1.95
Analyzes Portuguese policy in its various shapes of conquest, pacification, and colonization in the African territories of Angola, Moçambique, Portuguese Guiné and the islands of Cape Verde, São Tomé, and Principe over the last 500 years. An attempt is made to provide both the Portuguese and African historical perspectives. Includes a bibliography.

1034.
El Cid Campeador. THE EPIC OF THE CID. Translated by Gerald Markley. Indianapolis, Bobbs-Merrill, 1961. 132p. $1.45
The translator provides a concise introduction to the classic epic of Spain's national hero of the Middle Ages, Rodrigo Díaz de Vivar (1040?-1099). The name "El Cid" is derived from the Arabic title Sidi, meaning "lord." The epic appeared in 1140.

1035.
_____. POEM OF THE CID. Translated by W. S. Merwin. New York, New American Library, 1962. 301p. $0.95
This bilingual edition contains an English verse translation of the epic with the Spanish text of Ramón Menéndez Pidal.

1036.
_____. POEM OF THE CID. Translated by Lesley B. Simpson. Berkeley, University of California Press, 1965. 304p. $1.50
This textbook edition is a good translation of the epic depicting the legendary exploits of the soldier-hero Rodrigo Díaz de Vivar.

1037.

_____. POEM OF THE CID; a modern translation with notes, edited by G. Willbern; translated by Paul Blackburn. New York, R.D.M. Corp., 1966. 155p. $1.95

An abbreviated textbook edition of the Spanish epic.

1038.

Clarke, D. C. ALLEGORY, DECALOGUE, AND DEADLY SINS IN LA CELESTINA. Berkeley, University of California Press, 1969. 310p. $4.50

The author analyzes the allegories in this remarkable Spanish medieval drama.

1039.

Cohen, John Michael, ed. THE PENGUIN BOOK OF SPANISH VERSE. rev. ed. Harmondsworth, England, Penguin Books, 1960. 472p. $1.65

Ranging from El Cid to Claudio Rodriguez (b.1934) more than 100 poets are represented in the Anthology. Many Latin American poems are included. Each poem is presented in the original Spanish followed by a prose translation.

1040.

Colford, William E., ed. CLASSIC TALES FROM MODERN SPAIN. Woodbury, N. Y., Barron's Educational Series, 1964. 201p. $1.50

Contains 16 short stories from 19th century and 20th century authors, ranging from Gustavo Adolfo Bécquer to Vicente Blasco Ibañez.

1041.

Contreras, Alonso de. VIDA, NACIMIENTO, PADRES Y CRIANZA DEL CAPITAN ALONSO DE CONTRERAS. Philadelphia, Chilton Book Co., 1969. 200p. $0.90

A textbook edition of the autobiography of the famous Spanish adventurer and soldier of fortune of the 17th century.

1042.

Corredor, José María. CONVERSATIONS WITH CASALS. Translated by André Mangeot. New York, Dutton, 1957. 240p. illus. $1.55

The great Spanish musician gives his opinions of music, politics, and a variety of subjects. He emerges as a warm, intelligent, and direct human being. The French original, entitled Conversations avec Pablo Casals, was published in 1954.

1043.

Crabb, Daniel M. CRITICAL STUDY GUIDE TO CERVANTES' DON QUIXOTE. Totowa, N. J., Littlefield, Adams, 1966. 122p. map. $1.00

An introduction and and a chapter-by-chapter summary of the greatest of Spanish classics.

1044.

Corrigan, Robert Willoughby, ed. MASTERPIECES OF MODERN SPANISH THEATER. New York, Macmillian, 1967. 304p. $1.50

J. Benavente's Witches sabbath, G. Martínez Sierra's Cradle song; Federico García Lorca's Love of Don Perlimpín; A. Buero Vallejo's Death thrust are the plays included in this anthology.

1045.

Daix, Pierre. PICASSO. New York, Praeger, 1965. 271p. illus. $3.95

This is an illustrated edition which includes a good selection of Picasso's works as well as an introduction to the artist's life and work.

1046.

Damase, Jacques. PABLO PICASSO. Translated by Haydn Barnes, New York, Barnes and Noble, 622. 1965. 90p. Art series, illus. $0.95

Includes 72 illustrations, 24 of which are color reproductions. The introduction gives a concise survey of the life and work of the artist.

1047.
Davies, Reginald Trevor. THE GOLDEN CENTURY OF SPAIN, 1501-1621. New York,
Harper and Row, 1967. 325p. illus., maps. $2.75
   This is an excellent study of 16th century Spain by a noted English his-
torian, especially valuable for its emphasis on economic and social aspects.
Maps, illustrations, and a thorough bibliography enhance the text.

1048.
_____. SPAIN IN DECLINE, 1621-1700. New York, St. Martins
Press, 1968. 180p. maps. $2.50
   This is an important book about the Spanish Bourbon period which saw the
empire wane. Includes bibliographies.

1048A
Degand, León. GONZALEZ. New York, Universe Books, 1959. 135p. illus.
$1.95.
   The text introduces the work of the Spanish sculptor Julio González (1876-
1942). His work is an original epilogue to Cubism and marks a turning point
in modern sculpture. Thirty two black and white illustrations enhance this
attractive book.

1049.
Delibes, Miguel. EL CAMINO. Edited by José Amor y Vásquez, and Ruth H.
Kosoff. New York, Harcourt, Brace, and World. 1960. 244p. $2.95
   A textbook edition of Delibes' novel which appeared in 1950, is considered
among the best Spanish novels of the last two decades.

1050.
_____. LA PARTIDA. Philadelphia, Center for Curriculum Develop-
ment, 1954. 162p. $1.20
   First published in 1954, this is a widely read Spanish novel.

1051.
_____. VIEJAS HISTORIAS DE CASTILLA LA VIEJA. Philadelphia,
Center for Curriculum Development, 1964. 85p. illus. $1.20
   Describes the Spanish province of Castilla la Vieja. Attractive photo-
graphs enhance the text.

1052.
De Onís, Harriet, ed. CUENTOS Y NARRACIONES EN LENGUA ESPAÑOLA. New York,
Washington Square Press, 1961. 304p. $0.60
   Contains substantially the same collection of stories as appeared in
English translation in the editor's Spanish stories and tales ... first pub-
lished in 1954. See next entry.

1053.
_____. SPANISH SHORT STORIES AND TALES. New York, Washington
Square Press, 1964. 288p. $0.60
   These short stories have been selected for their literary value and their
intrinsic interest.

1054.
Díaz Plaja, Guillermo. HISTORY OF SPANISH LITERATURE. Translated by Hugh
Harter. New York, New York University Press, 1970. 320p. $3.45
   A comprehensive and up-to-date history of Spanish literature which will
be very useful in the classroom.

1055.
Diffie, Bailey W. PRELUDE TO EMPIRE: PORTUGAL OVERSEAS BEFORE HENRY THE
NAVIGATOR. Lincoln, University of Nebraska Press, 1960. 321p. $2.25
   Demonstrates the importance of the Portuguese overseas experience from
before 1415 to the subsequent period of the great discoveries. This is a
scholarly and interesting work with extensive annotations, an index, and a
brief bibliography.

1056.
Dixon, R. A. SPAIN. Chicago, Rand McNally, 1967. 96p. illus. maps. $1.00

1057.
Donini G., and G. B. Ford Jr., trans. ISIDORE OF SEVILLE'S HISTORY OF THE
KINGS OF THE GOTHS, VANDALS, & SUEVIANS. New York, Humanities Press, 1970.
320p. $4.00
    This is a very good translation of the Spanish historian's work.

1058.
Du Gue Trapier, E. EL GRECO: EARLY YEARS AT TOLEO. New York, Hispanic Society of America, 1969. 75p. illus. $2.25
    This is an attractive work about El Greco's early years at Toledo.

1059.
_____. EUGENIO LUCAS Y PADILLA. New York, Hispanic Society of
America, 1969. 99p. $1.00
    Presents the life and describes the work of Eugenio Lucas, a Spanish paint-
er of the 19th century who was a follower of Goya.

1060.
_____. VALDES LEAL: BAROQUE CONCEPT OF DEATH AND SUFFERING IN
HIS PAINTINGS. New York, Hispanic Society of America, 1970. 120p. illus.
$1.50
    Valdés Leal (1622-1690) was a Spanish painter who produced a great number
of religious and historical paintings.

1061.
Duffy, James. PORTUGAL IN AFRICA. Baltimore, Penguin Books, 240p. maps.
(Penguin African Library series) $0.95
    The author surveys Portuguese Africa from the explorations of the 15th
century to the growing colonial problems of the Salazar regime.

1062.
Durán, Manuel, ed. LORCA; A COLLECTION OF CRITICAL ESSAYS. Englewood Cliffs,
N. J., Prentice-Hall, 1962. 181p. $1.95
    Thirteen essays ranging from Angel del Río on "Lorca's Theatre" to Richard
Saez on "The Ritual Sacrifice in Lorca's Poet in New York," to William Carlos
Williams' discussion of Lorca the man. Includes bibliographies.

1063.
Durgnat, R. LUIS BUNUEL. Berkeley, University of California Press, 1969.
144p. $1.95
    This is a study of the acclaimed contemporary film director's work.

1064.
Dyckes, William. SPANISH ART NOW. New York, Wittenborn, 1967. 79p. illus.
$4.50
    Seventy seven contemporary artists from Spain are pictured and their work
described in brief biographical paragraphs. A representative black and white
photograph of their work, either painting or sculpture, completes the page.
[Charles Fleener]

1065.
Ebersole, Alva Vernon, comp. CINCO CUENTISTAS CONTEMPORANEOS. In collaboration with Jorge Campos. Englewood Cliffs, N. J., Prentice-Hall, 1969.
213p. Ports. $3.50
    Includes contemporary Spanish short stories by J. Campos, D. Sueiro,
C. Ianzo, M. Fraile, and F. García.

1066.
Elliot, John J. IMPERIAL SPAIN; 1469-1716. New York, New American Library,
1966. 406p. illus. $0.95
    This book by a prominent British Hispanist is of great interest to stu-
dents of history. It presents a synthetic account of the most important
years of the Spanish empire without detailed narrative. Includes a bibliography.

1067.
_____. THE OLD WORLD AND THE NEW, 1492-1650 (Wiles Lectures 1969).
New York, Cambridge University Press, 1970. 180p. $1.95
Prof. Elliott discusses the intellectual, economic, and social consequences
of the discovery and settlement of America for early modern Europe. He analyzes the way in which contact with new lands and peoples challenged a number of traditional assumptions about astronomy, geography, theology, history,
and the nature of man.

1068.
Enggass, R., and Jonathan Brown. ITALY AND SPAIN, 1600-1750. Englewood
Cliffs, N. J., Prentice-Hall, 1970. 256p. illus. $3.95
This college text consists of translations with introduction of important
source materials relevant to the art of Spain.

1069.
Eoff, Sherman Hinkle. THE MODERN SPANISH NOVEL: COMPARATIVE ESSAYS EXAMIN-
ING THE PHILOSOPHICAL IMPACT OF SCIENCE ON FICTION. New York, New York Uni-
versity Press, 1961. 280p. $1.95
A probing study of the philosophical influence of science on later 19th
century and modern European fiction. The Spanish novel occupies the greater
part of the discussion, reflecting important developmental phases in Spanish
fiction. The authors thoroughly studied in these essays include José María
Pereda, Leopoldo Alas, Emilia Pardo Bazán, Vicente Blasco Ibañez, Benito
Pérez Galdós, Pío Baroja, Miguel de Unamuno, and Ramón Sender.

1070.
Espronceda y Delgado, José de. EL DIABLO MUNDO: EL ESTUDIANTE DE SALAMANCA:
POESÍAS. Philadelphia, Center for Curriculum Development, 1970. 247p.
Contains a textbook edition of El diablo mundo, an unfinished poem; El
estudiante de Salamanca, a verse legend; and some of the poetry by Spain's
great romantic poet of the 19th century noted for his lyricism and emotional
power.

1071.
Fabian, Donald L. TRES FICCIONES BREVES. Boston Houghton, Mifflin, 1968.
162p. $2.50
Includes three short stories: "El tesoro del holandés" by Pío Baroja;
"Nada menos que todo un hombre" by Miguel de Unamuno; and "La cruz del diablo"
by Adolfo Bécquer. The book is intended for college level intermediate Spanish
courses.

1072.
Feis, Herbert. THE SPANISH STORY, FRANCO AND THE NATIONS AT WAR. New York,
Norton, 1966. 282p. $1.85
First published in 1948, this is a history of Spain's diplomatic and
economic relations with the allied and Axis powers during World War II,
written by a Pulitzer Prize winning historian.

1073.
Fernández de Moratín, Leandro. THE MAIDEN'S CONSENT. Translated by Harriet
de Onís. Great Neck, N.Y., Barron's Educational Series, 1962. 106p. $1.25
English translation of El sí de las niñas (1806), a prose comedy after the
manner of Molière by one of Spain's greatest dramatists.

1074.
Ferrater Mora, José. FILOSOFÍA ACTUAL. Philadelphis, Chilton Education Series,
1969. 188p. $0.90
The author outlines his thoughts on modern philosophy.

1075.
----------. UNAMUNO, A PHILOSOPHY OF TRAGEDY. Translated by Philip Silver.
Berkeley, University of California Press, 1962. 136p. $1.50
Presents Unamuno's philosophy. It is an English translation of Unamuno:
bosquejo de una Filosofía (1957).

1076.
Ferreira, Eusébio da Silva. MY NAME IS EUSÉBIO. Assisted by Fernando F.
Garcia. Translated by Derrik Low. New Rochelle, N.Y., Soccer Associates,
1968. 166p. illus. $2.50
   Entertainingly and accurately written story of the great Association Soccer
player from Moçambique. Well-chosen illustrations, including the World Cup.

1077.
Fitzmaurice-Kelly, James. ANTONIO PEREZ. New York, Hispanic Society of
America, 1922. 170p. $2.00
   Antonio Pérez (1534-1611) was a Spanish writer and politician who had been
secretary to Philip II. After a court scandal he fled to Aragón and died in
exile in France. He corresponded with major European political figures of his
era.

1078.
———————. CERVANTES IN ENGLAND. New York, Haskell House, 1970. 180p.
$1.95
   Studies the impact of Cervantes' work on Great Britain's intellectual life.

1079.
Flores, Ángel, ed. AN ANTHOLOGY OF SPANISH POETRY FROM GARCILASO TO GARCÍA
LORCA IN ENGLISH TRANSLATION WITH SPANISH ORIGINALS. New York, Doubleday,
1961. 516p. $1.45
   This edition contains poems by 17 Spanish and Spanish-American poets. The
editor has included succinct biographical sketches of each poet.

1080.
——————————, ed. GREAT SPANISH SHORT STORIES. New York, Dell, 1962. 304p.
$0.50
   The editor has included 17 short stories by Spanish and Latin American
writers, including Azorín, Valle-Inclán, López y Fuentes, Borges, and Rulfo.
Contains a good introduction.

1081.
——————————, ed. MASTERPIECES OF THE SPANISH GOLDEN AGE. New York, Harcourt,
Brace, and World, 1957. 395p. $2.25
   Includes the most important works of the classical period in Spanish
literature in English translation.

1882.
——————————, ed. MEDIEVAL AGE. New York, Dell, 1963. 606p. $0.95
   Contains a well-chosen selection of medieval ballads, poems, and epics.

1083.
——————————, ed. SELECCIONES ESPAÑOLAS. New York, Bantam Books, 1967. 231p.
   Included are selections from the works of Spanish and Spanish-American
writers such as Benito Lynch, Azorín, Jorge Luis Borges, Ricardo Palma, Luis
Taboada, José María Roa Bárcenas, and others.

1084.
——————————, ed. SPANISH DRAMA. New York, Bantam Books, 1962. 473p. $0.95
   This edition includes Olives, Peribañez, and Fuente Ovejuna by Lope de Vega;
The vigilant sentinel by Cervantes; The rogue of Seville by Tirso de Molina;
The truth suspected by Alarcón; Life is a dream by Calderón de la Barca; When
a girl says yes by Fernández de Moratín; The great Galeoto by Echegaray y
Eizaguirre; The bonds of interest by Benavente; and Blood wedding by García
Lorca.

1086.
——————————, ed. SPANISH STORIES; CUENTOS ESPAÑOLES....WITH NEW ENGLISH
TRANSLATIONS. New York, Bantam Books, 1960. 339p. $0.95
   This is a bilingual edition of stories by 13 masters of the Spanish
language, from both Spain and Latin America. It includes Cervantes, Alarcón,
Clarín, Borges, Cela, and Goytisolo, as well as an introduction by the editor.

1087.
Florit, Eugenio, ed. INVITATION TO SPANISH POETRY. New York, Dover, 1965.
143p. illus. ports. $4.95
Presents 30 Spanish poets in the original and in English translation,
ranging from the 12th to the 20th century. Portraits or photographs of many
of the poets are included. The poems are read in Spanish by Eugenio Florit
and Amelia Agostini de del Rio on an accompanying record.

1088.
Floyd, Troy S., ed. THE BOURBON REFORMERS AND SPANISH CIVILIZATION: BUILDERS
OR DESTROYERS? Boston, Heath, 1966. 87p. $1.75
The essays in this work attempt to analyze the complex and enduring
historical debate over the Bourbon rulers of Spain (1700-1808). The readings
are by Spanish and Latin American personalities of the 18th and 19th centuries.
All translations and footnotes are by the editor.

1089.
Fraker, C. F. STUDIES ON THE CANCIONERO DE BAENA. Chapel Hill, University
of North Carolina Press, 1970. 460p. $5.00
This is a thorough and very useful work on the Cancionero de Baena (1445),
an anthology of songs and lyric poetry. The Cancionero is one of the earliest
Castilian anthologies of this type.

1090.
Franco, Jean, ed. SHORT STORIES IN SPANISH; CUENTOS HISPÁNICOS. Baltimore,
Penguin Books, 1966. 203p. $0.95
This is a bilingual edition of eight short stories by Camilo José Cela,
and other contemporary Spanish writers.

1091.
Frank B. A. MAN CALLED CERVANTES. New York, Popular Library, 1970. 301p.
$0.60
A popular introduction to Miguel de Cervantes and his times.

1092.
Gagliardo, John G. ENLIGHTENED DESPOTISM. New York, Crowell, 1967. 118p.
$2.25
Surveys recent historical research concerning the era of enlightened
despotism in Western European history (1760-1790). Charles III of Spain and
the Marquis de Pombal of Portugal are examined.

1093.
Ganivet, Ángel. LOS TRABAJOS DEL INFATIGABLE CREADOR PÍO CID. Philadelphia,
Center for Curriculum Development, 1965. 398p. $2.34
This novel is a spiritual autobiography of Ganivet, published in 1898. It
analyzes the intrinsic mechanisms of Spanish character.

1094.
Gaquere, François. CHILDREN OF FATIMA. Boston, Daughters of St. Paul, 1970.
79p. illus. $0.35
Describes briefly Fatima in Portugal, and its history as a devotional
center.

1095.
García Lorca, Federico. FIVE PLAYS: COMEDIES AND TRAGICOMEDIES. Translated
by Richard L. O'Connell and James Graham-Lujan. Introd. by Francisco García
Lorca. New York, New Directions, 1968. 420p. $1.75
Includes the Shoemaker's Prodigious Wife; Don Perimplín; Doña Rosita, the
Spinster; Billy Club Puppets; and The Butterfly's Evil Spell. The last is an
incomplete play included here because it is Lorca's first play. It serves
as an appendix demonstrating the author's development. Prof. Francisco García
Lorca provides a good introduction to his brother's work.

1096.
----------. GYPSY BALLADS OF GARCIA LORCA. Translated by Rolfe Humphries.
Bloomington, Indiana University Press, 1968. 64p. $1.45
    Romancero gitano (1928) made García Lorca an immediate success. Many of
his ballads were soon recited everywhere, were sung by common people, and
enriched the treasure of traditional poetry. The poet took his subjects from
the people and incorporated then into his stream of living art.

1097.
----------. OBRAS ESCOGIDAS. Edited by Eugenio Florit. New York, Dell, 1967.
208p. $0.50
    Includes a selection of poems by Spain's most intense and original poet of
this century.

1098.
----------. POET IN NEW YORK. Translated by Ben Belitt, New York, Grove
Press, 1955. 192p. $1.95
    García Lorca's trip to the United States (1929-30) is reflected in his
Poeta en Nueva York (1940?). It describes the impression the modern city
made upon the poet, and shows the influence of many contemporary trends,
especially surrealism. The work exudes rich imagery, a sense of reality,
and the dramatic pace that is the hallmark of Lorca's work.

1099.
----------. THREE TRAGEDIES. Translated by James Graham-Luján and Richard
L. O'Connell. New York, New Directions, 1961. 212p. $1.75
    Contains Blood Wedding, Yerma, and The House of Bernarda Alba. An intro-
duction by the poet's brother, Francisco, provides an interesting personal
glimpse of Federico as a dramatist.

1100.
García Lorca, Federico. LA ZAPATERA PRODIGIOSA. Edited by E. F. Helman.
New York, Norton, 1968. 192p. illus. $2.35
    This play represents one of the highest attainments of contemporary poetic
theatre in the tradition of Spanish classic and romantic drama.

1101.
García-Mazas, José. EL POETA Y LA ESCULTORA; LA ESPAÑA QUE HUNTINGTON
CONOCIÓ. 2d ed. New York, Hispanic Society of America, 1962. 525p. illus.,
ports. $2.50
    An attractive volume about the lives of Archer Huntington and his wife,
founders of the magnificent library and museum, the Hispanic Society of
America. The work concentrates on the Huntingtons' sojourn in Spain.

1102.
Gasser, Manuel. JOAN MIRÓ. Translated by Haydn Barnes. New York, Barnes
and Noble, 1965. (Art series, 621) 90p. $0.95
    The Catalonian painter is represented by twenty-four excellent color re-
productions and a large number of black and white illustrations of his work.
The brief text is his life and work through the early 1960's. [Charles
Fleener].

1103.
Gel, Pieter. THE REVOLT OF THE NETHERLANDS. 1555-1609. 2nd ed. New York,
Barnes and Noble, 1966. 310p. maps. $2.50
    An outstanding European historian wrote this detailed history of the 16th
century Dutch revolt against Spain. Rather then interpreting the conflict in
terms of a contest between Protestantism and Catholicism, Geyl accounts for
the interplay of political, cultural, military, and religious forces. The
original title was Geschiedenis van de Nederlandsche Stam (1931).
[Charles Fleener].

1104.
Gilot, Francoise, and Carlton Lake. LIFE WITH PICASSO. New York, New
American Library, 1965. 350p. illus., $0.95
    One of Picasso's great loves describes her life with the artist, with
rare wit and insight.

1105.
Gironella, José María. LOS CIPRESES CREEN EN DIOS. New York, Harcourt, Brace, and World, 1969. 353p. $3.75
   In this novel about the Spanish Civil War, the author captures the enormous toll in human suffering and tragedy paid by the Spanish people during this crucial period of their history.

1106.
Goldston, Robert. THE CIVIL WAR IN SPAIN. Greenwich, Conn., Fawcett Publications, 1969. 221p. $0.75
   The author presents a brief, clear introduction to the Spanish tragedy of 1936-1939. Starting with "How war came" through eleven chapters to the "The fall of the Republic" he analyzes the war and the warring factions.

1107.
Gómez-Moreno, Carmen. MEDIEVAL ART FROM PRIVATE COLLECTIONS. Foreword by Thomas B. Hoving. New York, Metropolitan Museum of Art, 1968. chiefly illus. $7.95
   This is a very attractive illustrated book about medieval art in which the Luso-Hispanic world is well represented.

1108.
Góngora y Argote, Luis. POEMS OF CÓNGORA. Edited by R. O. Jones, New York, Cambridge University Press, 1966. 162p. $2.25
   Góngora (1561-1627) was the most complex poet of the Golden Age. His collected poems were first published in 1627. From 1580 to 1612 his poetry was chiefly lyrical. From 1612 on his work shows signs of increasing complexity which culminates in Góngora's unique baroque style. A third of this work serves as an introduction to the life and work of the poet.

1109.
Goya y Lucientes, Francisco. LOS CAPRICHOS. New York, Dover, 1969. 87 plates. $2.75
   Contains good reproductions of Goya's Los Caprichos.

1110.
----------. THE DISASTERS OF WAR. Introd. by Philip Hofer. New York, Dover, 1967. 106p. illus. $1.95
   Reproduces a collection of 80 plates by Goya that depict the Spanish nationalist uprising against the French puppet king. Joseph Bonaparte (1808-1814). Goya denounces war through his art. Philip Hofer's bilingual introduction examines the artist's work. Its original title was Los desastres de la guerra (1863).

1111.
----------. THE DISPARATES OR, PROVERBIOS. Introd. by Philip Hofer. New York, Dover, 1969. 64p. illus. $2.75
   In this over-sized volume the last of Goya's four main print series are reproduced. The 18 etchings, variously known as Los proverbios or Los disparates [follies] were probably executed in 1819. Includes three proofs and a preliminary drawing for a Disparates subject. First published in 1864.

1112.
----------. DRAWINGS OF GOYA. Edited by de Salas. Alhambra, Calif., Borden Pub. Co., 1969. illus. $1.75
   Includes representative drawings by the master.

1113.
----------. GOYA. Edited by E. L. Ferrari. New York, New American Library, 1970. 120p. illus. $0.95
   Illustrates the most important works of Goya.

1114.
----------. GOYA. Edited F. S. Wight. New York, H. F. Abrams, 1970. 110p. illus. $0.95
   Includes reproductions of a representative selection.

1115.
----------. LA TAUROMAQUIA AND THE BULLS OF BORDEAUX. Introd. by Philip
Hofer. New York, Dover, 1969. 120p. illus. $3.00
   Forty plates of La Tauromaquia and four lithographs of the Bulls of
Bordeaux are included in this splendid volume. This work is a great
addition to any collection of Spanish art.

1116.
Goytortúa Santos, Jesús. LLUVIA ROJA. Edited by Donald D. Walsh. New York,
Appleton-Century-Crofts, 1961. 195p. $2.45
   A textbook edition, with notes and vocabulary, of this contemporary Spanish
novel.

1117.
----------. PENSATIVA. Edited by Donald D. Walsh. New York, Appleton-
Century-Crosts, 1962. 202p. $2.45
   A textbook edition of this incisive contemporary Spanish novel.

1118.
Gracián y Morales, Baltasar. ART OF WORLDLY WISDOM. Translated by J. Jacobs.
New York, Ungar, 1960. 197. $1.25
   Arte de ingenio (1642) by the great Spanish prose stylist, explains the
literary theory of conceptismo.

1119.
----------. THE BEST OF GRACIÁN. Translated by T. Corvan. New York,
Philosophical Library, 1964. 84p. $0.95
   Contains selections from the essays and allegorical works of the great
Spanish moralist and stylist of the 17th century.

1120.
Green, Otis Howard. SPAIN AND THE WESTERN TRADITION: THE CASTILIAN MIND IN
LITERATURE FROM EL CID TO CALDERÓN. Madison, University of Wisconsin Press,
1963-66. 4 v. $2.95 each vol.
   This extensive work surveys Spanish literature within the Western tradition
from the Middle Ages to the Golden Age. It is most certainly a very important
contribution to the field.

1121.
Gris, Juan. GRIS:DESSINS AND GUACHES. Edited by Leiris Gallery. New York,
Wittenborn, 1965. 70p. illus. $3.50
   Attractive reproductions of representative works by the contemporary
Catalan painter, Gris.

1122.
Grismer, Raymond, and Doris Arjona. PAGEANT OF SPAIN. New York, Appleton-
Century-Crofts, 1967. 202p. illus. $2.45
   Introduces Spain to the student from a cultural and historical viewpoint.

1123.
Guillén, Claudio, ed. LAZARILLO DE TORMES. EL ABENCERRAJE. Introd. and
notes by Claudio Guillén. New York, Dell, 1966. 187p. $0.50
   La vida de Lazarillo de Tormes y sus fortunas (1554) gained instant success
and ushered in the picaresque novel. The book exudes good humor and
iconoclastic satire. El Abencerraje, a contemporary of the former, is a
poetic novel about the exploits of the chivalrous Moor. It fuses the traditions of medieval Morrish Spain and Renaissance themes of mythological
allusions. The editor presents the 1554 Antwerp text of Lazarillo and the
1565 Abencerraje of Antonio Villegas. The spellings has been modernized and
the texts have been divided into paragraphs.

1124.
Guillén, Jorge. CÁNTICO: A SELECTION. Edited by Norman Thomas di Giovanni.
Boston, Little, Brown, 1965. 291p. illus. $2.95
   The poet himself, who devoted 31 years to writing Cántico, chose the 50
poems for this edition. They appear in the original Spanish, with English
translation on the facing pages. Guillén said "Cántico is an act of

attentiveness. Despite many obstacles it tends toward serenity, toward joy, with wonder and with gratitude. Experience of being, affirmation of life, of this life on earth which has a value in itself..."

1125.
Guttman, A., ed. AMERICAN NEUTRALITY AND THE SPANISH CIVIL WAR. Boston, Heath, 1970. 243p. $2.25
　　Examines U.S. diplomacy during the 1936-1940 period.

1126.
Haggart, S. and D. Porter. DOLLAR-WISE GUIDE TO PORTUGAL. New York, A. Frommer, 1970. 225p. illus. $2.50
　　This travel guide emphasizes accomodations for the economy-minded tourist.

1127.
----------. SPAIN ON FIVE & TEN DOLLARS A DAY. 1969-1970. Rev. ed. New York, Essandess, 1970. 210p. illus. $2.50
　　Points out reasonably-priced accommodations and contains travel tips.

1128.
Halperin, Don A. ANCIENT SYNAGOGUES OF THE IBERIAN PENINSULA. Gainesville, University of Florida Press, 1969. 86p. illus. $2.00
　　Studies in detail ancient synagogues of Spain and Portugal. Includes a bibliography.

1129.
Hauben, Paul J., ed. THE SPANISH INQUISITION. New York, Wiley, 1969. 140p. $2.95
　　The editor's extensive introduction is followed by eight readings that are historiographical and descriptive in scope. The second set of selections includes sources and trial records of the Inquisition in Spain. This volume serves as an introduction to the nature and history of the Holy Office. [Charles Fleener]

1130.
Hawkes, John Ryder, and M. Hawkes. SPAIN. New Rochelle, N.Y., Soccer Associates, 1965. 100p. illus. maps. $1.00

1131.
Hemingway, Ernest. DEATH IN THE AFTERNOON. New York, Scribner, 1960. 487p. illus. $2.95
　　This is a paperback edition of Hemingway's splendid study on the Spanish bullfight. It explains the spectacle both emotionally and practically. First published in 1932.

1132.
----------. THE SUN ALSO RISES. New York, Scribner, 1970. 284p. $1.65
　　This is one Hemingway's earliest novels. It takes place in northern Spain and in Paris. Included are many elements and descriptions of landscapes of Spain, which surfaced with greater force in his subsequent novels.

1133.
----------. FOR WHOM THE BELL TOLLS. New York, Scribner, 1962. 352p. $1.95
　　Hemingway's classic novel about the Spanish Civil War will be of interest to all those interested in the period. The Nobel Prize winning novelist captured the essence of Spain during its bitter and agonizing struggle.

1134.
Herr, Richard. EIGHTEENTH-CENTURY REVOLUTION IN SPAIN. Princeton, N.J., Princeton University Press, 1969. 484p. maps, tables. $3.45
　　Scholarly and valuable guide to Spanish history in the late 18th and early 19th centuries. Professor Herr presents a view of the Spain of Charles III and Charles IV that includes the Peninsula's political, religious, and economic aspects as well as the social and cultural life. Includes bibliographies.

1135.
Hesse, Everett Wesley, and Harry F. William, eds. VIDA DE LAZARILLO DE
TORMES Y DE SUS FORTUNAS Y ADVERSIDADES. Introd. by Américo Castro. Rev.
ed. Madison, University of Wisconsin Press, 1960. 84p. $1.50
See Lazarillo de Tormes.

1136.
Hispanic Society of America, New York. STUDIES IN MEMORY OF RAMÓN MENÉNDEZ
PIDAL, by the Hispanic Society of America in cooperation with the editors of
the Hispanic Review. New York, 1971. 100p. plates $4.00
Contains articles on various aspects of the great Spanish scholar by Homero
Serís, Ciriaco Morón Arroyo, Theodore S.Beardsley, Samuel G. Armistead, and
others.

1137.
Holiday Editors. TRAVEL GUIDE TO SPAIN. Rev. ed. New York, Random House,
1966. 278p. illus. $1.65

1138.
Holt, Marion, ed. MODERN SPANISH STAGE: FOUR PLAYS. New York, Hill and Wang,
1970. 338p. $2.45
This anthology includes Antonio Buero Vallejo's The Concert at St. Ovide
(1958); Alfonso Sastre's Condemned Squad (1953); José López Rubio's The
Blindfold (1954); and Alejandro Casona's The Boat without a Fisherman (1945).

1139.
Honig, Edwin. GARCIA LORCA. Rev. ed. New York, New Directions, 1963. 239p.
$1.80
Professor Honig surveys Federico García Lorca's life and work, including
both poetry and drama. The introduction is excellent and sheds new light on
this important Spanish literary figure.

1140.
Houghton, Norris ed. GOLDEN AGE. New York, Dell, 1963. 349p. $0.75
Includes Lope de Vega's Sheep's Well, Calderón de la Barca's Life is a
Dream, and The Cid by Corneille.

1141.
Huntington, Archer M. TURNING PAGES. New York, Hispanic Society of America,
1950. 74p. $1.00
Includes poetry and essays by the prominent American Hispanophile.

1142.
----------. VERSOS. New York, Hispanic Society of America, 1952. 98p. illus.
$5.00
Selected poems by Huntington who spent his life disseminating the Spanish
cultural heritage.

1143.
Ignatius de Loyola, Saint. SPIRITUAL EXERCISES OF SAINT IGNATIUS. Translated by A. Mottola. Introd. by R. W. Gleason. New York, Doubleday, 1969.
251p. $0.95
English translation of St. Ignatius of Loyola's Ejercicios espirituales.

1144.
Iriarte Ruiz, Víctor, and Marion P. Holt. EL CARRUSEL. New York, Appleton-
Century-Crofts, 1970. 140p. $1.95
This is a college text of a two-act play written in the language of present-
day Madrid and dealing with contemporary problems. It includes a concise intro-
duction in Spanish, vocabulary, and exercises.

1145.
Isidore of Seville, Saint. ISIDORE OF SEVILLE'S HISTORY OF THE KINGS OF THE
GOTHS, VANDALS, AND SUEVI. Translated by Guido Donini and Gordon B. Ford Jr.
New York, Humanities Press, 1967. 46p. $4.00
This is the first translation into English of Isidore of Seville's
Chronicle of the history of the West Goths from 256 to 624 A.D. Historia de

regibus Gothorum, Vandalorum et Suevorum, (624 A.D.).

1147.
Jackson, Gabriel. THE SPANISH CIVIL WAR: DOMESTIC CRISIS OF INTERNATIONAL
CONSPIRACY. Boston, Heath, 1967. 112p. $2.45
     A careful and probing study of the Spanish Civil War, which points out the
international ramifications of a domestic upheaval. Includes a bibliography.

1148.
----------. THE SPANISH REPUBLIC AND THE CIVIL WAR, 1931-1939. Princeton,
N.J., Princeton University Press, 1967. 578p. illus., maps. $3.45
     Traces the history of Spain during the second Republic and through the
Civil War. The author analyzes modern Spain in order to discover the roots
of the disasters that overwhelmed the Republic. He also discusses the
structure of Spanish society. Includes a bibliography. [Charles Fleener]

1149.
Jiménez, E. and C. Puncel. CANCIONCITAS PARA CHIQUITINES. illus. by J.
Rupp. Glendale, Calif., Bowmar, 1970. 357p. $2.25
     Contains Spanish children's songs.

1150.
Jiménez, Juan Ramón. FORTY POEMS OF JUAN RAMON JIMENEZ. Translated by Robert
Bly. Madison, Minn., Sixties Press, 1969. 286p. illus. $1.00
     Includes excellent translations of representative poems by the Nobel-Prize
winning contemporary Spanish poet.

1151.
----------. PLATERO AND I. New translation by William H. and Mary Roberts
with an introd. by William H. Roberts. New York, New American Library, 1960.
231p. $0.75
     Jiménez was awarded the 1956 Nobel Prize in literature. He is considered
together with Antonio Machado, as the foremost lyric poet of contemporary
Spain.

1152.
----------. PLATERO Y YO; TRESCIENTOS POEMAS. Austin, University of Texas
Press, 1964. 310p. $1.75
     In addition to the classic prose poem, El Platero y yo, this attractive
volume contains 300 outstanding poems by Jiménez.

1153.
Johnson, Harold B., Jr., ed. FROM RECONQUEST TO EMPIRE; THE IBERIAN BACK-
GROUND TO LATIN AMERICAN HISTORY. New York, Knopf, 1970. 230p. $2.95
     This selection of readings includes essays ranging from medieval to modern
colonization, the elements of conquest and settlement to the ethos of medieval
Iberia. It provides a thorough background to the economic and social history
of the Iberic peninsula.

1154.
Jones, Joseph Ramón. UNA DECADA DE CESARES . Chapel Hill, University of
North Carolina Press, 1966. 527p. $12.00
     Antonio de Guevara (1480?-1545) of Spain was a courtier, writer, and
priest. His works were very popular in Spain and throughout Europe and
England. This is an exhaustive study on Guevara's work. Includes a biblio-
graphy.

1155.
Jones, Willis Knapp. SPANISH ONE ACT PLAYS IN ENGLISH. New York, Barron's
Educational Series, 1969. $1.95

1156.
Juan de la Cruz, Saint. ASCENT OF MOUNT CARMEL. Translated and edited with
a general introd. by E. Allison Peers. 3d. rev. ed. Garden City, N.Y.,
Doubleday, 1958. 386p. $1.45
     Translation of La subida del Monte Carmelo (1578-1583) by the purest lyric
poet and the most metaphysical among the European mystics. Ascent consists of

eight <u>canciones</u> each followed by prose commentaries in which the poet explains his verses.

1157.

----------. DARK NIGHT OF THE SOUL. Translated and edited, with an introd. by E. Allison Peers from the critical edition by P. Solverio de Santa Teresa. 3d rev. ed. Garden City, N.Y., Image Books, 1959. 193p. $0.85
 Translation of <u>Noche oscura del alma</u> (1579), which represents a pinnacle of mystic experience. Juan de la Cruz expresses the absolute union of the soul with the beloved. His poetry irradiates light, beauty, love, and it totally transcends the bounds of reality. In this latter aspect his writings differ from those of his great friend and mentor, Saint Teresa of Avila. Professor Peers has added a very good introduction to the present volume.

1158.

----------. DARK NIGHT OF THE SOUL. Translated, abridged, and edited by Kurt F. Reinhardt. New York, Ungar, 1957. 222p. illus. $1.75
 This edition of <u>Noche oscura del alma</u> (1579), has valuable notes by the translator and editor which explain the somewhat obscure imagery. The poem is accompanied by commentaries by the poet himself, clarifying his ecstatic and lyrical rhymes.

1159.

----------. LIVING FLAME OF LOVE. Translated, edited, and with an introd, by E. Allison Peers from the critical edition by P. Silverio de Santa Teresa. Garden City N.Y., Doubleday, 1962. 272p. $1.95
 Translation of <u>Oh llama de amor viva</u> (1954), and of San Juan's copious accompanying commentaries. The poem is an allegorical song, a categorical affirmation of absolute love and tenderness. San Juan's profound lyricism and metaphysical labyrinths have been compared to such great poets as Sappho, Cafavy, and Emily Dickinson. The editor's introduction and notes provide a thorough study of the poet.

1160.

----------. POEMS OF ST. JOHN OF THE CROSS. Translated by Roy Campbell. New York, Grosset and Dunlap, 1968. 90p. $1.95
 Includes all the known poems of Juan de la Cruz. The original texts are followed by poet Roy Campbell's excellent translations.

1161.

----------. THE POEMS OF ST. JOHN OF THE CROSS. Original Spanish texts and English versions newly revised and rewritten by John Frederick Nims, with an essay by Robert Graves. Rev. ed. New York, Grove Press, 1959. 157p. $1.95
 In his introductory essay Robert Graves notes that Juan de la Cruz had <u>duende</u>, or divine presence, to an unprecedented degree in his poetry. Graves agrees with the Spanish poet García Lorca that "no poem, whether written for love of God, or love of woman, is worth much if it lacks <u>duende</u>." The present volume contains all of Juan de la Cruz' poems. The translations by John F. Nims are excellent. The translator's essay at the end of the book explains succinctly the poet's background, and the various manuscripts which have been preserved.

1162.

----------. SPIRITUAL CANTICLE. 3d. rev. ed. Translated, edited, and with an introd. by E. Allison Peers, from the critical editions of P. Silverio de Santa Teresa. Garden City, N.Y., Doubleday, 1961. 520p. $1.45
 Translation of <u>El cántico espiritual</u> (1578) which was inspired by Solomon's <u>Song of songs</u> as translated from the Hebrew by another great Spanish mystic, Fray Luis de León. Part of <u>El cántico espiritual</u> was written while the poet was imprisoned in a Toledo dungeon. The last stanzas were completed in Baeza. <u>Cántico</u> constitutes San Juan's most ambitious poem. The poem is one of the most succesful long lyrics in literature. The sources include not only Hebrew folk culture, but also Spanish, Portuguese, and Moorish popular ballads.

1163.
Kamen, Henry Arthur Francis. SPANISH INQUISITION. New York, New American
Library, 1966. 339p. illus.,map. $1.25
    Interprets historically the role and impact of the activities of the Holy
Office in Spain.

1164.
Kanki, Keizo. GOYA. Palo Alto, Calif., Kodansha International, 1969. 154p.
illus. (part col.) $1.95
    Analyzes the style, techniques, and aims of Goya. The illustrations,
some in color, are very good.

1165.
Keller, John Esten, ed. THE BOOK OF THE WILES OF WOMEN. Chapel Hill, University of North Carolina Press, 1956. 60p. $3.50
    An English version of an anonymous collection of oriental tales about the
"deceits and wiles of women." It was translated from the Arabic into Spanish
in 1253 by order of the Infante Fadrique, younger brother of Alfonso X, king
of Spain. This work had a decisive influence on early Spanish medieval
literature.

1166.
-----------. ed. LIBRO DE LOS ENGANNOS ET LOS ASSAYAMIENTOS DE LAS MUGERES.
Chapel Hill, University of North Carolina Press, 1953. 56p. $3.50
    A collection of 24 oriental tales, translated from the Arabic into Spanish
in 1253, which became a part of Spanish literature. The plot revolved around
a charge of attempted seduction brought by a vindictive queen against her
stepson, who had spurned her advances. At his trial seven wise men speak in
his defense relating stories about the perfidy of women. This work has influenced the Arcipreste de Talavera's writings.

1167.
-----------. MOTIF-INDEX OF MEDIAEVAL SPANISH EXEMPLA. Knoxville, University
of Tennessee Press, 1949. 67p. $2.00
    Exemplum (in Spanish ejemplo or fábula) is a medieval didactic or moral
tale of the 13th through 15th centuries. They are usually grouped into a
series of stories within a story known as the "frame." The origin of most
of these tales can be traced to Sanskrit, Persian, Arabic, Greek and Latin
sources.

1169.
Kirkpatrick, Frederick Alexander. THE SPANISH CONQUISTADORES. Cleveland,
World Book Pub. Co., 1968. 366p. maps. $2.95
    Originally published in 1934, this work was the first single volume to
contain a succinct survey of the explorations and expeditions of the Spaniards
in the New World. It covers the period from Columbus' first voyage to Juan de
Garay's founding of Buenos Aires.

1170.
Kirsner, Robert. THE NOVELS AND TRAVELS OF CAMILO JOSÉ CELA. Chapel Hill,
University of North Carolina Press, 1963. 187p. (University of North Carolina
studies in romance languages and literature, 43) $5.00
    A major study of Cela's six novels: La familia de Pascual Duarte, Pabellón
de reposo, Nuevas andanzas y desventuras de Lazarillo de Tormes, La colmena,
Mrs. Caldwell habla consu hijo, and La Cátira, as well as his book of travels.
Cela describes his travels in Spain using a quasi-novelistic form with rare
artistic insight and objectivity.

1171.
Klingender, F. D. GOYA IN THE DEMOCRATIC TRADITION. New York, Schocken
Books, 1968. 235p. illus. tables. $2.95
    First published in 1948, this work attempts to define "the intimate inter-
action between life and art." It studies Goya's works in search of a key to
the interpretation of Spanish history during the regins of Charles III, Charles
IV, and Ferdinand VII. The author uses 122 figures to illustrate his work.
[Charles Fleener]

1172.
Lacy, Allen. MIGUEL DE UNAMUNO: THE RHETORIC OF EXISTENCE. New York,
Humanities Press, 1970p. 382p. $10.50
   This remarkable study analyzes the Spanish philosopher's work and art.

1173.
Laforet, Carmen. NADA. Edited by Edward R. Mulvihill and Roberto G. Sánchez.
New York, Oxford University Press, 1958. 269p. $2.95
   Nada was published in 1944 by an unknown young Spanish girl and it won its
author the first Eugenio Nadal Prize. It is an autobiographical novel narrated
by Andrea. What happens to Andrea among her uncles and aunts in a society
disintegrating after the Spanish Civil War is the story of the book.

1174.
La Souchère, Elena de. AN EXPLANATION OF SPAIN. Translated by Eleanor Ross
Levieux. New York, Random House, 1965. 373p. map, tables. $2.45
   This is an English translation of the original French title Explication de
l'Espagne (1962), an interesting book about modern Spain.

1175.
-----------. PICASSO: ANTIBES. New York, Tudor, 1962. illus. (Little art
library) $0.49
   A personal reminiscence of the author is included in the brief introduction
to these 15 color reproductions from the Picasso Museum in Antibes.

1176.
Lazarillo de Tormes. THE LIFE OF LAZARILLO DE TORMES. Translated by J.
Gerald Markley. Introd. by Allan G. Holaday. New York, Liberal Arts Press,
1954. 68p. $0.60
   A handy, compact English translation of the roguish anti-hero Lazarillo's
adventures, which has enjoyed uninterrupted success since its publication in
1554. This novel became the forerunner not only of the picaresque novel but
of the modern realistic novel as well.

1177.
-----------. THE LIFE OF LAZARILLO DE TORMES, HIS FORTUNES AND ADVERSITIES.
A modern translation with notes by James Parson. Introd. by Glen Wilbern.
New York, R.D.M. Corp., 1966. 96p. $0.95
   English translation of the 1554 Spanish picaresque novel in which the
roguish protagonist criticizes his times with mock-seriousness. The entire
tale is told by Lazarillo in a double perspective of self-concealment and self-
revelation.

1178.
-----------. THE LIFE OF LAZARILLO DE TORMES, HIS FORTUNES AND ADVERSITIES.
Translated by J. Gerald Markley. Introd. by Alan G. Holaday. Indianapolis,
Bobbs-Merril, 1960. 68p. $0.95
   An abridged English version of the classic Spanish picaresque novel which
ranks with the Celestina and Don Quijote as a realistic masterpiece.

1179.
-----------. THE LIFE OF LAZARILLO DE TORMES, HIS FORTUNES AND ADVERSITIES.
Translated by W. S. Merwin, with an introd. by Leonardo C. de Morelos. Garden
City, N.Y., Doubleday, 1962. 152p. $0.95
   The long introduction traces the historical and literary background of the
picaresque novel, a parody of the 16th century with the noblemen's exaggerated
notion of chivalry and honor, and the corruption which existed in high and low
places. This is a good edition for college courses.

1180.
-----------. THE LIFE OF LAZARILLO DE TORMES, HIS FORTUNES AND ADVERSITIES.
Translated with notes and an introd. by Harriet de Onís. Great Neck, N.Y.,
Barron's Educational Series, 1959. 74p. $0.95
   English translation of La vida de Lazarillo de Tormes y de sus fortunas
y adversidades (1554). Its authorship has been attributed to Hurtado de
Mendoza but modern scholarship conclusively rejects this theory.

1181.
----------. LA SEGUNDA PARTE DE LA VIDA DE LAZARILLO DE TORMES; SACADA DE LAS
CORONICAS ANTIGUAS DE TOLEDO. por H. de Luna. Edited by Elmer R. Sims.
Austin, University of Texas Press, 1958. 138p. $1.50
    This is a Spanish-language edition based on the first edition with notes.

1182.
----------. VIDA DE LAZARILLO DE TORMES Y DE SUS FORTUNAS Y ADVERSIDADES.
Edited by Everett W. Hesse and Harry F. Williams. Introd. by Americo Castro.
Rev. ed. Madison, University of Wisconsin Press, 1969. 84p. $1.50
    The notes and introduction in this Spanish-language version of Lazarillo
are scholarly and illuminate for the reader the background of 16th century
Spain, as well as facets in the character of Lazarillo and the various masters
he served.

1183.
Lea, Tom. BRAVE BULLS. Boston, Little, Brown, 1969. 224p. illus. $1.95
    Describes the art and techniques of bullfights.

1184.
Leiris, Michel. PICASSO AND THE HUMAN COMEDY. New York, Random House, 1971.
105p. illus. $1.95
    The author presents a witty and insightful work about the famous contempo-
rary artist.

1185.
Livermore, Harold V. A HISTORY OF SPAIN. 2d. ed., New York, Funk and Wag-
nalls 1967. 484p. maps. $2.95
    A thorough and valuable history of Spain intended for use in college courses.
Includes a good bibliography.

1186.
----------. A NEW HISTORY OF PORTUGAL. New York, Cambridge University Press,
1967. 363p. illus. maps. $2.95
    Traces the political history of Portugal, from pre-Roman Lusitania to the
republic's loss of Goa in 1962. It is a well-balanced, dispassionate, and
comprehensive survey. This is the best history of Portugal available in
English.

1187.
Longland, Jean R. SELECTIONS FROM CONTEMPORARY PORTUGUESE POETRY: A BILINGUAL
SELECTION. Ilus. by Anne Marie Jauss. Foreword by Ernesto Guerra Da Cal.
96p. illus. $2.95
    Through excellent English translations from as many as 28 modern and
nearly modern poets, along with the original versions, a little bibliographical
detail, and some delightful illustrations, Miss Longland provides a thorough
introduction to contemporary Portuguese poetry.

1188.
López Estrada, Francisco, and John Estep Keller. ANTONIO VILLEGAS' EL
ABENCERRAJE. Chapel Hill, University of North Carolina Press, 1964. 86p.
$3.50
    A study of this early 16th century narrative based on a theme from Moorish
romances.

1189.
Lott, Robert E. THE STRUCTURE AND STYLE OF AZORIN'S EL CABALLERO INACTUAL.
Athens, University of Georgia Press, 1963. 108p. (University of Georgia
monographs, 10) $2.75
    An attempt to provide a thorough interpretation of one of the most complex
novels of Azorín. The author also analyzes the work's significance and
aesthetic structure. [Charles Fleener]

1191.
Luis de Granada. WISDOM'S WORKSHOP. St. Louis, Mo., Herder, 1970. 267p.
$1.00
Luis de Granada (1504-1588) was a Spanish mystic, writer, and translator
who wrote in Latin, Portuguese, and Spanish. This work includes fragments
from his Suma de la vida cristiana.

1192.
Lyon, Richard Colton, ed. SANTAYANA ON AMERICA: ESSAYS, NOTES, AND LETTERS
OF AMERICAN LIFE, LITERATURE, AND PHILOSOPHY. New York, Harcourt, Brace,
and World, 1968. 307p. $3.75
These essays, notes, and letters were written over a 60-year period, 1890-
1951. The editor has divided them according to subject, thus the reader is
allowed to observe George Santayana discourse on "The American Intellect,"
"The American Will," and "The American Imagination."

1193.
McCrary, William Carlton. THE GOLDFINCH AND THE HAWK: A STUDY OF LOPE DE VEGA'S
EL CABALLERO DE OLMEDO. Chapel Hill, University of North Carolina Press, 1970.
362p. $5.00
This is a thorough critical edition of El caballero de Olmedo, a historical
play.

1194.
Machado y Ruiz, Antonio. JUAN DE MAIRENA: EPIGRAMS, MAXIMS, MEMORANDA, AND
MEMOIRS OF AN APOCRYPHAL PROFESSOR. Edited and translated by Ben Bellitt.
Berkeley, University of California Press, 1963. 135p. $1.50
A very good English translation of Juan de Mairena; sentencias, donaires,
apuntes y recuerdos de un profesor apócrifo (1936) which consists of philoso-
phic aphorisms and prose fragments by the great Spanish lyric poet.

1195.
Madariaga, Salvador de. DON QUIXOTE: AN INTRODUCTORY ESSAY IN PSYCHOLOGY.
Rev. ed. New York, Oxford University Press, 1968. 185p. $1.50
Madariaga wrote Guía del lector del Quijote in 1926, and published his own
English translation in 1934 in London. He is a product of three cultures and
writes in Spanish, English, and French; all translations of his books are his
own. He is the most cosmopolitan of Spain's 20th century intellectuals.

1196.
----------. THE FALL OF THE SPANISH EMPIRE. New rev. ed. New York, Collier
Books, 1963. 414p. $1.50
First published in 1947, this is the continuation of Rise of the Spanish
American Empire. Madariaga maintains that strife between brothers caused the
end of the Spanish empire, especially when the Creole brothers, restless under
a tyrannical Spanish father, turned to foreign but equally tyrannical in-
spiration for revolt.

1197.
Mahn, C. A. DENKMALER DER BASKISCHEN SPRACHE. New York, Humanities Press,
1971. 362p. $6.00
A study of Basque by a German philologist.

1198.
Marías, Julián. HISTORY OF PHILOSOPHY. Translated by Stanley Applebaum and
Clarence C. Strowbridge. New York, Dover, 1967. 505p. $2.75
A translation of the best-selling Spanish survey of western philosophy,
Historia de la filosofía (1966). The main topics treated are Greek, Christian,
Medieval, and Modern philosophy. Marías was a disciple of Ortega y Gasset.
A special preface to the English edition and a bibliography are included.

1199.
----------. MEDITACIONES SOBRE LA SOCIEDAD ESPANOLA. Philadelphia, Center
for Curriculum Development, 1971. 149p. $1.20
Textbook edition of a noted philosopher's description of Spanish society.

1200.
----------. MODOS DE VIVIR: UN OBSERVADOR ESPAÑOL EN LOS ESTADOS UNIDOS.
Edited by Edward R. Mulvihill and R. G. Sánchez. New York, Oxford University
Press, 1964. 182p. $2.50
   Spain's most influential philosopher of the second half of the 20th
century surveys the U.S. in a manner reminiscent of De Toqueville's famed
account.

1201.
Marquerie, Alfredo. NOVELAS PARA LEER EN UN VIAJE. Edited by Gustavus H.
Miller, and Jerónimo Mallo. New York, Scribner, 1962. 215p. $3.35
   Includes short stories by a Spanish writer.

1202.
Martínez Ruiz, José. DOÑA INÉS, by Azorín [pseud.] Edited by L. Living-
stone. New York, Appleton-Century-Crofts, 1969. 208p. $3.25
   Doña Inés appeared in 1925. It is an evocative vignette of people and
places and a criticism of Spanish life. The tone is personal, aesthetic,
and emotional. Includes notes and vocabulary.

1203.
----------. EXPERIENCIA DE LA VIDA, by Azorín [pseud.] Philadelphia, Center
for Curriculum Development, 1968. 200p. $1.20
   Azorín had a profound influence on Spanish literature during the first
20 years of this century. He understood Spanish spirituality and had a
feeling for the Castilian countryside.

1204.
----------. POLITICA Y LITERATURA by Azorin [pseud.] Philadelphia, Chilton
Books, 1967. 162p. $0.90
   Essays in criticism by the outstanding Spanish critic and writer.

1205.
Martinez Sierra, Gregorio. MAMA. Edited by Margaret S. Husson. New York,
Norton, 1964. 156p. $1.95
   This play was first published in 1912. Martinez Sierra's plays ushered
in the revival of modern Spanish theater.

1206.
----------. SUEÑO DE UNA NOCHE DE AGOSTO. Edited by D. Walsh. New York,
Norton, 1952. 189p. $1.95
   A noted play by Spain's well-known playwright.

1207.
Mattingly, Garrett. THE ARMADA. Boston, Houghton, Mifflin, 1962. 444p.
illus. $2.65
   This is an account of the 1588 Spanish attempt to conquer England, first
published in 1959. It provides a good background to 16th century Latin
America.

1208.
----------. CATHERINE OF ARAGON. New York, Random House, 1960. 415p.
$1.95
   An excellent and well-researched biography of the Spanish princess who
became Henry the Eighth's first wife.

1209.
----------. THE INVINCIBLE ARMADA AND ELIZABETHAN ENGLAND. Charlottesville,
University Press of Virginia. $1.25
   The author discusses the interpretations, which have been substantially
revised during the last half century, of the defeat of the Spanish Armada.

1210.
Matute, Ana María. DOCE HISTORIAS DE LA ARTAMILA DE ANA MARÍA MATUTE.
Edited by Robert A. G. Mead and Gloria Durán. New York, Harcourt, Brace,
and World, 1965. 172p. illus. $3.75

Ana María Matute is Spain's most gifted contemporary short story writer.
She depicts places, people, and events with humor and warmth.

1211.
Menéndez Pidal, Ramón. THE SPANIARDS IN THEIR HISTORY. Translated by Walter
Starkie. New York, Norton, 1966. 147p. maps. $1.65
A description of the Spanish character by Spain's leading humanist, this
is an important contribution to the study of Spanish civilization. It was
first published in 1950.

1212.
Mezerik, Avrahm G. GOA: PORTUGUESE COLONIAL POLICY, INDIAN CAMPAIGN, U.N.
RECORD, CHRONOLOGY. New York, International Review Service, 1962. 55p.
maps. $5.00
Reviews Portuguese colonial policy towards Goa.

1213.
Michel, Joseph, ed. VALLE-INCLÁN: PÁGINAS SELECTAS. New York, Prentice-
Hall, 1969. 198p. $2.95
The editor has selected a representative sampling from the works of the
great Spanish novelist.

1214.
Micheletti, Emma. VELASQUEZ. New York, Grosset & Dunlap, 1969. 120p. illus.
$1.25
A handsome edition about the work of the famous Spanish painter, illustrated
with 80 full-color drawings.

1215.
Michener, James A. IBERIA; SPANISH TRAVELS AND REFLECTIONS. Greenwich,
Conn., Fawcett Publications, 1968. 960p. illus. $1.95
A well-known American author gives his interpretation of that complex
and magnificent country which is Spain. He brings fresh insights to many
of the hidden places which tourists never seem to find. Photographs by
Robert Vavra enhance the text.

1216.
Mihura, Miguel. CARLOTA. Edited by Edith B. Sublette. New York, Odyssey
Press, 1963. 146p. $1.65
A contemporary play set in today's Spain by a young Spanish dramatist.

1217.
----------. MI ADORADO JUAN. Edited by John V. Falconieri and Anthony M.
Pasquariello. Boston, Ginn-Blaisdell, 1964. 110p. illus. $1.65
Textbook edition of a contemporary Spanish play.

1218.
Miller, Samuel J.T., and John P. Spielman, Jr. CRISTÓBAL ROJAS Y SPINOLA,
CAMERALIST AND IRENICIST, 1626-1695. Philadelphia, American Philosophical
Society, 1962. 108p. (Transactions of the American Philosophical Society,
new series, 52) $2.50
Rojas y Spinola was the bishop of Tina for most of the second half of the
17th century, and strove for the reunification of Protestants and Catholics.
The authors evoke the intellectual and social climate of the times through
the biography of their subject.

1219.
Miró Ferrer, Gabriel. EL HUMO DORMIDO. Introduction by Edmund L. King.
New York, Dell, 1967. 203p. $0.75
First published in 1919, this is one of Miró's descriptive works, in which
he presents the realities of Spain through its people, villages, and towns.

1220.
Mondragón Aguirre, Magdalena. PORQUE ME DA LA GANA. Edited by John Sarnacki.
New York, Odyssey Press, 1968. 108p. $1.65

1221.
Montoro, A. G. and S. A. Rigol. EN TORNO AL POEMA: DE BECQUER A MIGUEL HERNÁNDEZ. New York, Harcourt, Brace and World, 1969. 431p. $3.95
   A survey of Spanish poetry.

1222.
Nach, James. PORTUGAL IN PICTURES. Rev. ed. New York, Sterling Pub. Co., 1966. 64p. illus., maps. $1.00
   A popular, illustrated survey of Portugal, its people, and their culture, with handsome black and white photographs.

1223.
Nelson, Lowry, Jr., ed. CERVANTES; A COLLECTION OF CRITICAL ESSAYS. Englewood Cliffs, N.J., Prentice-Hall, 1969. 176p. $1.95
   A number of noted contemporary critics, such as Thomas Mann, Leon Spitzer, W. H. Auden,and the editor present their views on the great Spanish writer, analyzing Don Quixote, as well as his lesser-known works.

1224.
Norman, Barbara. THE SPANISH COOKBOOK. New York, Bantam, 1967. 197p. $0.75
   The author has selected representative recipes of Spanish food adapted for the U.S. kitchen.

1225.
O'Hara, Frank. NEW SPANISH PAINTINGS AND SCULPTURE. New York, Museum of Modern Art, 1960. 52p. illus. $1.95
   The catalog of an exhibition that surveyed the works of 16 contemporary Spanish artists. The director of the exhibition provides the text which is accompanied by 44 pages of black and white illustrations.

1226.
Ornstein, Jacob, ed. LUIS DE LUCENA: REPETICIÓN DE AMORES. Chapel Hill, University of North Carolina Press, 1954. 130p. $5.00
   This is annotated edition of Luis de Lucena's work.

1227.
Ortega y Gasset, José. CONCORD AND LIBERTY. New York, Norton, 1946. 182p. $1.95
   Essays by Spain's influential philosopher who embodied more than any other writer the spirit of the first three decades of the 20th century. He has commented on every important subject of our time.

1228.
----------. DEHUMANIZATION OF ART AND OTHER ESSAYS ON ART, CULTURE, AND LITERATURE. Rev. ed. Princeton, N.J., Princeton University Press, 1968. 204p. $2.45
   Five essays in which Ortega expresses his incisive views on the arts and literature in the 20th century. "Dehumanization of Art" and "Notes on the Novel" appeared in 1925; "On Point of View in the Arts" and "In Search of Goethe from Within" were first published in 1949; and "The Self and the Other" in 1952.

1229.
----------. HISTORY AS A SYSTEM. New York, Norton, 1961. 269p. $1.85
   Translation of Historia como sistema (1941) in which the outstanding Spanish philosopher expresses his views on history. To Ortega's thought and influence is added his extraordinary value as a writer.

1230.
----------. MAN AND CRISIS. Translated by Mildred Adams. New York, Norton, 1958. 217p. $1.75

1231.
----------. MAN AND PEOPLE. Translated by Willard Trask. New York, Norton, 1957. 272p. $1.95

1232.

----------. MEDITATIONS ON QUIXOTE. New York, Norton, 1961. 192p. $1.55

Ortega's first book, Meditaciones del Quijote (1914), outlines his philosophy, in which he conceives the ego as the first reality surrounded by circumstances and defines circumstances as silent things which are in one's immediate surroundings.

1233.

----------. MISSION OF THE UNIVERSITY. New York, Norton, 1967. 194p. $1.25

An essay on the aims and purposes of the university is presented in a systematic form.

1234.

----------. THE MODERN THEME. Introd. by José Ferrater Mora. New York, Harper and Row, 1961. 152p. $1.45

Translation of El tema de nuestro tiempo (1923) in which Ortega systematized his purely philosophical thought based on life itself. To the pure reason of idealism he opposed a "vital reason," constantly affected by the circumstances of life.

1235.

----------. ON LOVE. New York, World Pub. Co., 1969. 241p. $2.25

An essay on love by the Spanish philosopher who was very influential during the first half of the 20th century. He embodied more, perhaps, than any other writer or our time, the contemporary spirit. The original Spanish edition is entitled Estudios sobre el amor (1939).

1236.

----------. THE ORIGIN OF PHILOSOPHY. Translated by Toby Talbot. New York, Norton, 1967. 125p. $1.25

Essays on the origins of philosophy which had great impact on Latin American thought during the first half of the 20th century.

1237.

----------. LA REDENCIÓN DE LAS PROVINCIAS. Chilton Educational Series, 1967. 171p. $0.90

A series of essays, articles, and speeches published in 1931, in which Ortega expounded his ideas on current political events.

1238.

----------. THE REVOLT OF THE MASSES. New York, Norton, 1957. 190p. $1.50

First published in 1932 under the title La revolución de las masas, this is Ortega's most widely read book. In it he explains modern society as an inversion of values due to a crisis in European culture and to the preponderance of mass culture.

1239.

----------. SUS MEJORES PÁGINAS. Edited by Manuel Durán. Englewood Cliffs, N.J., Prentice-Hall, 1966. 250p. $3.95

Professor Durán has selected a representative series of essays by the great Spanish philosopher.

1240.

----------. WHAT IS PHILOSOPHY. New York, Norton, 1961. 252p. $1.85

1241.

Orwell, George. HOMAGE TO CATALONIA. New York, Harcourt, Brace and World, 1952. 232p. (Harvest book, 1962) $1.95

A memoir of the British novelist's experiences as a journalist and soldier in the Spanish Civil War. It is also a record of the author's disillusionment with totalitarian communism. Lionel Trilling, in his introduction to this edition, calls this work "one of the important documents of our time."
[Charles Fleener]

1242.
Palacio Valdés, Armando. JOSÉ. Translated by Harriet De Onís. Great Neck,
New York, Barron's Educational Series, 1961. $1.50
   Palacio Valdés (1853-1938) was a Spanish short story writer, novelist, and
essayist. He achieved fame in 1885 with José a novel of fishermen and the sea.

1243.
Pardo Bazán. Emilia. LOS PAZOS DE ULLOA. Philadelphia, Chilton Educational
Series, 1962. 102p. $1.20
   One of Prado Bazán best novels, it first appeared in 1886. It is a
Zolaesque study of social decay in a rural Galician setting.

1244.
Parker, Jack Horace, and Arthur M. Fox, eds. LOPE DE VEGA STUDIES, 1937-63;
A CRITICAL SURVEY AND ANNOTATED BIBLIOGRAPHY. Toronto, University of Toronto
Press, 1970. 366p. $6.00
   This is a thoroughly annotated bibliography of works about the great
Spanish Golden Age dramatist written between 1937 and 1962.

1245.
Parry, John Horace. THE AGE OF RECONNAISSANCE. New York, New American Library,
1964. 383p. illus. $1.25
   Excellent study of European expansion from 1450 to 1650 by an expert in
maritime history. Includes a good bibliography.

1246.
----------. THE ESTABLISHMENT OF EUROPEAN HEGEMONY 1415-1715; TRADE AND
EXPLORATION IN THE AGE OF THE RENAISSANCE. New York, Harper and Row, 1961.
202p. $1.45
   This is a succinct history of European expansion, emphasizing economic
motivations. Includes a good bibliography.

1247.
----------. ed. EUROPEAN RECONNAISSANCE. New York, Harper and Row, 1970.
219p. maps. $3.95

1248.
Paso Alfonso. LA CORBATA. Ed. by E.B. Sublette. New York, Odyssey Press,
1967. 146p. $1.65
   Alfonso Paso is a contemporary Spanish playwright. This is an annotated
edition of one of his most popular dramas.

1249.
Payne, Robert, ed. THE CIVIL WAR IN SPAIN, 1936-1939. New York, Fawcett
World Library, 1968. 336p. maps, tables. $0.95
   The editor has selected eye-witness accounts by participants including
George Orwell, John Dos Passos, and Arthur Koestler.

1250.
Paine, Stanley G. FALANGE: A HISTORY OF SPANISH FASCISM. Stanford, Calif.,
Stanford University Press, 1966. 316p. $2.95
   The author presents an excellent history of Spanish fascism from 1931 to
1959 with special emphasis on the 1936-1945 period. Includes bibliographies.

1251.
----------. FRANCO'S SPAIN. New York, Crowell, 1967. 142p. tables.
$1.95
   An analysis of Spain's evolution under Franco's regime, presenting the
country within the broader European context. The author includes a brief
biography of Franco, and also surveys to some extent the Spanish Civil War
which is used as the historical background for the development of the regime.
Includes bibliographies.

1252.
----------. THE SPANISH REVOLUTION. New York, Norton, 1970. 398p. maps.
$3.25

This is a thorough and important book on the Spanish Revolution. It traces
the forces that brought about the Revolution, such as the socialists, the
military, and other segments of society. It also analyzes the legacy of the
19th century within the broad political spectrum of Spain between World Wars
I and II. Includes bibliographies.

1253.
Paz, Elena, ed. FAVORITE SPANISH FOLKSONGS; TRADITIONAL SONGS FROM SPAIN AND
LATIN AMERICA. Compiled and edited by Elena Paz. New York, Oak Publications,
1965. 96p. illus. $2.45
This is a good selection of 49 Spanish songs with English translation and
music for voice. The text is enhanced with paintings, drawings, and woodcuts
by well-known Latin American and Spanish artists.

1254.
Penrose, Boies. TRAVEL AND DISCOVERY IN THE RENAISSANCE, 1420-1620. New York,
Atheneum, 1962. 463p. maps. $1.95
This is one of the first treatments of European expansion into Asia, Africa,
and America. The emphasis is on actual exploration, but two chapters deal
with cartography and geographical literature. It was first published in
1952. Includes a bibliography.

1255.
Penrose, Roland. PICASSO: HIS LIFE AND WORK. New York, Schocken Books, 1962.
410p. illus. $2.45
Explores the work and life of Pablo Picasso. The illustrations are representative of many periods of the artist's work.

1256.
----------. PICASSO. New York, Universe Books, 1961. 16p. 32 plates.
$1.95
A brief text explains 32 attractive reproductions of the artist's
paintings. [Charles Fleener]

1257.
Pérez Galdós, Benito. EL AMIGO MANSO. Edited by Denah Lida. New York,
Oxford University Press, 1963. 330p. $3.50
This is a realistic novel which centers around a Quixotesque personage.
It is written in a naturalistic style.

1258.
----------. COMPASSION: Translated by T. Talbot. New York, Ungar, 1962.
282p. $1.75
Deals with the decline of an aristocratic family in Madrid in the late
19th century and the rise of the new middle class.

1259.
----------. COMPASSION; a modern translation with notes by Joan MacLean.
New York, American R.D.M. Corp., 1966. 159p. $1.95
See above.

1260.
----------. LA DESHEREDADA. Philadelphia, Chilton Books, 1964. 246p.
$1.80
Perhaps Pérez Galdós'greatest novel, this work deals with the heroine's
delusions that she is of noble birth which eventually leads to her ruin.
It was first published in 1881.

1261.
----------. LA DE BRINGAS. Edited by R. Gullon. Englewood Cliffs, N.J.,
Prentice-Hall, 1971. 321p. $3.95

1262.
----------. DOÑA PERFECTA. Translated by Harriet de Onís. Great Neck, N.Y.,
Barron's Educational Series, 1960. 235p. $1.25
Pérez Galdós fought bigotry and radicalism in this novel published in
1876.

1263.
----------. DOÑA PERFECTA. Edited by Rodolfo Cardona. New York, Dell,
1965. 281p. $0.50
     See above.

1264.
----------. MARIANELA: A STORY OF SPANISH LOVE. Translated by H. W. Lester.
New York, Barnes and Noble, 1961. 295p. $1.50
     An English translation of Pérez Galdós' classic novel.

1265.
----------. MARIANELA. Edited by N. B. Adams. Boston, Ginn-Blaisdell, 1951.
197p. illus. $3.00
     An abridged version of Pérez Galdós' well-known and widely read novel.

1266.
----------. MARIANELA. Edited by A. Romo. New York, Regents Pub. Co., 1966.
200p. $1.25
     This is an abridged version of Pérez Galdós' naturalistic novel dealing
with social and psychological reality in Spain. It was first published in
1878.

1267.
----------. MIAU. Translated by John Michael Cohen. Baltimore, Penguin
Books, 1966. 282p. $1.75
     The great Spanish novelist displays his concern for the individual in
relation to society. The protagonist is a civil servant in Madrid who has
lost his post and is gradually driven to distraction and suicide. It was
first published in 1888.

1268.
----------. LA SOMBRA DE GALDÓS. Edited by Rodolfo Cardona. New York, Norton,
1964. 147p. $2.95
     Includes selections from Pérez Galdós works.

1269.
----------. TORMENTO. Philadelphia, Chilton Books, 1967. 175p. $0.90
     This novel was first published in 1886; it is written in the style of
literary realism for which Pérez Galdós became well-known.

1270.
----------. TORQUEMADA EN LA HOGUERA. TORQUEMADA EN LA CRUZ. TORQUEMADA
EN EL PURGATORIO. TORQUEMADA Y SAN PEDRO. Philadelphia, Chilton Books,
1969. 392p. $1.80
     This is an annotated textbook edition of the Torquemada series published
between 1889 and 1895. These works deal with the ethical decay resulting
from avarice.

1271.
----------. TRISTANA. Translated by R. Selden Rose. Peterborough, N.H.,
W.L. Bauhan, 1961. 143p. $1.95
     This short novel is a masterful study of possessiveness carried to the
point of vice. It presents a microcosmic view of Spanish culture and values.

1272.
Picasso, Pablo. DESIRE CAUGHT BY THE TAIL: A PLAY. Translated by Bernard
Frechtman, New York, Citadel Press, 1962. 60p. illus. $0.95
     This is a unique play written in three days during the German occupation
of Paris. Included are line drawings by the author. Originally published
under the title Le désir attrapé par la queue.

1273.
----------. DRAWINGS OF PICASSO. Edited by Arthur Millier. Alhambra, Calif.,
A. Borden, 1961. 48p. (chiefly illus.) $1.75
     Excellent reproductions of Picasso's most representative works at a
reasonable price.

1274.
----------. EYE OF PICASSO. Introd. by Sir Roland Penrose. New York,
New American Library, 1967. 27p. illus. $1.25

1275.
----------. SCULPTOR'S STUDIO; ETCHINGS BY PICASSO. Introd. by William S.
Lieberman. New York, Museum of Modern Art, distributed by the New York
Graphic Arts Society. illus. $2.50
    Contains etchings by Picasso.

1276.
Pike, David Wingeate. CONJECTURE, PROPAGANDA AND DECEIT AND THE SPANISH
CIVIL WAR. Stanford, California, Institute of International Studies, 1968.
$4.00
    A study of the Spanish Civil War based on French archival materials
which have only recently became available to the public.

1277.
----------. LA CRISE ESPAGNOLE DE 1936. Stanford, California, California
Institute of International Studies, 1966. 214p. $2.50
    Analyzes the political crisis in Spain in 1936.

1278.
----------. VAE VICTIS: LOS REPUBLICANOS ESPAÑOLES REFUGIADOS EN FRANCIA,
1939-1944. Paris, Ruedo Ibérico, 1969. $1.25
    Traces the history of the Spanish Republican refugees from Spain to
France starting with 1939 up to the liberation of France in 1944. It is
based on many original sources, although the author states that all the
archives have not yet been opened to the public.

1279.
Pitt-Rivers, Julian A. THE PEOPLE OF THE SIERRA. Chicago, University of
Chicago Press, 1971. 274p. $1.95
    This excellent monograph studies the people of Alaclá de la Sierra in
Andalusia, Spain. It covers daily living and patterns of life style, and
thus provides insight into the social life of southern Spain.

1280.
Plaidy, J. THE SPANISH INQUISITION: ITS RISE, GROWTH AND END. New York,
Citadel Press, 1970. 341p. $3.95
    A diffusely organized superficial study of the Spanish Inquisition.

1281.
Prestage, Edgar D. FRANCISCO MANUEL DE MELLO. New York, Hispanic Society
of America, 1969. 110p. illus. $2.00
    Studies the life and works of Francisco Mello [i.e. Melo] a Portuguese
literary figure of the 17th century who also spent a considerable part of
his life in Spain. He became famous for his voluminous historical and
literary writings.

1282.
Puhl, Louis J. THE SPIRITUAL EXERCISES OF ST. IGNATIUS: BASED ON STUDIES IN
THE LANGUAGE OF THE AUTOGRAPH. Chicago, Loyola University Press, 1968.
216p. $2.00
    A clear, idiomatic translation of the Spiritual Exercises of the Spanish
saint and founder of the Jesuit order. This edition was first published in
1955.

1283.
Puzzo, Dante Anthony. THE SPANISH CIVIL WAR. Edited by L. L. Snyder.
New York, Van Nostrand, 1969. 191p. $1.95
    A brief historical study of the Spanish Civil War, which is intended for
classroom use. It relies of some documents as well as on newspaper report.

1284.
Ramboz, Ina W. CANCIONES DE NAVIDAD. Edited by the National Textbook Corp.
Skokie, Ill., National Textbook Corp., 1969. 45p. $1.00; 5 or more $0.85 each
    Includes Christmas carols from Spain and Latin America.

1285.
Rennert, Hugo Albert. THE SPANISH STAGE IN THE TIME OF LOPE DE VEGA. New
York, Dover, 1963. 403p. $2.75
    A scholarly study of the various aspects of Spanish drama, including staging,
costumes, and actors, during the 16th and 17th centuries. [Charles Fleener]

1286.
Rey, Agapito, and A. G. Solalinde. ENSAYO DE UNA BIBLIOGRARÍA DE LAS
LEYENDAS TROYANAS EN LA LITERATURA ESPAÑOLA. Bloomington, Indiana University
Press, 1969. 103p. $1.00
    First published in 1942 by the prominent Spanish medievalist who has been
residing in the U.S. for the past 30 years, this is an annotated bibliography
of Trojan legends in Spanish literature.

1287.
----------. EL LIBRO DE LOS CIEN CAPITULOS. Bloomington, Indiana University
Press, 1960. 92p. $4.00
    A new edition of the medieval work Libro de los çient capitulos.

1288.
Rexroth, Kenneth, ed. THIRTY SPANISH POEMS OF LOVE AND EXILE. San Francisco,
City Lights Books, 1968. 31p. $1.00
    Included are Rafael Alberti, Jorge Guillén, Pablo Neruda, Federico García
Lorca, and Antonio Machado. The editor says that "only some of these poets
were born in Spain. None of them lives there today." [Charles Fleener]

1289.
Ricart, Domingo. JUAN DE VALDÉS Y EL PENSAMIENTO RELIGIOSO EUROPEO EN LOS
SIGLOS 16 y 17. Lawrence, University of Kansas Press, 1971. 223p. $2.50
    Juan de Valdés was a philosopher,religious writer, and literary critic in
16th century Spain. His writings were controversial and fearing the Inquisition he went to Rome in 1531. This work studies Valdés influence on European
philosophy.

1290.
Rikhoff, Jean ed. A QUIXOTE ANTHOLOGY. New York, Grosset and Dunlap, 1961,
372p. $2.45

1291.
Rincón, E. COPLAS SATÍRICAS Y DRAMÁTICAS DE LA EDAD MEDIA. Philadelphia,
Center for Curriculum Development, 1967. 187p. $1.20
    Contains a very good selection of Spanish medieval satiric and dramatic
ballads.

1292.
Río, Amelia Agostini de del, ed. FLORES DEL ROMANCERO. Englewood Cliffs ,
N.J., Prentice-Hall, 1970. 288p. $3.95
    The editor has assembled outstanding ballads from their origins to the
present to illustrate the development in theme, technique, style, and length.
The text also indicates the influence of ballads on other literary genres.

1293.
Rivers, Elías L., ed. THIRTY-SIX SPANISH POEMS. Boston, Houghton Mifflin,
1957. 72p. $1.75

1294.
----------. RENAISSANCE AND BAROQUE POETRY OF SPAIN WITH ENGLISH PROSE
TRANSLATIONS. New York, Dell Pub. Co., 1966. 351p. $0.95
    This is a bilingual edition of Spanish poetry of the 15th and 16th
centuries with a good introduction by the editor.

1295.
Rodriguez, Alfred and William Rosenthal, eds. THE MODERN SPANISH ESSAY.
Waltham, Mass., Blaisdell Pub. Co., 1969. 129p. $1.95
    An annotated anthology of contemporary Spanish essays intended for inter-
mediate and advanced Spanish courses. The editors provide an introduction and
notes on the writers and their works. Included are Miguel de Unamuno, José
Ortega y Gasset, Salvador de Madariaga, Azorín, Eugenio D'Ors, Gregorio
Marañón, Francisco Ayala, Pedro Laín Entralgo, and Julian Marías.

1296.
Rojas, C., ed. DE CELA A CASTILLO-NAVARRO; VEINTE AÑOS DE PROSA ESPAÑOLA
CONTEMPORÁNEA. Englewood Cliffs, N.J., Prentice-Hall, 1969. 271p. $3.95
    Includes selections of Spanish prose written from 1945 to 1965.

1297.
Rojas, Fernando de. LA CELESTINA; A NOVEL IN DIALOGUE. Translated by
Lesley Bird Simpson. Berkeley, University of California Press, 1962.
162p. illus. $1.25
    This is a very good modern translation of the classic Spanish drama.

1298.
----------. CELESTINA; A PLAY IN TWENTY-ONE ACTS ATTRIBUTED TO FERNANDO DE
ROJAS. Translated by Mack Hendricks Singleton. Madison, University of
Wisconsin Press, 1962. 299p. $1.95
    This is a scholarly version of the Spanish drama that includes all the
original editorial sources, such as letters, prologues, a modern preface,
and a critical bibliography.

1299.
----------. LA CELESTINA: TRAGICOMEDIA DE CALISTO Y MELIBEA. Prologue by
Stephen Gilman. Edited by Dorothy Severun. Philadelphia, Center for
Curriculum Development, 1970. 274p. $1.20
    This is an analytical presentation of the classic Spanish 15th century
masterpiece which many critics consider second only to Don Quijote. It was
first published in 1499. Celestina is the central character who with her
devious ways persuades Melibea to respond to Calisto, her suitor.

1300.
----------. CRITICAL EDITION OF THE FIRST FRENCH TRANSLATION, 1527, OF THE
SPANISH CLASSIC LA CELESTINA. Edited by J. G. Brault. Detroit, Wayne State
University Press, 482p. $8.00
    A thoroughly analyzed and annotated edition of the first French translation
of the Tragicomedia de Calisto y Melibea, which will be of great interest to
students of medieval Spanish literature.

1301.
----------. THE SPANISH BAWD: LA CELESTINA; BEING THE TRAGICOMEDY OF CALISTO
AND MELIBEA. Translated and edited by John Michael Cohen. Baltimore, Penguin
Books, 1964. 248p. $1.25
    This is a very good English translation of this great work of Spanish
literature.

1302.
Rojas Zorrilla, Francisco de. DEL REY ABAJO NINGUNO. Translated by Raymond
R. MacCurdy. Englewood Cliffs, N.J., Prentice-Hall, 1970. 128p. $2.95
    Rojas Zorrilla (1607-1648) was one of the outstanding dramatists of the
Spanish Golden Age. This play was first published in 1650. It deals with
the conflict between two national ideals, loyalty to the king and personal
honor. The introduction explains the Spanish code of honor.

1303.
Roth, Cecil. THE SPANISH INQUISITION. New York, Norton, 1964. 316p. illus.
$1.95
    First published in 1937, this book attempts to trace the history of the
Spanish Inquisition. Appendices provide transcripts of a trial for heresy.

1304.
Roy, Gregor. CERVANTES' DON QUIXOTE. New York, Monarch Press, 1965. 106p.
$1.00
    A guide for the college student. The plot is discussed, characters
analyzed, and possible examination questions are suggested and answered.
[Charles Fleener]

1305.
Salinas Pedro. EL DEFENSOR. Philadelphia, Chilton Educational Division,
1969. 195p. $0.90
    Salinas (1892-1951) was one of the most outstanding Spanish lyric poets
of the 20th century. In 1936 he established residence in the U.S. and taught
at the Johns Hopkins University, the University of Puerto Rico, and Wellesley
College. He wrote an intellectual type of poetry in which outward simplicity
was arrived at through complex mental processes.

1306.
----------. REALITY AND THE POET IN SPANISH POETRY. Introd. by Jorge Guillén.
Baltimore, Johns Hopkins Press, 1940. 165p. $1.95
    A lucid critical work in which Salinas states that "the poet places himself
before reality... in order to create something else." Included are critical
essays on El Cid, Calderón de la Barca, Garcilaso, Góngora, and San Juan de
la Cruz. Jorge Guillén's 30 p. introduction on his good friend and fellow
poet is excellent.

1307.
Sallese, Nicholas Francis, and J. A. Perez. ESPAÑA: VIDA Y LITERATURA.
New York, Van Nostrand, 1969. 271p. $4.95
    Includes a brief outline of Spanish culture and literature for students
of intermediate Spanish.

1308.
Salter, Cedric. INTRODUCING SPAIN. Rev. ed. New York, Transatlantic Arts,
1971. 210p. $2.45
    Describes Spain in general terms.

1309.
Sánchez, José ed. NINETEENTH CENTURY SPANISH VERSE. New York, Appleton-
Century-Crofts, 1949. 374p. $3.25
    The editor presents selections from 19th century Spanish poets such as
José Espronceda, Gustavo Adolfo Bécquer, Rosalía de Castro, and others.

1310.
Sánchez-Cantón, Francisco Javier. PRADO. New York, New American Library,
1969. 207p. illus. $4.95
    Attractive illustrations from the rich collections of Spain's Prado
Museum are the core of this handsome book.

1311.
Sánchez Silva, J. M. MARCELINO PAN Y VINO. Edited by E. R. Mulvihill and
R. G. Sánchez. New York, Oxford University Press, 1967. 121p. $1.95
    A book based on the Spanish folk tale which became an internationally
acclaimed, award-winning motion picture of Spain.

1312.
Santayana, George. CHARACTER AND OPINION IN THE UNITED STATES. New York,
Norton, 1967. 233p. $1.65
    Santayana (1863-1952) was born in Spain but lived most of his life in
Boston. In this work he deals with conflict of materialism and idealism
in American life. Mid-19th century New England is his point of departure
for a penetrating analysis of American civilization.

1313.
----------. THE LAST PURITAN: A MEMOIR IN THE FORM OF A NOVEL. New York,
Scribner's 1964. 602p. $2.45
    This fictionalized autobiography, first published in 1936, is the only

novel written by Santayana. In it he analyzes the New England character and comments on the moral and material idols of the 20th century. [Charles Fleener]

1314.
----------. PERSONS AND PLACES:THE BACKGROUND OF MY LIFE. New York, Scribner's 1944. 262p. $1.45
The great Spanish-born philosopher writes of his early years in Spain, his arrival in the U.S., and ends with his graduation from Harvard. The book contains many interesting comments on late 19th-century Spain. [Charles Fleener]

1315.
----------. THE SENSE OF BEAUTY: BEING THE OUTLINE OF AESTHETIC THEORY. New York, Dover, 1955. 168p. illus. $1.00
First published in 1896, the author discusses here "why, when, and how beauty appears, what conditions an object must fulfill to be beautiful, what elements of our nature make us sensitive to beauty." The book is written in an elegant literary style. [Charles Fleener]

1316.
----------. SOLILOQUIES IN ENGLAND AND LATER SOLILOQUIES. Ann Arbor, University of Michigan Press, 1967. 264p. $2.25
Contains 55 essays written from 1914 to 1921 when Santayana was at Oxford. The essays show the thoughts of a detached philosopher and a superb stylist. [Charles Fleener]

1317.
Schapiro, J. Salwyn. ANTICLERICALISM; CONFLICT BETWEEN CHURCH AND STATE IN FRANCE, ITALY, AND SPAIN. New York, Van Nostrand, 1967. 207p. $1.75
The author outlines the history of Roman Catholic anti-clericalism through the modern periods of Spain, France, and Italy. Included also are 44 readings, six of which deal exclusively with Spain. Includes bibliographies. [Charles Fleener]

1318.
Schierbeek, Bert. SPAIN. Chicago, Follett Pub. Co., 1967. 128p. illus. $1.65
A general description of Spain.

1319.
Scholberg, Kenneth R. PIERRE BAYLE AND SPAIN. Chapel Hill, University of North Carolina Press, 1958. 40p. $3.50
Pierre Bayle (1647-1706) was an erudite and controversial French philosopher and theologian, and one of the most interesting men of his time. This book explores Bayle's impact on Spanish thought of the period.

1320.
----------. ed. and trans. SPANISH LIFE IN THE LATE MIDDLE AGES. Chapel Hill, University of North Carolina Press, 1965. 180p. (University of North Carolina. Studies in the Romance languages and literatures, 57) $4.00
This collection of prose writings from 15th-century Castile focuses on the court of Juan II. The pieces describe the land and the people, political and intellectual life, warfare, knighthood, and daily life.

1321.
Schonberg, Jean Louis. A LA RECHERCHE DE LORCA. Port Washington, N.Y., Paris Publications, 1971. $8.50
An important study about the life and work of the great Spanish poet.

1322.
Sender, Ramón José. CRÓNICA DEL ALBA. Edited by Florence H. Sender. New York, Appleton-Century-Crofts, 1970. 212p. $2.65
Textbook edition of the contemporary Spanish novelist's work which was published in 1942. The novel goes back to Sender's childhood days in Aragón, portraying with humor and tenderness the unfolding of a boy's character.

1323.
----------. JUBILEO EN EL ZÓCALO. Edited by Florence H. Sender. New York, Appleton-Century-Crofts, 1964. 215p. map. $2.65
Sender's vigorous novelistic style is well represented in this novel.

1324.
----------. SEVEN RED SUNDAYS. New York, Collier-Macmillan, 1967. 192p. $0.95
This is an English translation of Siete domingos rojos (1932) which deals with an abortive workers' revolution in Madrid.

1325.
----------. TRES EJEMPLOS DE AMOR Y UNA TEORÍA. Philadelphia, Center for Curriculum Development, 1969. 181p. $2.00

1326.
Seneca, Lucius Annaeus. THYESTES. Translated by Moses Hadas. Indianapolis, Bobbs-Merrill, 1957. 32p. (Library of liberal arts series, 76) $0.50
The Hispanic-born philosopher, spokesman for Roman stoicism, is here represented by one of his finest tragedies. The late Moses Hadas' translation is excellent. [Charles Fleener]

1327.
Seris, Homero. MANUAL DE BIBLIOGRAFÍA DE LA LITERATURA ESPAÑOLA. New York, Hispanic Society of America, 1962. 2 v. $3.50
Originally published in 1954, this is an extensive bibliography of Spanish literature organized by subjects.

1328.
Shaw, L., and C. Ibañez. CARTAS DE ZARAGOZA. New York, St. Martin's Press, 1971. 321p. illus. $1.80

1329.
Simon and Schuster. Editorial Staff. PORTUGAL. New York, 1971. 245p. illus., maps. $3.50
Covers all there is to see in Portugal. The various points of interest are rated with one, two, or three stars. Includes maps and very good illustrations.

1330.
Smith, C. Colin, ed. SPANISH BALLADS. New York, Pergamon Press, 1964. 220p. $2.95
After a 50-page introduction to the literary background, the editor presents 70 ballads in the original Spanish, each explained in accompanying notes. The ballads, ranging from the 8th to the 16th century, fall into three categories: historical, Carolingian, and novelesque. [Charles Fleener]

1331.
Spaulding, Robert K. HOW SPANISH GREW. Berkeley, University of California Press, 1962. 259p. $1.50
First published in 1943, this is an interesting history of the evolution and structure of the Spanish language.

1332.
Stansky, Peter, and William Abraham. JOURNEY TO THE FRONTIER; THE ROADS TO THE SPANISH CIVIL WAR. New York, Norton, 1970. 430p. illus. $2.45
Julian Bell and John Cornford, the subjects of this dual biography, were among the thousands of Europeans and Americans who made their way to Spain in the 1930's to fight for the Republic. It is a striking account of life and death in the Spanish Civil War.

1333.
Strongin, Theodore, comp. CASALS. Illustrated by Vytas Valaitis. New York, Grossman, 1966. 112p. illus. $3.50
Vytas Valaitis photographed Pablo Casals, the great Spanish cellist, at work and at play. Theodore Strongin provided the introduction and a biography of Casals.

1334.
Sturman, Marianne. DON QUIXOTE NOTES. Lincoln, Nebr., Cliff's Notes, 1964. 89p. $1.00
This essay presents a discussion of the action and thought of Don Quixote and a concise interpretation of its artistic merits and significance. Chapter summaries and selected questions are included.

1335.
Suárez, Francisco. DISPUTATION SIX ON FORMAL AND UNIVERSAL UNITY. Translated by J. F. Ross. Milwaukee, Wis., Marquette University Press, 1964. 123p. $3.50
Francisco Suárez (1548-1617), the Spanish theologian and philosopher, was the most important figure of the second flowering of Scholasticism. His principal work, Disputationes Metaphysicae (of which the present work is a portion) was used for over a century as the textbook in philosophy in most European universities, Protestant and Catholic alike.

1336.
----------. ON THE VARIOUS KINDS OF DISTINCTIONS. Translated by Cyril Vollert. Milwaukee, Wis., Marquette University Press, 1947. 67p. $1.50
This is a work dealing with philosophy by the influential Spanish philosopher of the late 16th century.

1337.
Sutton, Denys. DIEGO VELASQUEZ. New York, Barnes and Noble, 1967. 89p. illus. $0.95
Contains over 50 illustrations, almost half in color. The accompanying text is concise and it describes the life and work of this great Spanish painter of the 17th century.

1338.
Tardy, William Thomas, ed. DOS NOVELAS PICARESCAS. Skokie, Ill., National Textbook Corp., 1968. 129p. $1.00; five or more $0.85 each.

1339.
Téllez, Gabriel de. EL BURLADOR DE SEVILLA; LA PRUDENCIA EN LA MUJER, by Tirso de Molina [pseud.] New York, Dell, 1965. 288p. $0.50
Tirso de Molina (1584-1648) was a famous Spanish dramatist of the Lope de Vega school. El burlador de Sevilla y convidado de piedra (1630), his most acclaimed play, was the first Don Juan drama in world literature. La prudencia en la mujer (1633) is a historical play.

1340.
Thompson, C., ed. CINCO COMEDIAS. Skokie, Ill., National Text-book Corp., 1969. 162p. $1.00, 5 or more $0.85 each
Includes annotated, abridged editions of five Spanish plays.

1341.
Thomas, Hugh. THE SPANISH CIVIL WAR. New York, Harper and Row, 1963. 720p. illus., maps, tables. $3.45
A comprehensive account, with a good summary of the historical antecedents of the war. It is amply illustrated with maps and photographs. Includes a bibliography. [Charles Fleener]

1342.
Traverso, Edmundo. THE SPANISH-AMERICAN WAR: A STUDY IN POLICY CHANGE. Boston, Heath, 1968. 140p. $1.80
Reexamines the Spanish-American war and U.S. policy.

1343.
Trend, John Brande. THE CIVILIZATION OF SPAIN. 2d. ed. New York, Oxford University Press, 1967. 138p. maps. $1.85
In six essays Prof. Trend outlines the history of Spain and her cultural achievements. This is a scholarly and lucid survey ranging from the Phoenicians to the Falange. The text stops at the Civil War, but a revised bibliography by Henry Kamen lists the principal secondary sources for the study of Hispanic history and culture into the 1960's. [Charles Fleener]

1344.

----------. LUIS MILÁN AND THE VIHUELISTAS. New York, Hispanic Society of
America, 1969. 170p. illus. $2.00
   The vihuela is an ancient Spanish musical instrument used by troubadours,
similar to the Spanish guitar. The vihuela was especially popular in 16th
century Spain. Luis Milán wrote a definitive work on vihuela history and
music: Libro de música de vihuela de mano.... (1536)

1345.
Turnbull, Eleanor L. TEN CENTURIES OF SPANISH POETRY; AN ANTHOLOGY IN ENGLISH
VERSE WITH ORIGINAL TEXTS FROM THE 11th CENTURY TO THE GENERATION OF 1898.
Introd. by Pedro Salinas. Baltimore, Johns Hopkins Press, 1969. $2.95
   This is an anthology in English translations tracing the original Spanish
texts of the vast panorama of Spanish poetry from its origins in the Mozarabic
ballads of the 11th century to the leading figures of the Generation of 1898.
A very important and useful work.

1346.
Turner, Raymond. GONZALO FERNÁNDEZ DE OVIEDO Y VALDÉS. Chapel Hill, University of North Carolina Press, 1967. 61p. $3.50
   This monograph studies an early chronicle of Spanish exploration and conquest in the New World.

1347.
Unamuno y Jugo, Miguel de. ABEL SÁNCHEZ AND OTHER STORIES. Translated by
Anthony Kerrigan. Chicago, Regnery,1956. 216p. $1.45
   Includes three stories by the Spanish Basque philosopher essayist, poet,
and novelist: Abel Sánchez; (1917) The madness of Doctor Montarco; and
Saint Emmanuel the Good, Martyr (1933).

1348.
----------. THE AGONY OF CHRISTIANITY. Translated by Kurt F. Reinhardt.
New York, Ungar, 1960. 155p. $1.45
   English translation of La agonía del cristianismo (1925), an important
essay on ethics and the modern world.

1349.
----------. DOS NOVELAS CORTAS. Edited by James Russell Stamm and Herbert
E. Isar. Boston, Ginn, 1961. 127p. illus. $3.25

1350.
----------. RELATOS DE UNAMUNO. Edited by E. K. Paucker. New York,
Appleton-Century-Crofts, 1969. 199p. illus. $3.25
   This is an annotated textbook edition of essays and short stories by one
of Spain's most important literary figures.

1351.
----------. THREE EXEMPLARY NOVELS. Edited by Angel Flores. New York, Grove
Press, 1956. 227p. $1.95
   Includes English translations of Tres novelas ejemplares, comprising The
Marquis of Lumbria, Two mothers, and Nothing less than a man. This work was
first published in 1920. Unamuno dissects the Spanish psyche and characterizes
intrinsic Spanish values.

1352.
----------. TRAGIC SENSE OF LIFE. Translated by J. C. Flitch. New York,
Dover, 1967. 311p. $2.50
   This is Unamuno's most highly regarded essay, in which he states "my work
... is to combat all those who live resigned, be it to Catholicism, to
rationalism, or to agnosticism; it is to make everyone live fearfully and
hungrily." The original title is Del sentimiento trágico de la vida (1913).

1353.
----------. UNAMUNO: SUS MEJORES PÁGINAS. Edited by P. Metzidakis. Englewood Cliffs, N.J., Prentice-Hall, 1970. 395p. $3.95
   This edition includes selections from Unamuno's incomparable essays, novels,
and poetry.

1354.
Valdés, Mario J. DEATH IN THE LITERATURE OF UNAMUNO. Urbana, University of
Illinois Press, 1964. 173p. $1.25
   This monograph is an important study of death in Unamuno's works.

1355.
Valera y Alcalá Galiano, Juan. PEPITA JIMÉNEZ. Edited by A. Romo. New York,
Regents Pub. Co., 1970. 210p. $1.25
   This is an abridged textbook edition in Spanish of a novel originally pub-
lished in 1874.

1356.
----------. PEPITA JIMÉNEZ. Translated by Harriet De Onís. Great Neck, N.Y.,
Barron's Educational Series, 1964. 181p. $1.25
   Juan Valera (1824-1905) was one of Spain's best 19th century regional
novelists. Pepita Jiménez was his first and most famous novel, published in
1874. It is a psychological study of the victory of passionate love over
divine aspirations.

1357.
Valle-Inclán, Ramón del. LUCES DE BOHEMIA; DIVINAS PALABRAS. New York, Dell,
1969. 244p. $0.60
   Valle-Inclán (1866-1936) was a Galician novelist, poet, and dramatist of
the generation of 1898. Luces de Bohemia (1921) deals with the literary and
Bohemian world that the author loved. Divinas palabras (1919) is a novel.

1358.
Vega y Carpio, Lope Félix de. CASTIGO SIN VENGANZA. Edited by C. A. Jones.
New York, Pergamon Press, 1966. 136p. $2.95
   This is a Spanish-language edition of a popular romantic comedy by Lope de
Vega.

1359.
----------. EL DUQUE DE VISEO. Philadelphia, Center for Curriculum Develop-
ment, 1969. 120p. $1.20
   This is an annotated textbook edition of a play by Spain's most acclaimed
dramatist of the Golden Age, and its greatest literary figure after Cervantes.
Lope de Vega was born in 1562 and died in 1635.

1360.
----------. FIVE PLAYS: PERIBAÑEZ; FUENTE OVEJUNA; THE DOG IN THE MANGER;
THE KNIGHT FROM OLMEDO; JUSTICE WITHOUT VENGEANCE. New York, Hill and Wang,
1967. 345p. $1.95
   English versions of a selection of five dramas and comedies.

1361.
----------. FUENTE OVEJUNA. Translated by William E. Colford. Woodbury,
N.Y., Barron's Educational Series, 1968. 201p. $1.50
   A bilingual edition of this historical drama which deals with the epic
revenge of an entire village of hard-working peasants against their feudal
lord.

1362.
----------. FUENTE OVEJUNA; LA DAMA BOBA. Introd. and notes by Everett
Hesse. New York, Dell Pub. Co., 1965. 288p. $0.50
   This is a Spanish edition of the historical play Fuente Ovejuna, and the
comedy La dama boba. In the latter Lope satirizes Spanish customs.

1363.
----------. FUENTE OVEJUNA. Edited by Alberto Romo. New York, Regents
Pub. Co., 1963. 124p. $1.25
   This is an abridged Spanish edition of Lope de Vega's celebrated historical
drama.

1364.
Watson, Foster. LUIS VIVES, EL GRAN VALENCIANO. New York, Hispanic Society
of America, 1969. 195p. illus. $2.00

Vives (1492-1540) was a Spanish philosopher and humanist from Valencia. The works which brought Vives most fame in his own century were concerned with education. This work is a brief outline of his life and works.

1365.
Weber, F. W. LITERARY PERSPECTIVES OF RAMÓN PÉREZ DE AYALA. Chapel Hill, University of North Carolina Press, 1970. 245p. $5.00
   This monograph analyzes the works of the novelist, poet, and critic,Ramón Pérez de Ayala of Spain. He was a consummate master of characterization and of novelistic technique.

1366.
Weelen, Guy. MIRÓ; 1940-1955. New York, Tudor Pub. Co., 1960. 87p. illus. $0.49
   Contains a few drawings and 14 color prints of the Barcelona-born surrealist painter. The author provides a background sketch of Joan Miró's life and work.

1367.
Welsh, Doris Varner, ed. CATALOG OF THE WILLIAM B. GREENLEE COLLECTION OF PORTUGUESE HISTORY AND LITERATURE AND THE PORTUGUESE MATERIALS IN THE NEWBERRY LIBRARY. Chicago, Newberry Library, 1959. 179. $3.00
   This is a useful catalog of an exceptional collection of Portuguese literature and history at the Newberry Library in Chicago.

1368.
Wentinck, Charles. EL GRECO. Translated by Albert J. Fransella. New York, Barnes and Noble, 1964. 89p. illus. $0.75
   The author has selected 54 excellent color reproductions of the great Spanish master's paintings. A brief text explains El Greco's difficult life and the artistic influences on it.

1369.
Whelpton, Peter. PORTUGAL. Chicago, Rand McNally, 1967. 96p. illus. maps. $1.00
   This is an attractively illustrated travel guide to Portugal.

1370.
Wilson, F. POLITICAL THOUGHT IN NATIONAL SPAIN. Champaign, Ill., Stipes Pub. Co., 1970. 282p. $2.30
   Outlines political philosophy in Spain's national history,concentrating on the last two centuries.

1371.
Winks, Robin W. AGE OF IMPERIALISM. New ed. Englewood Cliffs, N.J. Prentice-Hall, 1969. 192p. $2.45
   Includes the writings of the most influential European imperialists from the Reformation to the 20th century with accounts by their colonial subjects. This volume provides material with which to evaluate the impact of 500 years of Western colonial expansion. Includes bibliographies.

1372.
Young, Howard Thomas. JUAN RAMÓN JIMÉNEZ. New York, Columbia University Press, 1967. 48p. $1.00
   This brief study analyzes the life and work of Spain's Nobel Prize winning poet who became famous as a leading Modernist and great lyricist.

1373.
----------. THE VICTORIOUS EXPRESSION: A STUDY OF FOUR CONTEMPORARY SPANISH POETS: UNAMUNO, MACHADO, JIMÉNEZ, AND LORCA. Madison, University of Wisconsin Press, 1964. 223p. $1.95
   This is an excellent study of the four most important contemporary Spanish poets.

1374.
Zayas y Sotomayor, Maria de. NOVELAS EJEMPLARES Y AMOROSAS. Philadelphia, Chilton Books, 1969. 202p. $0.90

1375.
Zobel de Ayala, Fernando. CASA COLGADAS, CUENCA MUSEUM: SPANISH ABSTRACT
ART. New York, Wittenborn, 1967. 151p. illus. $4.50
    A brief bilingual introduction describes this collection of abstract art
housed in the Hanging Houses of Cuenca. Sculptures and paintings comprise
the greater part of this work. The more than 80 illustrations are in black
and white. [Charles Fleener]

1376.
Zorrilla y Moral, José. DON JUAN TENORIO. Edited by N. B. Adams. New York,
Appleton-Century-Crofts, 1970. 221p. $2.25
    Zorilla (1817-1893) was a Spanish romantic dramatist and lyric poet who
wrote Don Juan Tenorio in 1844. This play became his greatest stage success.
Zorrilla made his Don Juan into a warm and sympathetic character.

1377.
Zunzunegui, Juan Antonio de. CUENTOS Y PATRAÑAS DE MI RÍA. Edited by Rex
Edward Ballinger. New York, Appleton-Century-Crofts, 1966. 203p. $2.65
    This is a textbook edition of a novel by the Basque writer who was born
in 1901. The book was published in 1935. It deals with the north of Spain
and it has sharply drawn characters.

DICTIONARIES, GRAMMARS, READERS,

AND TEXTBOOKS

1378.
Abreu, Maria Isabel, and Cléa Rameh. PORTUGUESE CONTEMPORANEO. Edited by
Richard J. O'Brien. Washington, Georgetown University Press, 1967. 2 v.
illus. $3.95 each
  The authors have prepared a linguistically based grammar of Brazilian
Portuguese emphasizing everyday speech patterns.

1379.
Andújar, Julio I. MASTERING SPANISH VERBS. New York, Regents, Pub. Co.,
1968. 229p. tables $1.50
  This thorough text describes Spanish verbs and contains drills and exercises.

1380.
----------., and Robert James Dixson. SOUND TEACHING; A LABORATORY MANUAL
OF EVERYDAY SPANISH. New York, Regents Pub. Co., 1969. 306p. tables $1.75

1381.
----------. WORKBOOK IN EVERYDAY SPANISH. New York, Regents Pub. Co., 1968.
2 v. $1.25 each

1382.
Angel Juvenal Lodoño, and Robert James Dixson. MÉTODO DIRECTO DE CONVER-
SACIÓN EN ESPAÑOL. New York, Regents Pub. Co., 1966. 2 v. $1.50 each
  The authors have prepared a thorough guide to Spanish conversation. This
will be most useful for beginning and intermediate Spanish classes.

1383.
----------. TESTS AND DRILLS IN SPANISH GRAMMAR. New York, Regents Pub.
Co., 1966. 280p. $1.50
  This is a bilingual review of Spanish grammar.

1384.
Auerbach, Erich. INTRODUCTION TO ROMANCE LANGUAGES AND LITERATURE. Translated by Guy Daniels. New York, Capricorn Books, 1961. 291p. $1.65
  An introductory book to the romance languages and a brief outline of each
language's literature.

1385.
Ayllón, Cándido, and Paul Smith. SPANISH COMPOSITION THROUGH LITERATURE.
Englewood Cliffs, N.J., Prentice-Hall, 1968. 350p. $5.95
  Includes the Spanish Academy's norms for accentuation, a vocabulary, and
an index.

1386.
Boggs, Ralph Stelle. BASIC SPANISH PRONUNCIATION. New York, Regents Pub.,
1967. 195p. $1.25

1387.
Bolinger, Dwight L., et al. WRITING MODERN SPANISH; A STUDENT MANUAL FOR
MODERN SPANISH. 2d ed. New York, Harcourt, Brace and World, 1969. $1.50
  Teacher's manual is sent free on request. This manual contains rules for
writing Spanish.

1388.
Bowen, J. D., and, Stockwell R. P. PATTERNS OF SPANISH PRONUNCIATION.
Chicago, University of Chicago Press, 1969. 279p. $2.75

1389.
Brener, Edin. CONVERSEMOS. New York, Appleton-Century-Crofts, 1952. 146p.
plates $2.50
   Intended for review purposes of Spanish conversation.

1390.
Brown, Charles Barrett, and Milton L. Shane. BRAZILIAN-PORTUGUESE IDIOM
LIST. Selected on the basis of range and frequency of occurence. Nashville,
Tenn., Vanderbilt University Press, 1961. 118p. $2.00
   This is a useful list of the most frequently used Portuguese idioms in
Brazil.

1391.
Bruton, J. G. EJERCICIOS DE ESPAÑOL. New York, Pergamon Books, 1968.
119p. $2.50
   A compilation of drills and exercises intended for intermediate Spanish
classes.

1392.
Burnett, J. CRUCIGRAMAS PARA ESTUDIANTES. Skokie, Ill., National Textbook
Corp., 1969. 92p. $1.00
   Contains crossword puzzles which help a student to learn Spanish and
acquire a wider vocabulary.

1393.
Cabat, Louis, and J. Goodwin. SPANISH: HOW TO PREPARE FOR COLLEGE BOARD
ACHIEVEMENT TESTS. Woodbury, N.Y., Barron's Educational Series, 1968.
107p. illus. $1.95
   This is a bilingual edition to prepare a student for college board Spanish
language requirements.

1394.
Cabat, Luis and Robert Cabat. UNIFIED SPANISH; A REVIEW TEXT FOR GRAMMAR AND
CIVILIZATION. Enl. ed. New York, Oxford Books, 1963. 331p. $1.60
   In addition to the text of the author's The Hispanic World (1961), this
volume contains a Spanish grammar.

1395.
Castillo, Carlos, and Otto F. Bond, eds. UNIVERSITY OF CHICAGO SPANISH
DICTIONARY: ENGLISH-SPANISH, SPANISH-ENGLISH. Chicago, University of Chicago
Press, 1968. 226p. $1.85

1396.
----------. UNIVERSITY OF CHICAGO SPANISH- ENGLISH, ENGLISH- SPANISH
DICTIONARY. New York, Washington Square Press, 1968. 220p. $0.75
   A compact and useful reference for the student of Spanish or the traveler.

1397.
Caycedo de Naber, Cecilia. PASATIEMPOS PARA AMPLIAR EL VOCABULARIO. Skokie,
Illinois, National Textbook Corp., 1968. 4 v. illus. $3.00 each
   This is a compilation of useful exercises to enlarge the students'
Spanish vocabulary.

1398.
Cohen, Leon J., and A. C. Rogers. SAY IT IN ENGLISH FOR SPANISH-SPEAKING
PEOPLE. New York, Dover, 1957. 134p. illus. $0.75

1399.
----------. SAY IT IN SPANISH. New York, Dover, 1954. 128p. illus.
$0.75
   An exercise book with vocabulary to learn Spanish.

1400.
Cortina Academy. BRAZILIAN-PORTUGUESE CONVERSATION COURSE. Rev. ed. New
York, Cortina, 1969. 250p. $2.00

1401.
Dixson, Robert James. THE BLUE BOOK OF SPANISH. New York, Regents Pub. Co.,
1960. 192p. $1.00

1402.
-----------. DINER'S CLUB BASIC SPANISH FOR TRAVELERS. New York, Regents Pub.
Co., 1962. 186p. $0.85

1403.
Dobrian, Walter A., and C. R. Jefferson. SPANISH READERS FOR CONVERSATION.
Boston, Houghton, Mifflin, 1970. 212p. $3.40

1404.
Duff, Charles. SPANISH FOR BEGINNERS. New York, Barnes and Noble, 1958.
334p. $1.95
    A teaching aid for beginning Spanish students.

1405.
Durán, Manuel. PROGRAMMED SPANISH DICTIONARY. Englewood Cliffs, Prentice-
Hall, 1965. 216p. $1.75

1406.
Eaton, H. ENGLISH, FRENCH, GERMAN, SPANISH WORD FREQUENCY DICTIONARY. New
York, Dover, 1960. 440p. $3.00
    This book was originally published under the title Semantic frequency list.

1407.
Fabian, Donald L. ESSENTIALS OF SPANISH. Boston, Houghton, Mifflin, 1957.
140p. $2.50
    A basic book for beginning Spanish students.

1408.
Falconieri, John Vincent, ed. DUENDES DETERMINISTAS Y OTROS CUENTOS.
Englewook Cliffs, N.J., Prentice-Hall, 1965. 192p. $3.95
    Includes short stories designed to teach Spanish language courses, with
an extensive vocabulary of words and idioms.

1409.
Feldman, D.M. and G. L. Boarino, eds. LECTURAS CONTEMPORANEAS. Boston, Ginn-
Blaisdell, 1970. 180p. $3.75

1410.
Flores, Ángel, ed. FIRST SPANISH READER: A BEGINNER'S DUAL LANGUAGE BOOK.
New York, Bantam Books, 1964. 167p. $0.75
    A bilingual edition of Spanish and Spanish-American writings.

1411.
Friar, John G., and G. W. Kelly. PRACTICAL SPANISH GRAMMAR. New York,
Doubleday 1960. 184p. $2.95

1412.
Fucilla, Joseph Gurin. SPANISH DICTIONARY; SPANISH-ENGLISH, ENGLISH-SPANISH.
Rev. ed. New York, Bantam Books, 1964. 2 v. in 1. $0.95

1413.
-----------. WORLD-WIDE SPANISH DICTIONARY. New York, Fawcett, 1964. 2 v.
in 1 $1.25
    This dictionary includes words used in different Spanish dialects.

1414.
Gallego Blanco, E. VERBOS ESPAÑOLES REGULARES E IRREGULARES. Chicago,
Loyola, 1970. 89p. $1.30

Contains exercises and exhaustive explanations about regular and irregular Spanish verbs.

1415.
García-Prada, Carlos, and William E. Wilson, eds. CUENTOS DE ALARCÓN. Boston, Houghton, Mifflin, 1970. 210p. $2.95
Contains short stories by Pedro Antonio de Alarcón for Spanish courses.

1416.
---------------. ENTENDÁMONOS: MANUAL DE CONVERSACIÓN. 2d ed. Boston, Houghton, Mifflin, 1970. 250p. $2.95

1417.
---------------. TRES CUENTOS. 2d ed. Boston, Houghton, Mifflin, 1959. 193p. $2.95

1418.
Gerrard, A. B. and J. D. Heras. CASSELL'S BEYOND THE DICTIONARY IN SPANISH: A HANDBOOK OF EVERYDAY USAGE. New York, Funk & Wagnalls, 1968. 325p. $1.95
Bilingual, English and Spanish handbook for proficiency in Spanish everyday speech.

1419.
Gillhoff, G. A. UNIVERSITY SPANISH-ENGLISH AND ENGLISH-SPANISH DICTIONARY. New York, Apollo, 1966. 1261p. $4.49
Orginally published in hard cover under the title Crowell's Spanish-English and English-Spanish Dictionary. (1963). This is a new edition of a useful reference tool.

1420.
Gode, Alexander. PORTUGUESE AT SIGHT. New York, Ungar, 1962. 102p. illus. $1.25
A succinct grammar for beginners.

1421.
Gómez-Gil, Orlando, and Irene E. Stanslawczyk, eds. TIERRAS, COSTUMBRES Y TIPOS HISPÁNICOS. New York, Odyssey Press, 1970. 377p. maps $2.75
The editors have compiled a literary reader for Spanish language students.

1422.
Gooch, Anthony. DIMINUTIVE, AUGMENTATIVE AND PEJORATIVE SUFFIXES IN MODERN SPANISH. Elmsford, N.Y., Pergamon Press, 1970. 385p. $14.50
Provides and exhaustive examination of suffixes used in Spanish.

1423.
Gorostiza, Celestino. EL COLOR DE NUESTRA PIEL. Edited by Luis Soto-Ruiz, and Samuel S. Trifilo. New York, Macmillan, 1966. 119p. $2.25
Textbook edition of the Mexican novelist's most celebrated work published in 1952. The theme in the color of skin of the mestizo seen as a social problem.

1424.
Goytisolo, Juan. FIESTAS. Introd. by K. Schwartz. New York, Dell, 1964. 255p. $0.50
Textbook edition of a Spanish novel

1425.
Greenfield, Eric Viele. SPANISH GRAMMAR. 4th ed. New York, Barnes & Noble, 1942. 236p. $1.50

1426.
Gruber, Edward C., ed. SPANISH GRAMMAR WITH EASE. New York, Arco, 1967. 186p. $1.95

1427.
Herzfeld, A. NOTAS Y EJERCICIOS DE COMPOSICIÓN. Edited by L. D. Mills. Englewood Cliffs, N.J., Prentice-Hall, 1970. 349p. $3.95

This is a valuable exercise book for the study of Spanish.

1428.
Hirschhorn, Howard H. SPANISH-ENGLISH AND ENGLISH-SPANISH MEDICAL GUIDE.
Chicago, Regents Pub. Co., 1968. 120p. $1.00

1429.
Holder, Preston ed. INTRODUCTION TO THE HANDBOOK OF AMERICAN INDIAN
LANGUAGES, by Franz Boas. INDIAN LINGUISTIC FAMILIES OF AMERICA NORTH OF
MEXICO, by J. V. Powell. Lincoln, Neb., University of Nebraska Press, 1966.
221p. $1.85
    These two remarkable articles study American Indian languages from the
linguistic and geographic points of view.

1430.
Hughes, D. CONCHITA DE CUBA. Francestown, N.H., Marshall Jones, 1970.
$1.40

1431.
----------. NIÑOS DE ESPAÑA. Francestown, N.H., Marshall Jones, 1970.
275p. $1.40
    This attractive reader is intended for Spanish language classes.

1432.
----------. PEDRO: INTRODUCCIÓN AL ESPAÑOL. Francestown, N. H., Marshall
Jones, 1969. 260p. $1.40
    A delightful text of elementary Spanish.

1433.
Ibarra, Francisco. SPEAK EVERYDAY SPANISH. Translated by Dorothy Crispo.
New York, Dell, 1966. 191p. $0.50
    A basic course of Spanish with a bibliography.

1434.
Iriarte, R. JUEGO DE NIÑOS. Edited by I. M. Schevill. Englewood Cliffs,
N. J., Prentice-Hall, 1970. 324p. $3.95

1435.
Jassey, William. ADVANCED TESTS FOR THE GRADUATE RECORD EXAMINATION: SPANISH.
New York, Arco, 1968. 300p. $3.95
    This is a useful book to prepare for the Spanish language graduate record
examination.

1436.
Johnson, J. L. SPANISH PROSE TODAY: COMPOSITION AND CONVERSATION. New York,
Barnes and Noble, 1970. 275p. $1.75
    Contains numerous examples and exercises to perfect the students' skills
in Spanish composition and conversation.

1437.
Jones, Malcoom Bancroft. SPANISH IDIOMS. Boston, Heath, 1955. 87p. $1.95
    Contains listings, explanations, and guides to usage of a large number of
commonly used Spanish idioms.

1438.
Kany, Charles Emil. ADVANCED SPANISH CONVERSATION. Boston, Heath, 1969.
320p. $1.25
    Originally published in 1939, this is a new edition of a book on advanced
Spanish conversation.

1439.
----------. SPOKEN SPANISH FOR STUDENTS AND TRAVELERS. Rev. ed. Boston,
Heath, 1961. 296p. illus. $2.50
    A convenient guide for students of Spanish, to which the author has added
vocabularies intended for travelers.

1440.
Kendris, Christopher. DICCIONAIRE DE 201 VERBES ESPAGNOLES CONJUGÉS A TOUTES LES PERSONNES. Great Neck, N.Y., Barron, 1968. 224p. $1.25
A review of Spanish verbs intended for the use of French-speaking students. Useful in simultaneous translation drills.

1441.
----------. DICCIONARIO DE 201 VERBOS FRANCESES CONJUGADOS EN TODOS SUS TIEMPOS Y PERSONAS. Great Neck, N.Y., Barron, 1968. 224p. $1.25
The author has assembled a review of the most frequently used French verbs for Spanish-speaking students. This work may also be helpful in courses in simultaneous translation. Also published in hard cover.

1442.
Kepple, Ella Huff. THREE CHILDREN OF CHILE. New York, Freindship Press, 1961. 127p. illus. $1.75

1443.
Kercheville, F. M. PRACTICAL SPOKEN SPANISH. 7th ed. rev. Albuquerque, University of New Mexico Press, 1969. 258p. $1.75
First published in 1959, this is a practical guide to Spanish conversation.

1444.
Larra, Mariano José de. EN ESTE PAÍS Y OTROS ARTÍCULOS. With notes by J. Campos. Philadelphia, Center for Curriculum Development, 1969. 195p. $1.20
Includes a selection of articles by Larra in which he describes Spanish manners and customs.

1445.
Lastra, Yolanda. COCHABAMBA QUECHUA SYNTAX. New York, Humanities Press, 1968. 104p. $8.00
This is an important work which summarizes Quechua syntax as it is used in Bolivia. It will be of great interest to linguists and to students of Quechua.

1446.
Lopes, Albert R. BOM DIA! ONE MINUTE DIALOGUES IN PORTUGUESE. New York, Appleton-Century-Crofts, 1964. 33p. $1.25
This is a supplementary text containing dialogues in Portuguese.

1447.
López-Morillas, Juan. NEW SPANISH SELF-TAUGHT. Rev. ed. New York, Funk and Wagnalls, 1959. 340p. $1.95

1448.
López Rubio, José. OTRA ORILLA: COMEDIA EN TRES ACTOS. Edited by Anthony M. Pasquariello and John V. Falconieri. New York, Appleton-Century-Crofts, 1958. 137p. $2.25

1449.
----------. UN TRONO PARA CRISTY. Edited by Gerald E. Wade. New York, Dodd, Mead, 1960. 146p. $2.95

1450.
----------. VENDA PARA LOS OJOS. Edited by Marion P. Holt, New York, Appleton-Century-Crofts, 1966. 131p. $2.25

1451.
Marín, Diego and Neale H. Taylor. VIDA ESPAÑOLA. Rev. ed. New York, Appleton-Century-Crofts, 1955. 235p. illus. $3.25

1452.
Marín, Diego. VIDA ESPAÑOLA. 3d ed. New York, Appleton-Century-Crofts, 1970. 238p. illus. $3.75

1453.
Martín-Gaite, Carmen. BALNEARIO. Philadelphia, Chilton Books, 1969. 129p.
$0.90

1454.
Martinez, A. LA FORJA DE LOS SUEÑOS. Edited by C. R. Linsalata and F.
Sedgwick. Boston, Houghton, Mifflin, 1969. 241p. $2.25

1455.
Mason, K. L. J. ADVANCED SPANISH COURSE. New York, Pergamon Press, 1967.
377p. $5.00
    A thorough and useful Spanish course for the student with knowledge of the
language.

1456.
Medio, Dolores. EL FUNCIONARIO PÚBLICO. Edited by Beatrice P. Patt and
Martin Nozick. New York, Oxford University Press, 1963. 295p. $2.95

1457.
Milor, J. H. HISTORIETAS EN ESPAÑOL. Skokie, Ill., National textbook Corp.,
1969. 267p. $2.75

1458.
Modern Language Association. WRITING MODERN SPANISH: A STUDENT MANUAL FOR
MODERN SPANISH. 2d ed. New York, Harcourt, Brace, and World, 1966. 256p.
$2.95
    Frederick S. Richard and Guillermo Kurtzfeld prepared this useful volume.

1459.
Narváez, Ricardo A. INSTRUCTION IN SPANISH MORPHOLOGY: DERIVATIONAL LISTS.
St. Paul, Minn., EMC Corp., 1969. 74p. tables. $4.75
    This is a well-prepared and convenient aid to the study of Spanish.

1460.
----------. INSTRUCTION IN SPANISH PRONUNCIATION: SEGMENTALS. Rev. ed.
St. Paul, Minn., EMC Corp., 1970. 64p. illus., tables $3.00
    A useful aid in studying Spanish pronunciation.

1461.
Newmark, Maxim. DICTIONARY OF SPANISH LITERATURE. Paterson, N.J., Little -
field, Adams, 1963. 352p. $2.25
    This convenient reference work greatly simplifies basic data on authors,
titles, technical terminology, and literary currents.

1462.
Nitti, John J. TWO HUNDRED AND ONE PORTUGUESE VERBS FULLY CONJUGATED IN ALL
THE TENSES. Great Neck, N.Y., Barron's 1968. 212p. $2.95
    A valuable study aid for Portuguese verbs.

1463.
Olmo, Lauro. LA CAMISA. Edited A. K. Ariza and I. F. Ariza. New York,
Pergamon Press, 1968. 125p. illus. $2.50

1464.
Pei, Mario Andrew, and Eloy Vaquero. GETTING ALONG IN SPANISH. New York,
Bantam Books, 1957. 225p. illus. $0.75

1465.
Pittaro, John Michael. CUENTECITOS. Chicago, Regents Pub. Co., 1969. 224p.
$1.25
    Contains short stories and folk tales.

1466.
Prado, C. del, and J. Calvo. PRIMERAS LECTURAS: UNA HISTORIA INCOMPLETA.
New York, Odyssey Press, 1970. 282p. $1.95

1467.
Prista, Alexander. ESSENTIAL PORTUGUESE GRAMMAR. New York, Dover Publications, 1966. 114p. $1.25
    This is a well designed grammar which includes vocabularies.

1468.
Ramondine, Salvatore, ed. NEW WORLD SPANISH-ENGLISH, ENGLISH-SPANISH DICTIONARY. Introd. by Mario A. Pei. New York, New American Library, 1969. 257p. $1.50

1469.
Reedy, Daniel R., and Joseph R. Jones, eds. NARRACIONES EJEMPLARES DE HISP-ANOAMÉRICA. Englewood Cliffs, N.J., Prentice-Hall, 1967. 241p. $3.95

1470.
Riccio, Guy J. INTRODUCTION TO BRAZILIAN PORTUGUESE. Annapolis Md., U.S. Naval Institute, 1957. 299p. $4.50
    A thorough introduction to Portuguese as it is spoken in Brazil.

1471.
Rice, Frank A., ed. STUDY OF THE ROLE OF SECOND LANGUAGES IN ASIA, AFRICA, AND LATIN AMERICA. Washington, Center for Applied Linguistics, 1962. 123p. $2.50
    An important analysis of how important second languages have become in the third world.

1472.
Robles, José. CARTILLA ESPAÑOLA. New York, Appleton-Century-Crofts, 1935. 110p. illus. $1.95

1473.
Rodriguez, Mario B. CUENTOS DE AMBOS MUNDOS. Boston, Houghton, Mifflin, 1960. 161p. $1.50

1474.
----------. CUENTISTAS DE HOY. Boston, Houghton, Mifflin, 1952. 208p. illus. $2.95

1475.
Rodriguez, P. César. BILINGUAL DICTIONARY OF THE GRAPHIC ARTS. Edited by George A. Humphrey. Rev. ed. Farmingdale, N.Y., G.A. Humphrey, 1966. 448p. $15.00
    A useful and welcome compilation of Spanish and English terms used in the graphic arts.

1476.
Rodriguez, T. Manuel, et al. SPANISH VERBS AND REVIEW OF EXPRESSION PATTERNS; VERB KEY METHOD. New York, D. McKay Co., 1966. 1 v. (unpaged) $1.50

1477.
Schulz, Charles. HAY QUE AYUDARTE CHARLIE BROWN. Cartoons by the author. New York, Holt, Rinehart and Winston, 1970. 128p. illus. $1.50
    This is the Spanish version of You Need Help Charlie Brown, featuring the characters of the peanuts comic strip.

1478.
Spaulding, Robert K. SYTAX OF THE SPANISH VERB. New York, Harcourt, Brace, and World, 1970. 225p. $2.80
    This is an exhaustive study about Spanish verbs.

1479.
U.S. Dept. of Defense. THE ARMED FORCES DICTIONARY OF SPOKEN SPANISH WORDS; WORDS, PHRASES, SENTENCES. New York, Doubleday, 1968. 384p. $2.45
    This is a very useful dictionary.

1480.
U.S. Dept. of Defense. DICTIONARY OF SPOKEN SPANISH: SPANISH-ENGLISH,
ENGLISH-SPANISH. New York, Dover, 1967. 349p. $2.00
    This dictionary will be very useful for students.

1481.
Valdman, Albert. BASIC COURSE IN HAITIAN CREOLE. New York, Humanities
Press, 1971. 345p. $15.75
    Analyzes common features of Creole and the West European languages
(Spanish, English, Dutch, and French). Creole is a hybrid of lower class
French and Afro-Portuguese Pidgin. The book contains vocabularies of regular
usage. It is intended for the professional linguist and language teacher.

1482.
Vallejo, A. B. CARTAS BOCA ABAJO. Edited by F. Illaraz. Englewood Cliffs,
N.J., Prentice-Hall, 1970. 302p. $3.25
    A convenient Spanish reader for classroom use.

1483.
Vasi, Susan, and Joseph Tomasino. AUDITORY AND READING COMPREHENSION
EXERCISES IN SPANISH. New York, Regents Pub. Co., 1968. $1.95
    Contains Spanish reading exercises.

1484.
Warren, Virgil Alexander, and Nelson August Cavazos, eds. UNA MADEJA DE LANA
AZUL CELESTE. Englewood Cliffs, N.J., Prentice-Hall, 1969. 192p. $2.95
    A Spanish language reader.

1486.
Willes, Burlington. GAMES AND IDEAS FOR TEACHING SPANISH. Palo Alto, Calif.,
Fearon Publishers, 1967. 33p. illus. $1.50
    An imaginative and creative manual for teaching Spanish which will be very
useful for teachers.

1487.
Williams, Edwin B. NEW COLLEGE SPANISH AND ENGLISH DICTIONARY. New York,
Bantam Books, 1969. 532p. $0.95
    This is one of the most complete Spanish-English, English-Spanish
dictionaries.

1488.
Wofsy, Samuel Abraham. DIÁLOGOS ENTRETENIDOS. New York, Scribner, 1962.
207p. illus. $2.95
    Contains sparkling dialogues intended for Spanish language courses.

1489.
Arjona, Doris King, and Carlos Vázquez Arjona, eds. QUINCE CUENTOS DE LAS ESPAÑAS. New York, Scribner's, 1971. 258p. illus. $2.50
    An anthology of 15 Spanish and Spanish American stories suitable for inter-mediate Spanish classes. Stories by Ricardo Palma, Gregorio López y Fuentes, Miguel de Cervantes, Vicente Blasco Ibañez, Pío Baroja, Ana María Matute, Jorge Luis Borges, among others, are included in this excellent selection.

1490.
Clark, Margaret. HEALTH IN THE MEXICAN-AMERICAN CULTURE: A COMMUNITY STUDY. Berkeley, University of California Press, 1971. 253p. $2.45
    This is a very interesting study of the pattern of community life, language, literacy, education, religion, and family life of a Mexican-American community near San Jose, California. The author presents data which will be useful to sociologists and health practicioners working with the largest Spanish-speaking minority in the United States.

1491.
Johnson, Kenneth F. MEXICAN DEMOCRACY: A CRITICAL VIEW. Boston, Allyn and Bacon, 1971. 190p. $1.95
    A thorough analysis of Mexican politics. The author relies on clandestine literature of protest as well as on the more traditional sources, and on numerous interviews. The work starts with the historical development of Mexican politics, analyzes the PRI as a power organism, and then proceeds to outline the political dimemmas faced by other political groups.

1492.
Smith, Thomas Lynn, ed. AGRARIAN REFORM IN LATIN AMERICA. New York, Knopf, 1965. 218p. tables. $2.50
    19 essays and the editor's introduction survey the development of concern about agrarian reform and current programs being undertaken in Latin America. Brazil and Colombia receive special emphasis. Include a good bibliography.

1493.
----------. LATIN AMERICAN POPULATION STUDIES. Gainesville, University of Florida Press, 1960. 83p. maps. tables. $2.00
    The author presents a thorough compilation and analysis of demographic data for Latin America as a whole, amply supported by graphs and tables. The principal topics treated are the number and distribution of inhabitants, age and sex composition, rate of reproduction, rural-urban migration, and population growth.

1494.
----------. THE PROCESS OF RURAL DEVELOPMENT IN LATIN AMERICA. Gainesville, University of Florida Press, 1969. 87p. illus. map. $2.00
    An important study about recent rural developments in Latin America which will be of great interest to area specialists.

1495.
----------. STUDIES OF LATIN AMERICAN SOCIETIES. New York, Doubleday, 1969. 281p. $1.95
    The emphasis is on societal structures and the rapid changes that are taking place.

1496.
Soustelle, Jacques. THE DAILY LIFE OF THE AZTECS ON THE EVE OF THE CONQUEST. Translated by Patrick O'Brian. Baltimore, Penguin Books, 1964. 302p. **illus.**, **maps.** $2.95
English translation of <u>La vie cótidienne des Azteques á la veille de la</u> <u>conquête espagnole</u> (1955), which is an ethnology of Aztecs at the time of contact, largely as described in native codices and early histories.

1497.
Spratling William. A SMALL MEXICAN WORLD. Boston, Little, Brown, 1964. 198p. illus. $1.95
Originally published in 1932, this is the account of a trip through rural Mexico in 1931 by a man who was a longtime resident in that country. It is an interesting narrative punctuated by sharp insights. Includes charcoal drawings by the author.

1498.
Stastny, Francisco. BREVE HISTORIA DEL ARTE EN EL PERU. New York, Wittenborn, 1967. 57p. illus. $2.00
This is a succinct Spanish-language survey of Peruvian art with attractive illustrations.

1499.
STATISTICAL ABSTRACTS OF LATIN AMERICA. Los Angeles, University of California, Latin American Center, 1955- . (annual) tables. $10.00
The latest edition is 1968-1969. This is an excellent source for comparative statistical data on Latin America. It also includes a good bibliography of statistical sources.

1500.
Stavenhagen, Rodolfo, ed. AGRARIAN PROBLEMS AND PEASANT MOVEMENTS IN LATIN AMERICA. Garden City, N.Y., Doubleday, 1970. 583p. tables. $2.45
Includes papers by anthropologists, economists, political scientists, and sociologists, from a wide range of nationalities. The essays provide the reader with aspects of the agrarian problems and the situation in which more than 100,000,000 peasants find themselves in Latin America.

1501.
Stavrianos, Leften Stavros, <u>and</u> George I. Blanksten. LATIN AMERICA; A CULTURE AREA IN PERSPECTIVE. Boston, Allyn and Bacon, 1964. 76p. **illus.**, map. $1.40
This concise review of Latin America's cultural background is intended for the general reader. Includes a brief bibliography.

1502.
Stein, Stanley J., <u>and</u> Barbara H. Stein. THE COLONIAL HERITAGE OF LATIN AMERICA; ESSAYS ON ECONOMIC DEPENDENCE IN PERSPECTIVE. New York, Oxford University Press, 1970. 222p. $1.50
The authors present a series of essays with a social and economic approach trying to pinpoint the coordinates of sustained backwardness in a dependent colonial area. They have selected broad chronological periods to achieve their aim. Includes a bibliography.

1503.
----------. VASSOURAS: BRAZILIAN COFFEE COUNTY, 1850-1900. New York, Atheneum, 1971. 289p. tables $3.25
A survey of coffee production in Vassouras.

1504.
Steiner, Stanley. LA RAZA: THE MEXICAN-AMERICANS. New York, Harper & Row, 1970. 432p. $1.95
The author has drawn skillful portraits of many of the more influential Mexican-American leaders, such as César Chavez, Rodolfo "Corky" Gonzales, Reies López Tijerina, and others. He describes in a journalistic style the cultural, social, and economic environment of the Chicanos in the Southwest.

1505.
Sterling, Phillip and Maria Brau. QUIET REBELS: FOUR PUERTO RICAN LEADERS:
JOSÉ CELSO BARBOSA, LUIS MUÑOZ MARÍZ, JOSÉ DE DIEGO, AND LUIS MUÑOZ RIVERA.
New York, Doubleday, 1968. 118p. illus. map. $2.95
Biographical sketches of four prominent Puerto Rican leaders.

1506.
Stephens, John Lloyd. INCIDENTS OF TRAVEL IN YUCATÁN. New York, Dover, 1963.
2 v. illus., maps. $2.50 each vol.
Originally published in 1841 as Incidents of travel in Central America,
Chiapas, and Yucatan, this is an abridged edition which deals with the portions
devoted to Yucatán. It is a classic travelogue by a well-known American
traveler and amateur archaeologist of the 19th century, and is a major
contribution to modern Maya research.

1507.
----------. INCIDENTS OF TRAVEL IN CENTRAL AMERICA, CHIAPAS, AND YUCATÁN.
Illus. by Caterwood. New York, Dover, 1969. 2 v. illus., maps. $3.00 each
vol.
This is another complete edition of the famous travelogue by a prominent
American traveler and amateur archaeologist. The roiginal edition appeared
in 1841. Catherwoods' beautiful illustrations have been reproduced in the
present edition.

1508.
Stimson, Frederick S. CUBA'S ROMANTIC POET; THE STORY OF PLACIDO. Chapel
Hill, University of North Carolina Press, 1964. 150p. (Studies in Romance
languages and literatures,) $5.00
This is a scholarly biography of one of the most popular Cuban poets,
Gabriel de la Concepción Valdés, better known by his pseudonym "Plácido."
Professor Stimson describes Plácido's Cuba, the main events of the poet's
life (1809-1844), and his work.

1509.
Stoetzer, O.C. THE ORGANIZATION OF AMERICAN STATES: AN INTRODUCTION. New
York, Praeger, 1965. 213p. illus., tables. $1.95
This is a historical overview of the OAS. Over half of the book consists
of the texts of pertinent documents through which the OAS operates. The
work was originally published for German university students under the title
Panamerika: Idee und Wirklichkeit; die Organisation der Amerikanischen
Staaten (1964)

1510.
Strout, Richard Robert. RECRUITMENT OF CANDIDATES IN MEMDOZA PROVINCE,
ARGENTINA. Chapel Hill, University of North Carolina Press, 1968. 159p.
$4.50
This monograph investigates how different parties in Mendoza, Argentina,
recruited their legislative-gubernatorial candidates from 1962 to 1965. The
aim is to test certain assertions about the social backgrounds of the candidates, the role of the oligarchy, and emerging changes in the political
process. [Charles Fleener]

1511.
Stycos, J. Mayone. CHILDREN OF THE BARRIADA. New York, Grossman, 1970.
196p. illus. $3.95
The author illustrates through interviews and photographs the conditions
in a Latin American slum, making a strong case for serious efforts at improved birth control.

1512.
Turner, Paul, and Shirley Turner, comps. CHONTAL TO SPANISH-ENGLISH;
SPANISH TO CHONTAL. Tucson, University of Arizona Press, 1971. 364p. $3.25
Chontal is a Mexican Indian language. The Highland Chontal Indians of the
southeastern corner of the state of Oaxaca are the ones who speak the language
which is the object of this dictionary. It differs markedly from Lowland
Chontal, that communication between their respective speakers is in Spanish
rather than in the two Chontal languages.

LIST OF PUBLISHERS AND ADDRESSES

ABC-Clio (American Bibliographical Center-Clio Press), Riviera Campus,
    2010 Alameda Padre Serra, Santa Barbara, Calif. 93103.
Harry N. Abrams, Inc., 110 E. 59th St., New York, N.Y. 10022
Academy Guild Press, Box 655 Sausalito, Calif. 94965
Airmont Pub. Co., Inc.,
    Orders to Associated Booksellers, 147 McKinley Ave., Bridgeport, Conn.
    06606
Aldine Pub. Co., 529 S. Wabash Ave., Chicago, Ill. 60605
Allyn and Bacon, Inc., Rockleigh, N.J. 07647
American Philosophical Association, Philadelphia, Penn. 19106
American R. D. M. Corp., 148 Lafayette St., New York, N.Y. 10013
American Universities Field Staff, Inc., 3 Lebanon St., Hanover, N.H. 03755
Amsco Music Book Pub. Co., 33 W. 60th St., New York, N.Y. 10023
Ancient City Book Shop, Box 1986, Santa Fe, N.M. 87501
Antheneum Publishers, 162 East 38th Street, New York, N.Y. 10016
Apollo Editions, Thomas Y. Crowell Co., 201 Park Ave., S., New York, N.Y.
    10003
Appleton-Century-Crofts, Inc., 440 Park Avenue, New York, N.Y. 01016
Arco Pub. Co., Inc., 219 Park Ave., S., New York. 10003
Arizona State University Press, Tempe, Arizona. 85281
Associated Bookseller, 147 McKinley Ave., Bridgeport, Conn. 06606
Atheneum Pubs., Inc., 122 E. 42nd St., New York, N.Y. 10017
Avon Book Div., the Hearst Corp., 959 Eight Ave., New York, N.Y. 10019
Ballantine Books, Inc., 101 Fifth Ave., New York, N.Y. 10003
Barnes & Noble, Inc., 105 Fifth Ave., New York, N.Y. 10003
Bantam Books, Inc., 666 Fifth Ave., New York, N.Y. 10019
Barron's Educational Series, Inc., 113 Crossways Park Dr., Woodbury N.Y.
    11797
William L. Bauhan, Inc., Noone House, Peterborough, N.H. 03458
    (Imprint: Noone House)
Beacon Press, Inc., 25 Beacon St., Boston, Mass. 02108
Between Hours Press, 29 E. 63rd St., New York, N.Y. 10021
Binfords & Mort, 2505 S.E. Eleventh Ave., Portland, Ore. 97242
B'nai B'rith Great Book Series, 1640 Rhode Island Ave., N.W. Washington,
    D.C. 20036
Bobbs-Merrill Co., 4300 W. 62nd St., Indianapolis, Ind. 42668
Bookman Associates--See Twayne Publishers
Borden Pub. Co., 1855 W. Main St., Alhambra, Calif. 91801
R. R. Bowker Co., 1180 Avenue of the Americas, New York, N.Y. 10036
Rowmar Pub. Co., 622 Rodier Dr., Glendale, Calif. 91201
George Braziller Inc., 1 Park Ave., New York, N.Y. 10016
The Brookings Institution, 1775 Mass. Ave., N.W., Washington, D.C. 20036
Charles E. Tuttle Co., Inc., 28 S. Main St., Rutland, Vt. 05701
California State College Press, 6101 East 7th Street, Long Beach, Calif.
    90801
Cambridge Book Co., 488 Madison Ave., New York, N.Y. 10022
Capricorn Books--See Putnam
Carnegie Endowment for International Peace, United Nations Plaza at 46th
    St., New York, N.Y. 10017
Chandler Pub. Co., An Intext Publisher, 124 Spear St., San Francisco, Calif.
    94105
Chilton Book Co., 401 Walnut St., Philadelphia, Pa. 19106
The Citadel Press, 222 Park Ave., S. New York, N.Y. 10003
City Lights Books, 1562 Grant Ave., San Francisco, Calif. 94133

Clarion Books--See S & S
Collier Books--See Macmillan
Columbia University Press, 440 W. 110th St., New York, N.Y. 10025
Compsco Pub. Co., 663 Fifth Ave., New York, N.Y. 10022
Corinth Books, Dist. by Citadel Press
Cornell University Press, 124 Roberts Place, Ithaca, N.Y. 14850
Cornerstone Library, Inc., 630 Fifth Ave., New York, N.Y. 10003
Creative Press, P.O. Box 89, Claremont, Calif. 91711
Center for Applied Linguistics, Office of Information & Publications 1717
    Massachusetts Ave., Washington, D.C. 20036
Dell Pub. Co., Inc., 750 Third Ave., New York, N.Y. 10017
Dodd, Mead & Co., 79 Madison Ave., New York, N.Y. 10016
Doubleday & Co., Inc., 277 Park Ave., New York, N.Y. 10017
Dover Pubns., Inc., 180 Varick St., New York, N.Y. 10014
Dow Jones & Co., Book Div., Box 300, Princeton, N.J. 08540
Dufour Editions, Inc., Chester Springs, Pa. 19425
Dumbarton Oaks, 1703 32nd Street, N.W. Washington, D.C. 20007
E. P. Dutton & Co., Inc., 201 Park Ave., S., New York, N.Y. 10003
Education and World Affairs, New York, N.Y. 10036
William B. Eerdmans Pub. Co., 255 Jefferson Ave., S.E. Grand Rapids Mich.
    49502
EMC Corp., 180 E. 6th St., St. Paul, Minn. 55101
Essandess Special Editions, Simon & Schuster, Inc., 630 Fifth Ave., New York,
    N.Y. 10020
Facts on File, Inc., 119 W. 57th St., New York, N.Y. 10019
Fawcett World Library, 67 W. 44th St., New York, N.Y. 10036
Fearon Pubs., Inc., 2165 Park Blvd., Palo Alto, Calif. 94306
Fernhill House, Ltd., 162 E. 23rd St., New York, N.Y. 10010
Fides Pubs., Inc., P.O. Box F. Notre Dame, Ind. 46556
Follett Pub. Co., 201 N. Wells St., Chicago, Ill. 60606
Free Press Paperbacks, 866 Third Ave., New York, N.Y. 10022
Friendship Press, 475 Riverside Dr., New York, N.Y. 10027
Frommer-Pasmantier Pub. Corp., 70 Fifth Ave., New York, N.Y. 10011
Frontier Book Co., Box 253, Fort Davis, Tex. 70734
Farrar, Straus & Giroux, Inc., 19 Union Square, W., New York, N.Y. 10003
Funk & Wagnalls Co., Inc. 330 Madison Ave., New York, N.Y. 10017
Grosset & Dunlap, Inc., 51 Madison Ave., New York, N.Y. 10010
Gary Press, Box 655, Brownsville, Tex. 78520
Ginn & Co., 275 Wyman St., Waltham, Mass. 02154
Green Mountain Press, Box 16628, Denver, Colo. 80216
Grossman Pub., 125A E. 19th St., New York, N.Y. 10003
Grove Press, Inc., 214 Mercer St. New York, N.Y. 10012
Hafner Publishing Co., Inc., 31 E. 10th St., New York, N.Y. 10003
Harcourt, Brace, Jovanovich, Inc., 757 Third Ave., New York, N.Y. 10017
Harper & Row, Pubs., 49 E. 33rd St., New York, N.Y. 10016
Harian Pubns., Dist. by G & D
D.C. Heath, 125 Spring St. Lexington, Mass. 02173
Herder & Herder, Inc., 232 Madison Ave., New York, N.Y. 10016
Hill & Wang, Inc., 72 Fifth Ave., New York, N.Y. 10011
The Hispanic Society of America, 613 W. 155th St., New York, N.Y. 10032
Houghton Mifflin Co., 2 Park St., Boston, Mass. 02107
Hoover Institution On War, Revolution & Peace, Stanford University, Stanford
    Calif. 94305
Holt, Rinehart & Winston, Inc., 383 Madison Ave., New York, N.Y. 10017
Humanities Press, Inc., 303 Park Ave., S., New York, N.Y. 10010
George A. Humphrey, Box 81 Farmingdale, N.Y. 11735
Henry E. Huntington Library & Art Gallery, 1151 Oxford Rd., San Marino,
    Calif. 91108
Institute for Cross-Cultural Research, 4000 Albermarle St., N.W. Washington,
D.C. 20016
Image Books--See Doubleday and Co.
Indiana University School of Business, Bureau of Business Research, Blooming-
    ton, Indiana. 47401
Institution for Comparative Studies of Political Problems--See Operations and
    Policy Research

International Pubs. Co., Inc., 381 Park Ave., S., New York, N.Y. 10016
International Review Service, 15 Washington Place, New York, N.Y. 10003
Island Press, 175 Bahia Ave., Fort Myers Beach, Fla. 33931
Jenkins Pub. Co., Texas Pemberton Press, 1 Pemberton Pkwy., Austin, Tex.
  78703
John Knox Press, 801 E. Main St., Box 1176, Richmond, Va. 23209
The Johns Hopkins Press, 5820 York Rd., Baltimore, Md. 21218
Kallman Pub. Co., Box 14076, Gainesville, Fla. 32601
Kent State University Press, Kent, Ohio 44240
Dale Stuart King, Pub., 875 Crista Loma Rd., Tucson, Ariz. 85704
Robert R. Knapp, P.O. Box 7234, San Diego, Calif. 92107
Alfred A. Knopf, Inc., 201 E. 50th St., New York, N.Y. 10022
Kodansha International U.S.A., 577 College Ave., Palo Alto, Calif. 94306
Kraus Reprints, 16 East 46th Street, New York, N.Y. 10017
Los Angeles County Museum of Art, 5905 Wilshire Blvd., Los Angeles, Calif.
  90036
La Siesta Press, Box 406, Glendale, Calif. 91209
Las Americas Publishers, 152 East 23rd Street, New York, N.Y. 10010
J. B. Lippincott Co., E. Washington Square, Philadelphia, Pa. 19105
Little, Brown & Co., 34 Beacon St., Boston, Mass. 02106
Littlefield, Adams & Co., 81 Adams Dr., Totowa, N.J. 07512
Liveright, 386 Park Ave., S., New York, N.Y. 10016
Loyola University Press, 3441 N. Ashland Ave., Chicago, Ill. 60657
Marshall Jones Co., Francestown, N.H. 03043
Macfadden-Bartell Corp., 205 E. 42nd St., New York, N.Y. 10036
Laurence McGilvery, Box 852, La Jolla, Calif. 92037
McGraw-Hill Book Co., 330 W. 42nd St., New York, N.Y. 10036
David McKay Co., Inc., 750 Third Ave., New York, N.Y. 10017
Macmillan Co., 866 Third Ave., New York, N.Y. 10022
McNally & Loftin, Pubs., Box 1316, Santa Barbara, Calif. 93102
Marquette University Press, 1131 W. Wisconsin Ave., Milwaukee, Wis. 53233
Maryknoll Pubns., Maryknoll, N.Y. 10545
Marzani & Munsell, 260 W. 21st St., N.Y. 10011
Meridian Books of World Publishers, 2231 West 110 St., Cleveland, Ohio. 44102
Merit Publishers--See Path Press Inc.
Metropolitan Museum of Art, New York Graphic Society Ltd., 140 Greenwich Ave.,
  Greenwich, Conn. 06830
Metropolitan Press, Binfords & Mort Pubs., 2505 S.E. 11th Ave., Portland, Ore.
  27242
Michigan State University Press, Box 550, East Lansing, Mich. 48823
M.I.T. Press, 50 Ames St., Massachusetts Institute of Technology, Cambridge,
Mass. 02142
Monarch Press, Inc. 650 5th Ave., New York, N.Y. 10020
Monthly Review Press 35 W. 19th St., New York, N.Y. 10011
Moody Press, 820 N. LaSalle St., Chicago, Ill. 60610
Museum of Primitive Art, 15 West 54th St., New York, N.Y. 10019
New American Library, Inc., 1301 Ave. of the Americas, New York, N.Y. 10019
National Academy of Sciences, National Research Council, 2101 Constitution
  Ave., N.W. Washington, D.C. 20418
National Textbook Corp., 8259 Niles Center Rd., Skokie, Ill. 60076
Natural History Press, American Museum of Natural History, Central Park West
  & 79th St., New York, N.Y. 10024
Newberry Library, 60 West Walton St., Chicago, Ill. 60610
New York Teacher's College, New York, N.Y. 10027
Martinus Nijhoff, The Hague, Netherlands
W.W. Norton & Co., 55 Fifth Ave., New York, N.Y. 10003
New York Graphic Soc., 140 Greenwich Ave., Greenwich, Conn. 06830
New York York University Press, Washington Square, New York, N.Y. 10003
Oak Pubns., 33 W. 60th St., New York, N.Y. 10023
Oceana Pubns., Inc., 75 Main St., Dobbs Ferry, N.Y. 10522
October House, Inc., 55 W. 13th St., New York, N.Y. 10011
Office of International Affairs, Iniversity of Houston, Johnson City, Texas
  78636
Ohio State University Press, Hitchcock Hall, 2070 Neil Ave., Columbus, Ohio.
  43210
Operations and Policy Research Inc., Institute for the Study of Political
  Systems, 4000 Albemarle Street, N.W. Washington, D.C. 20016

Oregon State University Press, 101 Waldo Hall, P.O. 689, Corvallis, Oreg. 97331

Oxford Book Co., Inc., 387 Park Ave., S., New York, N.Y. 10016

Oxford University Press 200 Madison Ave., New York, N.Y. 10016

Prentice-Hall Inc., Englewood Cliffs, N.J. 07632

Pacific Coast Pubs., 4085 Campbell Ave., at Scott Dr., Menlo Park Calif. 94025

Pathfinder Press, Inc., 873 Broadway, New York, N.Y. 10003

Pocket Books, Inc., 630 Fifth Ave., New York, N.Y. 10020

Pegasus, 850 Third Ave., New York, N.Y. 10022

Pemberton Press—See Jenkins Pub. Co.

Penguin Books, Inc., 39 W. 55th St., New York, N.Y. 10019

Pergamon Press Inc., Maxwell House Fairview Park, Elmsford, N.Y. 10523

Philosophical Library, Inc., 15 E. 40th St., New York, N.Y. 10016

Pioneer Publications; Merit Pubns, 73 Broadway, New York, N.Y. 10003

Pittsburgh University Press, 4200 5th Avenue, Pittsburg, Pa. 15213

Frederick A. Praeger, Inc., 11 Fourth Ave., New York, N.Y. 10003

Princeton University Press, Princeton, N.J. 08540

G. P. Putnam's Sons, 200 Madison Ave., New York, N.Y. 10016

Pyramid Pubns., 444 Madison Ave., New York, N.Y. 10022

Quadrangle Books, Inc., 12 E. Delaware Pl. Chicago, Ill. 60611. Orders to Random House, Inc. Westminster, Md. 21157

Rand McNally & Co. P.O. Box 7600, Chicago, Ill. 60680

Random House, Inc., Random House Bldg., 201 E. 50th St., New York, N.Y. 10022

Redwood City Tribune, Redwood, California. 94062

Regents Pub. Co., Inc., 630 Fifth Ave., New York, N.Y. 10020

Henry Regnery Co., 114 W. Illinois St., Chicago, Ill. 60610

The Ward Ritchie Press, 3044 Riverside Dr., Los Angeles, Calif. 90039

Simon & Schuster, Inc. 630 Fifth Ave., New York, N.Y. 10020

Savile Bookshop 3236 P. St. N.W., Washington, D.C. 20007

Schenkman Pub. Co., 1 Story St., Harvard Square, Cambridge Mass. 02138

Schocken Books, Inc., 67 Park Ave., New York, N.Y. 10016

Abner Schram, 1860 Broadway, New York, N.Y. 10023

Charles Scribner's Sons 597 Fifth Ave., New York, N.Y. 10017

Sixties Press, Odin House, Madison, Minn. 56256

Soccer Associates, P.O. Box 634, New Rochelle, N.Y. 10802

Southern University Press, 130 S. 19th St., Birmingham, Ala. 35233

St. Johns University Press, Grand Central & Utopia Parkway, Jamaica N.Y. 11432

St. Louis University Press, 220 N. Grand Boulevard, St. Louis, Mo. 63103

St. Martin's Press, Inc., 175 Fifth Ave., New York, N.Y. 10010

Stanford University Press, Stanford, Calif. 94305

Stein & Day, 7 E. 48th St., New York, N.Y. 10017

Sterling Pub., Co., 419 Park Ave., S., New York, N.Y. 10016

Stipes Pub. Co., 10-12 Chester St., Champaign, Ill. 61820

Stryker Post Pubns., 888 17th N.W. Washington, D.C. 20006

South-Western Pub. Co., 5101 Madison Rd., Cincinnati, Ohio. 45227

Swallow Press, Inc., 1139 S. Wabash Ave., Chicago, Ill. 60605

Taplinger Pub. Co., 29 E. 10th St., New York, N.Y. 10003

The Tate Gallery Pubns., Box 428, Truchas, N. Mex. 87578

Press of the Territorian, Box 1847, Santa Fe., N.M. 87501

Texas Christian University Press, T.C.U. Station, Fort Worth, Texas. 76129

Texas Western Press, University of Texas at El Paso, El Paso, Tex. 79999

Trail-R Club of America, Box 1376, Beverly Hills, Calif. 90213

Transatlantic Arts, Inc., North Village Green, Levittown, N.Y. 11756

Travel Digest (Paul, Richmond & Co.) 1100 Glendon Ave., Suite 1517, West Los Angeles, Calif. 90024

Tudor Pub. Co., 572 Fifth Ave., New York, N.Y. 10036

Twayne Publishers, 31 Union Square, W., New York, N.Y. 10003

Twentieth Century Fund, Inc., 41 E. 70th St., New York, N.Y. 10021

University of Alaska Press, University Campus, College, Alaska. 99735

University of Arizona Press, Box 3398, College Station, Tucson, Ariz. 85700

University of California, Art Museum, Berkeley, Calif. 94720

University of California Press, 3333 Fulton St., Berkeley, Calif. 94720

University of Florida Press, 15 N. W. 15th St., Gainesville, Fla. 32601

University of Georgia Press, Waddel Hall, Athens, Ga. 30601

University of Illinois Press, Urbana, Ill. 61801
University of Kansas Press, Lawrence, Kan. 66044
University of Michigan Press, 615 E. University, Ann Arbor, Mich. 48106
University of Minnesota Press, 2037 University Ave., S.E., Minneapolis, Minn. 55455
University of North Carolina Press, Box 2288, Chapel Hill, N.C. 27514
University of New Mexico Press, Albuquerque, N.M. 87106
University of Notre Dame Press, Notre Dame, Ind. 46556
University of Oklahoma Press, 1005 Asp Ave., Norman, Okla. 73069
University of Oregon Books, Eugene, Oreg. 97403
University of Puerto Rico, Institute of Caribbean Studies, Rio Piedras, Puerto Rico. 00928
University of Texas Press, P.O. Box 7819, Univ. Station, Austin, Texas. 78712
University of Toronto Press, Toronto 181, Canada; or 33 E. Typper St., Buffalo N.Y. 14208
University of Wisconsin Press, P.O. Box 1379, Madison, Wis. 53701
University Press of Kansas, 358 Watson Library, Lawrence, Kansas. 66044
University Press of Virginia, P.O. Box 3608, Univ. Station, Charlottesville, Va. 22903
Frederick Ungar Co., 250 Park Ave., S., New York, N.Y. 10003
University Place Book Shop, 840 Broadway, New York, N.Y. 10003
Universe Books, Inc., 381 Park Ave., S., New York, N.Y. 10016
U.S. Naval Institute, Annapolis, Md. 21402
Vanderbilt University Press, Nashville, Tenn. 37203
Van Nostrand Reinhold Co., 450 W. 33rd St., New York, N.Y. 10001
Viking Press, Inc., 625 Madison Ave., New York, N.Y. 10022
Walker & Co., 720 Fifth Ave., New York, N.Y. 10019
Washington Square Press, 620 5th Avenue, New York, N.Y. 10020
Wayne State University Press, Wayne State University Press, Wayne State Univ., 5980 Cass Ave., Detroit, Mich. 48202
John Wiley & Son, Inc., 605 Third Ave., New York, N.Y. 10016
George Wittenborn, Inc., 1018 Madison Ave., New York, N.Y. 10021
William C. Brown Co., Pubs., 135 So. Locust St., Dubuque, Iowa. 52001
World Pub. Co., 110 E. 59th St., New York, N.Y. 10022
Yale University Press, 92A Yale Station, New Haven, Conn. 06520

California, 234; history, 225, 253, 339, 691
Camões, Luiz, 954
Cancionero de Baena, 1089
Caribbean, 318, 380, 418; economic integration, 555
Casals, Pablo, 1042, 1333
Casas, Bartolomé de las, 48-49, 376, 383
Castro Ruz, Fidel, 491, 543, 586, 904
Catherine of Aragón, 1208
Catholicism, 229
  colonial Latin America, 352; national period, Latin America, 174, 243,
  846, 894; Mexico, 223, 348-350; Spain, 1218; Spanish borderlands, mis-
  sions, 32, 83-84, 339, 547, 672
Cattle raising, 551, 889
Cela, Camilo José, 1170
Celso Barbosa, José, 793
Central America
  bibl., 735; history, 734
Cernuda, Luis, 173
Cervantes Saavedra, Miguel de, 922, 944, 950, 1043, 1078, 1091, 1190, 1223,
  1290, 1304, 1334
Charles V, emperor, 100, 1047, 1066
Chicanos, 114, 302, 401-402, 405, 566, 577, 691, 756, 1504; education, 408;
  social customs, 813-815, 818, 1490
Chile, 72; history, independence, 898; national period, 118, 498, 789;
  politics and government, 161, 322, 684
Christian Democrats, 161, 182, 684
Christophe, Henri, 157, 171
Church and state, Latin America, 511, 590, 688, 811; Spain, 1317
Coffee, Brazil, 1503
Colombia, foreign relations, with the U.S., 121; politics and government,
  70, 221, 276
Columbus, Christopher, 167, 610, 804, 827
Communism, bibl., 754; Cuba, 149, 151-153, 155, 220, 227-228, 426, 450, 801;
  Dominican Republic, 220; Latin America, 4, 155, 536, 571, 694, 792;
  Venezuela, 10
Cookery
  Mexican, 18, 267-268, 655, 816, 905-906; New Mexican, 267-268; Spanish,
  947A, 1224
Copyright laws, 662
Coronado y Valdés, Francisco Vásquez de, 82, 206
Cortés, Hernán, 126, 332
Costa Rica, 120
Cross-cultural studies, Afro-Latins, 703
Cuba
  bibl., 667, 844; description and travel, 403, 686; economic conditions,
  85, 656; foreign relations, with the U.S., 1, 16, 490, 507-508, 596-597,
  658, 799; with the U.S.S.R., 1, 16, 257, 570; history, 608, 798; politics
  and government, 145-147, 149-151, 207, 227-228, 260, 287, 347, 542-543,
  747, 801, 883; social conditions, 656

Dalí, Salvador, 972
Dances, Latin America, 517
Daniels, Josephus, 192
Darío, Rubén, 235
Demography, 37-38, 177, 1493
Denuclearization of Latin America, 308
Díaz del Castillo, Bernal, 345
Diego, José de, 793
Dominican Republic
  foreign relations, with the U.S., 573, 821; politics and government, 260,
  573, 879
Dutch Caribbean, 29, 313
Duvalier, François, 219, 260

Economic integration
    Caribbean, 555; Central America, 258, 384, 649; Latin America, 585, 837
Ecuador, 105, 568, 623
Education
    Brazil, 397; Cuba, 259; Latin America, 265, 386; Mexico and Central
    America, 129, 204; West Indies, 866, 885
Elites in Latin America, 331, 538
Ethnohistory, Latin America, 123, 867. See also, Anthropology
    Aztecs, 805, 843, 856, 1496; Guatemala, 494; Incas, 309, 472, 474, 858;
    Mayas, 165, 324, 611, 805, 822-823, 859; Mesoamerica, 97, 166, 442, 500,
    890; Mexico, 217, 283, 355, 476, 520, 784; Peru, 250, 323, 496, 509, 580,
    594, 857-858; Spanish borderlands, 634
Ethnology
    Arawaks, 261; Brazil, 421; Central Garibs, 262; Comanches, 458; Cubeos,
    330; Guiana, 443; Kaingángs, 407; Mapuches, 263-264, Mayas, 132, 619,
    651, 712-713, 715, 720, 855; Mixtecans, 743; North American Indians, 277;
    Pokomanes, 720; Pueblos, 547; Sirionos, 419; Tzotzil, 696; Urubus, 441;
    Yaquis, 139, 661.

Fatima, Portugal, 1094
Fauna, Caribbean, 761
Fernández de Oviedo y Valdés, Gonzalo, 1346
Festivals, Latin America, 603
Fish and shellfish, 657, 853
Flora, Mexico, 682
Florida, 33, 771
Folklore, bibl. 131; New Mexico and Arizona, 266
Foot and mouth disease, 34
Foreign researchers in Latin America, 76
Franciscan missions, 83, 547
Franco y Bahamode, Francisco, 1251
French Caribbean, 28

Galápagos Islands, 108
Games, 461-462, 493, 854
García Lorca, Federico, 1139, 1321, 1373
Gauchos, 141
Geography
    Latin America, 693, 730; Middle America, 556; South America, 557
Ginés de Sepúlveda, Juan 953
Godoy Alcayaga, Lucila, see Mistral, Gabriela [pseud.]
González, Julio, 1108A
Goya y Lucientes, Francisco de, 909, 1164, 1171
Gracián y Morales, Baltasar, 948
Graphic arts, dictionaries, 1475
Guatemala
    description and travel, 278, 615; history, 896; politics and government,
    237, 304, 470; social conditions, 619
Güemes, Martín, 369
Guerrilla movements
    Bolivia, 336, 358; Guatemala, 224; Latin America, 132, 360, 694; poetry,
    224
Guevara, Antonio de, 1154
Guevara, Ernesto (Che), 13, 148, 336, 456, 739-740, 792

Haiti
    history, 171, 455, 499, 534; politics and government, 219, 260; social
    conditions, 99, 722
Huntington, Anna Vaughn (Hyatt), 1101
Huntington, Archer Milton, 1101

Industrialization, 519
Inquisition, Spain, 1129, 1163, 1280, 1303
Inter-American conferences, 445
Inter-American Development Bank, 591
Inter-American relations, 637, 781, 795, 821

Interior decorating, Spain, 992-993
Isidore of Seville, 1057

Jamaica, 768
Jesuit missions, 84, 606
Jiménez, Juan Ramón, 1372-1373
Juárez, Benito, 40

Kino, Eusebio Francisco, 83
Kon-Tiki, 409-411

Labor conditions
    Cuba, 193, 904; Latin America, 115; Spanish colonies, 48-49
Language
    Basque, 1197; Guatemala, 589; Haiti, 1481; North American Indians, 1429;
    Quechua, 1445; romance languages, 1384
Latin America, 197, 317, 501, 504, 601, 626, 680, 776, 807, 819, 882
    bibl., 20-21, 109, 475, 481; biographies, 14, 95, 721, 808; civilization,
    164, 321, 404, 485, 574, 674, 687, 725, 775, 874, 877, 897, 1501,
    description and travel, 45, 180; economic conditions, 24, 71, 286, 297,
    299, 326, 341, 412, 414, 565, 588; foreign relations, 66, 130, 308;
    politics and government, 4, 11-12, 23, 119, 211, 232, 333, 386, 428,
    466, 502, 505, 659, 826, 850-851; social conditions, 2, 5, 30, 46, 65,
    178, 182, 371, 394, 463-464, 497, 522, 598, 1495, 1511
Latin American history, 73, 77, 84, 256, 377, 382, 484, 690, 748
    discovery and exploration, 7, 47,75, 80, 82, 102, 167, 179, 198, 610,
    647, 1169; conquest, 32, 49, 126, 187-188, 215, 269, 271, 424, 430, 1169
    colonial period, 48, 95, 320-321, 378, 383, 390, 564, 762, 833, 875,
    1502, 1511-1512; independence period, 81, 439, 729, 830; national period,
    375, 379, 748, 876
Latin American literature
    anthologies, 27, 35, 168-169, 235, 248, 828, 887, 926; bibl., 247, 437-
    438, 524, 1489; essay, Argentina, 91-93, 765; essay Mexico, 676-677;
    history and criticism, 26, 249, 338, 391, 396, 446, 526, 829; novel,
    Argentina, 25, 186, 189, 213, 307, 365-366, 432-435, 545, 575, 753;novel,
    Brazil, 196, 552-553, 852; novel, Colombia, 127, 231; novel, Guatemala,
    660; novel, Mexico, 26, 42-44, 110, 294-295, 368, 750-752, 899; novel,
    Paraguay, 282; novel, Venezuela, 305, 670, 842; poetry, anthologies, 89
    107, 222, 224, 636; poetry, Caribbean, 780; poetry, Chile, 604-605, 627-
    632, 669; poetry, Cuba, 576, 1508, 812; poetry, Peru, 718, 845; poetry,
    Uruguay, 907; short story, anthologies, 135, 172, 175, 212, 252; short
    story, Argentina and Uruguay, 88, 90-91, 136, 185, 284; short story,
    Brazil, 372, 554; short story, Mexico and Nicaragua, 183, 210; short
    story, Spanish America, 106, 736, 900-901; short story, Venezuela, 284;
    short story, West Indies, 616
Latin American studies, 755
Latin American theatre
    bibl., 440; Brazil, 802; Spanish America, 134, 199, 757, 802, 838-840;
    West Indies, 157
Literary societies, Mexico, 759
López, Fernán, 951
Loyola, Ignacio de, Saint, 1282
Lucas y Padilla, Eugeno, 1059
Lucena, Luis de, 1226

Machado, Antonio, 1373
Manuscripts
    Huntington Library, San Marino, Calif., 774; Mesoamerican pictorial
    material, 217, 324, 500; Portuguese medieval manuscripts, 923
Martinez Ruiz, José, 1189
Mello, Francisco Manuel de, 1281
Menéndez Pidal, Ramón, 1136
Mexico
    civilization, 516, 668, 791; description and travel, 98, 274, 278-279,
    310, 370, 417, 422, 451, 513-514, 562, 612, 758, 895, 1497; economic
    conditions, 327, 477, 779; foreign relations, with the U.S., 163, 192,

Spanish literature, cont'd.
1309; poetry, 20th century, 920, 1096-1098, 1150-1152, 1288, 1321; short
story, 1052-1053, 1080, 1083, 1086; short story, 19th century, 1040, 1071;
short story, 20th century, 927, 930, 937-938, 1005, 1040, 1065, 1071,
1090, 1201, 1210, 1347, 1349, 1357
Spanish mysticism, 935, 946, 1156-1162, 1191
Spanish theatre, anthologies, 960-961, 1340; medieval, 977, 1038, 1082, 1291-
1292; Golden Age, 924, 940, 994-1000, 1081, 1084, 1140, 1193, 1285, 1302,
1339, 1358-1363; 18th and 19th centuries, 1073, 1084, 1376; 20th century,
932-933, 957-959, 982-987, 1001, 1007-1009, 1044, 1084, 1095, 1099-1100,
1138, 1144, 1155, 1205-1206, 1216-1217, 1248, 1272
Statistics
Cuba, 593; Latin America, 834, 1499
Stock Exchange, 239
Surinam, 313
Synagogues, Spain and Portugal, 1128

Taxco, Mexico, 281
Teresa of Avila, Saint, 935
Textiles, Peru, 22, 496, 766
Theotocopuli, Dominico, called El Greco, 976, 1058, 1368
Torres, Camilo, 132
Transportation, 399
Treaties, Latin America, 544, 653, 663-665
Trinidad and Tobago, 255, 416, 886
Trujillo, Rafael, 879

Unanumo y Jugo, Miguel, 947, 1075, 1172, 1354, 1373
United States
foreign relations, with Argentina, Brazil and Chile, 238; with Colombia, 121; with Cuba, 1, 257, 490, 507-508, 596-597, 622, 658, 799; with
the Dominican Republic, 573, 821; with Latin America, 3, 18, 226, 231A,
300, 537, 587, 592, 708, 710, 744, 847, 871, 876, 893; with Panama, 539;
with Spain, 35, 342A, 698, 872, 956, 1125; War with Mexico, 225, 540, 560,
709, 749; War with Spain, 698, 745, 1342
Urbanization
bibl., 706; pre-Columbian America, 387; contemporary Latin America, 388

Valdés, Gabriel de la Concepción, also known as Plácido [pseud.], 1508
Valdés Leal, Juan de, 1060
Valle Caviedes, Juan del, 718
Valle-Inclán, Ramón del, 1213
Vallejo, César, 629
Vega y Carpio, Lope Félix de, 1193, 1244
Valázquez, Diego Rodriguez de Silva, 1214
Venezuela, 70, 292, 578, 817
Vicente, Gil, 952
Vives, Juan Luis, 1364

West Indies, 41, 60, 128, 205, 254, 413, 671, 678, 783
Wilson, Woodrow, 704

Zapata, Emiliano, 602, 892

☆ U.S. GOVERNMENT PRINTING OFFICE:1972 O—449-137